EX LIBRIS
CARL VAN DUYNE

# The Making of
# United States International
# Economic Policy

D1502944

# Stephen D. Cohen

## foreword by
## C. Fred Bergsten

The Praeger Special Studies program—
utilizing the most modern and efficient book
production techniques and a selective
worldwide distribution network—makes
available to the academic, government, and
business communities significant, timely
research in U.S. and international economic, social, and political development.

# The Making of United States International Economic Policy

## Principles, Problems, and Proposals for Reform

PRAEGER SPECIAL STUDIES IN INTERNATIONAL BUSINESS, FINANCE, AND TRADE

Praeger Publishers     New York     London

Library of Congress Cataloging in Publication Data

Cohen, Stephen D
    The making of United States international economic
policy.

    (Praeger special studies in international business,
finance, and trade)
    Includes bibliographical references and index.
    1.  United States—Foreign economic relations.
I.  Title.
HF1455.C576   1977      382.1'0973          77-7469
ISBN 0-03-021926-4
ISBN 0-03-021921-3 student ed.

PRAEGER SPECIAL STUDIES
200 Park Avenue, New York, N.Y. 10017, U.S.A.

Published in the United States of America in 1977
by Praeger Publishers
A Division of Holt, Rinehart and Winston, CBS, Inc.

3-1303-00060-4026

789 038 987654321

© 1977 by Praeger Publishers

*All rights reserved*

Printed in the United States of America

382.3
C678m

To My Mother and Father

lolol/r

# FOREWORD
## C. Fred Bergsten

International economic policy has become one of the central concerns of the government of the United States. External events increasingly determine the fate of our domestic economy. Economic considerations increasingly dictate the focus of our foreign policy. Indeed, U.S. officials must think increasingly in terms of contributing to the management of a single world economy, rather than simply of the economic relations among nations.

Yet the U.S. government has never found a way to manage its own international economic policy effectively. Each administration has tried at least one new approach. Leadership has been centered in the Department of State, the Treasury Department, and several parts of the White House. But no effort to date has found the key to success: consistent fusion of the economic and foreign policy roots from which international economic policy must spring. Further delay in doing so could levy extremely heavy costs on the United States, and on the other countries around the world whose dependence on external forces is even greater than our own.

Stephen D. Cohen brings to this issue a background that combines experience in academia, the private sector, and the government itself. He has devoted long study to the issue as the staff member responsible for international economic policy to the Commission on the Organization of the Government for the Conduct of Foreign Policy. His book is thus of cardinal importance.

Cohen's analysis of the content of international economic policy, and of past efforts to organize it, provides the essential backdrop. His proposals are creative, constructive, and controversial. I recommend this volume highly to all Americans as a guide against which to judge the success of their government in dealing with some of the most crucial issues of the last quarter of the twentieth century.

# ACKNOWLEDGMENTS

I would be remiss if I did not express at the outset my gratitude for the assistance received during the writing of this book. First and foremost, I am indebted to the Rockefeller Foundation's Conflict in International Relations Program for its generous funding of my research. In extending the grant to me, the Foundation exerted absolutely no supervision or control, directly or indirectly, over the book's contents or conclusions. The cooperation and assistance provided to me by John J. Stremlau, of the Conflict in International Relations Program, could not have been better.

A collective thank you is extended to the numerous civil servants in the governments of the United States and Western Europe, and in the Canadian and Australian embassies in Washington, D.C., who provided invaluable information and insights on a not-for-attribution basis.

Special thanks are due William Diebold, Jr. and Robert Hormats who read the entire initial draft of my manuscript and provided numerous suggestions. The chapter on comparative international economic policy making benefited considerably from the helpful critiques provided by Helen and William Wallace, Wolfgang Hager, Gene Kaplan, and Hiroya Ichikawa. Additional comments were received from Edward G. Sanders. All opinions and errors, of course, remain the sole responsibility of the author.

I am also grateful to Teri L. Teel for a masterful job of quickly and accurately typing the original manuscript, despite my handwriting. Thanks also to Glenda Bennett, Cynthia A. Teel, and Cecelia Jones for additional typing help.

Finally, I wish to express a deeply-felt personal appreciation to my wife, Linda, and my children, Sondra and Marc, for their toleration and acceptance of my devoting all too many evenings to my research and writing efforts.

# CONTENTS

# LIST OF ACRONYMS

| | |
|---|---|
| AID | Agency for International Development |
| CCC | Commodity Credit Corporation |
| CCIEP | Cabinet Committee for International Economic Policy (proposed in this book) |
| CEA | Council of Economic Advisers |
| CEP | Council on Economic Policy |
| CFEP | Council on Foreign Economic Policy |
| CIA | Central Intelligence Agency |
| CIEC | Conference on International Economic Cooperation |
| CIEP | Council on International Economic Policy |
| CPCC | Commodities Policy Coordinating Committee |
| DCC | Development Coordination Committee |
| DIBA | Domestic and International Business Administration |
| DICP | Department of International Commercial Policy (proposed in this book) |
| DITC | Department of Industry, Trade, and Commerce (Canadian) |
| DREE | Direction des Relations Économiques Extérieures (French) |
| EC | European Communities |
| EEC | European Economic Community |
| EPB | Economic Policy Board |
| Eximbank | Export-Import Bank |
| FAS | Foreign Agricultural Service |
| FCO | Foreign and Commonwealth Office (British) |
| FEA | Federal Energy Administration (also Foreign Economic Administration during World War II era) |
| FRG | Federal Republic of Germany |
| GAO | General Accounting Office |
| GATT | General Agreement on Tariffs and Trade |
| IEA | International Energy Agency |
| IMF | International Monetary Fund |
| ITC | International Trade Commission |
| LDC | less developed country |
| MITI | Ministry of International Trade and Industry (Japanese) |
| MTNs | multilateral trade negotiations |
| NAC | National Advisory Council (on International Monetary and Financial Policies) |
| NSC | National Security Council |

| | |
|---|---|
| OASIA | Office of the Assistant Secretary for International Affairs |
| OECD | Organization for Economic Cooperation and Development |
| OMB | Office of Management and Budget |
| OPEC | Organization of Petroleum Exporting Countries |
| SGCI | Secretariat General of the Interministerial Committee for Questions of European Economic Cooperation (French) |
| UHD | Utrikes Handels Departementet (Swedish) |
| UNCTAD | United Nations Conference on Trade and Development |
| USDA | United States Department of Agriculture |

Not everything that is faced can be changed. But nothing can be changed until it is faced.

Anonymous

The importance of U.S. international economic policy has increased more rapidly than the quality of its content, the efficiency of its conduct, or the quantity of knowledge about it. This situation is a reflection of an inherent dilemma: international economic policy* straddles the fields of economic policy and foreign policy. The paradox of its being more important than the concern for, or understanding of, it is explained by the tendency of most economists and political scientists to view international economic relations as a disaggregated subordinate to either domestic economic or foreign policy priorities, respectively.

The spiraling dynamic of global interdependence suggests that a second- or third-best U.S. international economic policy already is a burden too costly for anyone to bear graciously. The global challenges of the 1980s may elevate mediocre U.S. policy in this field from the category of burden to one of disaster. One method of preventing such a contingency is to raise levels of knowledge and consciousness concerning it. Another is to assure the best possible organization and procedures to formulate and implement this policy.

This study was initiated because of five assumptions made about the organizational process by which the international economic policy of the United States is planned, decided, and implemented:

1. It is an important factor in shaping the substance of that policy: organizational issues in this area are mainly struggles for power, that is, the ability to successfully pursue certain values and priorities. The substance of the

---

*The term "international economic policy" is used throughout this book in lieu of the more commonly used phrase "foreign economic policy." The former is the preferable term because in today's world, policy making in this area must take account of too many questions of domestic economic and political policy to be considered "foreign." For example, certain changes in the U.S. tax code could have a major impact on U.S. corporations operating overseas, thereby affecting foreign investment policy. Certain internal programs—for example, adjustment assistance—owe their existence exclusively to the vicissitudes of international economic intercourse. Lobbying in Washington by such key interest groups as organized labor and multinational corporations affects the legislative process and hence international economic relations. Moreover, the term "foreign economic policy" usually connotes a subdivision of foreign policy as a whole and is therefore an oversimplification.

policy is important to the domestic economic policy and the foreign policy of the United States, as well as to the policies of most other countries.

2. A unique organizational process is, in a sense, the thing that makes international economic policy a separate phenomenon, not simply a subordinate of other broader policy areas. The inherent multifaceted nature of the subject requires delicate, permanent trade-offs among its four basic elements: domestic and foreign aspects of both economic and political factors. It is due to the inherent nature of the subject, not an accident of organization, that conflicting priorities are reconciled.

3. The decision-making phase of the process is working poorly: at times it is dilatory and inadequate in coping with exigencies.

4. The shortcomings of the process can and should be remedied; improvements would reduce some of the obstacles to achieving better and more responsive policy.

5. The absence heretofore of any independent, all-encompassing study of organizational arrangements concerned with international economic relations is one reason for the continuance of existing policy shortcomings. A properly executed study of this type should increase understanding and should stir thinking in the short term and actual change in the medium term.

## THESIS AND OBJECTIVES

The basic thesis of this study is that there are three prerequisites for a more constructive, effective, coherent, clear, and consistent U.S. international economic policy. The first is a precise understanding of what this policy phenomenon is all about. The second is knowledge of the major variables and constants weighed in the policy-making process as competing domestic and foreign priorities are reconciled by government officials. The last prerequisite is an end to the organizational status quo in favor of initiating an overdue reorganization of, and introducing innovations in, the decision-making process.

The objective of this book is straightforward: to supply the facts, concepts, and proposals to meet these three prerequisites. Consequently, the first task is to project a better understanding of the content and implications of U.S. international economic policy by exploring the extent to which global economic interdependence has blurred distinctions between U.S. and foreign economies, changed the nature of international political relations, and in the process created a new, separate policy phenomenon. The second is to explain why and how the policy-making process functions. Finally, the book will provide original recommendations for creating an optimal set of organizational arrangements by which to orchestrate this policy, the assumption being that better organization will encourage better policy substance.

If the first two of these objectives are fulfilled successfully, an important scholarly contribution will have been made to the still nascent effort to accord the subject of international economic policy the place of importance and the separate identity it deserves. If the third objective is realized, the initial step will have been taken in rectifying the problem of an inadequate, inappropriate governmental organization. The central problem of improving organization in this field is to successfully cope with the inherent value struggle in international economic policy: domestic economic versus foreign political considerations. The very few would-be administrative reformers have been reflective of the dilemma of organizational thinking being filtered through prisms shaped by values and personal experience. Few innovations or genuine solutions have been forthcoming. The necessary organizational remedies remain to be articulated where it counts: White House leadership and control; a systematic, impartial means of coordination; a rationalized trade policy-making apparatus; and a host of procedural reforms.

The time has come to think of the effect of international economic relations on U.S. policy making as being revolutionary, not evolutionary. The unique characteristics and burgeoning importance of international economic policy need to be studied and analyzed as a separate and distinct phenomenon. For too long, it has been viewed as either stepchild by foreign-policy officials or as foreign cousin by domestic economic policy practitioners.

The pervasive intellectual failure to respect international economic policy as a distinct entity has been a critical factor in shaping the substance of that policy. Caught between the domestic economic and foreign-policy machines, it has frequently been inconsistent, defensive, inadequate, and botched. Failure to appreciate the unique nature of international economic policy has hindered the development of a fully rational organization and decision-making procedure. Organization is not merely an ornament in the U.S. international economic policy equation. Control of it has been a prize coveted by two rival bureaucratic factions living together in uncertain harmony. Until domestic economic considerations and foreign-policy considerations are united, policy substance will continue to suffer from internal power struggles.

## TERMS OF REFERENCE

When classified as a comprehensive study aimed specifically at the international economic policy-making organization, written without any link whatsoever with government institutions or funds, this book is without precedent. Why should this vacuum exist? There are probably several reasons. One is the two-cultures syndrome whereby economists are uninterested in organizational dynamics, while political scientists are baffled by the complexity and breadth of economic policy. As illustration, one need look only to published case studies of the bureaucratic politics paradigm; here one will typically find only traditional national security issues analyzed. A second reason is the relatively recent emergence of U.S. international economic policy as a major force that deserves special consideration. A third reason is that the few published organizational studies that have included references to international economic policy have been done by governmental bodies, for example, congressional committees and the 1975 report of the Commission on the Organization of the Government for the Conduct of Foreign Policy (often referred to as the Murphy Commission, in deference to its chairman, Robert Murphy). These brief references have been based largely on the recommendations of senior policy officials, past and present, whose views are inextricably linked with their individual bureaucratic experiences. There are, admittedly, few independent sources to turn to for quick, sage advice.

Since the ultimate purpose of this study is to make proposals for improving the organizational process by which international economic policy is made, it is proper first to explain exactly what that system is and what it is dealing with. "Policy making," a term repeated throughout this book, is used as a generic term to collectively describe a multifaceted process. Its mechanics consist of planning, data assessment, identification of problems, articulation of options, the making of specific decisions, implementation of those decisions, and evaluation of existing policies. The output of the process is fourfold: actions (such as imposition of a tariff surcharge, rejection of U.S. participation in an international commodity agreement); postures (for example, the European Community's system of variable levies on food imports should be denounced as injurious to U.S. interests, the monetary role of gold should be phased out); negotiating positions (for example, proposing termination of a specific U.S. trade barrier in exchange for a trade liberalization measure by a trading partner); and programs (such as bilateral foreign aid, export promotion, currency swaps).

The process is dealing with economic and quasi-economic issues that transcend national boundaries and are of concern to governments and private sectors alike. It is a broad field, involving many subsectors of policy issues. Some, like dollar devaluation, are of extraordinary importance to the entire U.S. economy and have worldwide repercussions. Other policy issues are of monumental importance only to a limited group, for example, adjustment assistance funds being made available to unemployed U.S. automobile workers, or the negotiation of textile export restraint agreements with other countries. Still others are of a fairly routine nature involving no clashes of interests or values, such as a bilateral loan for rural development or routine bilateral consultations. In some cases, policy must be decided on quickly under a crisis situation; sometimes, it must be decided on in order to meet a timetable decided long in advance (congressional hearings, an international conference); and in other cases, policy may be discussed with relative leisure.

The presumption of heterogeneity is the central standard by which this study approached the subject of policy making. Generalizations are minimized. Neat compartmentalizations (such as who takes the policy initiatives, how good was planning, what was the impact of public opinion) are eschewed. The central assumption about the policy-making process parallels that made by William Wallace in his pioneer study of the British foreign policy process: the system involved "is less one of a series of discrete and identifiable decisions than of a continuous flow of policy, in which successive messages received about the international environment, the interpretation given to the information received, the preconceptions of those responsible for policy, their assessment of possible alternatives in terms of their competing and often incompatible objectives, and the organizational context within which they make policy, all combine to shape the direction of that flow."[1]

If this is the system, what exactly is it dealing with? The answer lies in a broad number of issues that, first, must be compatible with broad doctrines (democracy and capitalism) and, second, must be able to reconcile the policy objectives of domestic economic policy management (for example, full employment and price stability) with those of national security (for example, stable, prosperous world order and strong alliances). There actually are very few isolated and finite decisions that write the history of U.S. international economic policy. In most cases, policy changes evolve from accumulations of small decisions, of adjustments to circumstances and gut reactions to evolving situations.

The making of U.S. international economic policy is occasionally the function of the personal initiatives or whims of the president and his senior advisers. A degree of irrationality in the system is inevitable. It occasionally is a decisive reaction to a real or perceived crisis. These are the exceptions, however. The normal process of policy making is a mundane, but a rational process of reconciling organizational conflicts. More often than not, policy evolves slowly and subtly within a given organizational framework in which personalities, the roles officials are called upon to play, the objectives they pursue, and perceived domestic and international pressures all interact to give the exaggerated impression of a series of individual attempts to divine the national interest.

## METHODOLOGY

A disaggregated, iconoclastic approach complements the overall design of the study: to present scholarly examination by a nonparticipant looking in from outside the system. A totally dispassionate view towards the merits of any individual bureaucratic perspective or special-interest viewpoint hopefully is maintained throughout. The hoped-for objective of an outsider has been molded to extensive research and to interviews with many of the past and present senior participants in the process. The subsequent critique of the organizational process and the recommendations for change represent no particular constituency. They emanate from these three principles:

1. International economic policy must be viewed as being a separate phenomenon, not a tool for use by either foreign policy or domestic economic policy officials.
2. The structure of international economic policy making, like any governmental function, should not be modeled after a profit-making organization; exclusive emphasis on managerial efficiency would be deleterious to assuring a balanced domestic policy.
3. It is folly to ignore the need to tailor any policy-making organization to the informal "flow of confidence" from the president to his chief advisers, a flow which is individualistic and thus dynamic.

The most realistic approach to recommending organizational reforms was deemed to be the middle ground that attempts to walk a fine line between flexibility and the need to regularize and strengthen the decision-making process. The regularity of the presidential electoral process and the inevitability of the American cult of personality mean that no single utopian model is feasible. No master system can be designed realistically merely by rearranging boxes on an organization chart. It is also foolhardy to recommend any basic changes without first appreciating what international economic policy is and then how it has been made in this country.

Existing organizational arrangements are unnecessarily disjointed and ineffective. They should be changed. Yet they are not. The reasons for this situation, as well as the means of effecting reforms, are rooted in the fact that most observers view the substance of international economic policy either in a one-dimensional, narrow-minded way or with bewilderment. The first part of this book, therefore, develops the theme that it must be viewed as an entity unto itself, despite its inevitable roots in domestic economic and foreign policy considerations. This initial part concludes by examining the links between substance and organizational considerations. Without this link, the question of organization would be irrelevant and research would then logically be limited to technical and theoretical economic studies. In fact, substance is frequently shaped by organizational considerations and by bureaucratic actors with varying perspectives and interests they seek to enhance.

The next step in the process is to examine empirically the organizational process at work, that is, the procedures of international economic policy making. Such an assignment is more difficult than it would appear. A truly representative selection of case studies would require literally dozens of studies and a massive effort far beyond the scope of this work. The tendency for international economic decisions to be made in an extraordinary and idiosyncratic manner creates sampling difficulties. A small, but representative list would be extremely difficult to design with objectivity as the objective. A list chosen on a completely random basis would probably provide few lessons on any permanent or universal basis. On the other hand, a carefully chosen selection could stack the deck in favor of a preordained conclusion.

The means out of this research dilemma is adoption of a varied, eclectic approach. The policy-making system is examined first by moving from the general to the specific: from basic models of decision making to employing case studies to illustrate the models in practice. Next, a few individual events are examined, more because of special interest than the precedents they set. Finally, a detailed examination is made of the key functional question of coordination. This empirical exercise then leads to a critical evaluation of what is good, bad, and immutable in the U.S. system.

A final assumption of this phase of the study is that the means by which the principal economic partners of the United States are organized to formulate and implement international economic policy should be examined. Not only are there possible lessons and techniques to be learned, but U.S. organization must be reasonably compatible with its counterparts.

After an exposition of how an optimal system would function in practice, the raw materials are now ready to be blended together to produce the final product: suggested changes in organizational arrangements. Some are perhaps too far-reaching or idealistic for it to be assumed that they would be quickly or easily embraced by key bureaucratic actors. However, if probability of immediate enactment were the central criterion, this book would more appropriately take the form of a brief letter from the author to his congressman. Some proposals involve structural change in the means by which policy options are considered. Others are more modest, producing only a better-oiled engine, not a radically different motor. Suggested changes are offered in terms of practicality and intellectual soundness, not on the basis of projected popularity in the bureaucracy.

All in all, this study is more a beginning than a definitive statement. The literature on international economic policy is still relatively primitive. Its quantity and quality do not do justice to the distinctness and importance of the subject. The gulf must be narrowed in the case of foreign policy practitioners' lack of appreciation of the forces of economics in international economic policy. The gulf must be narrowed in the lack of appreciation of the global political impact of U.S. international economic policy. Acceptance of the latter as a distinct policy area is the best and quickest way of closing both gaps. This policy is too gigantic a fusion of political and economic factors to be a subordinated phenomenon.

Reasonable people may disagree with this thesis. They may also disagree with the recommendations. Second only to actual acceptance of most of the recommended reforms, the success of this effort should be measured by its ability to provoke thought and thereby engender a lengthy and provocative debate about the making of the international economic policy of the United States.

## NOTE

1. William Wallace, *The Foreign Policy Process in Britain* (London: Royal Institute of International Affairs, 1975), pp. 5–6.

# SUBSTANCE

# 1

## THE CONTENT OF
## U.S. INTERNATIONAL
## ECONOMIC POLICY

The plain fact is that the United States now has no discernible foreign economic policy.

*Wall Street Journal* editorial

## SCOPE AND DEFINITION

The international economic policy of the United States encompasses the means by which the government influences and controls how the private sector and certain governmental programs interact with the economies of other countries. This process is managed unilaterally, bilaterally, and multilaterally. Private international interactions occur in a number of sectors: trade, finance, investment, transportation, tourism, and so on. Governments intrude in these operations of commercial origin to set the general ground rules (for example, tariffs) and to assure that international economic intercourse does not conflict with domestic economic policy or foreign-policy priorities, that is, the economic and physical security of their citizens. Some policies involve government actions on behalf of the private sector. Other portions of international economic relations consist of exclusively government-to-government actions.

International economic relations, narrowly defined, embrace the full spectrum of transnational business techniques: merchandise trade transactions, services (for example, transportation), foreign investment, and financial flows. Also included are governmental discussions involving official economic policy considerations, such as monetary reform and foreign economic aid, as well as issues where economics covers the surface of sensitive political-national security concerns, such as energy and oceanic resources. A broad definition would encompass most of the new generation of interdependence issues: joint scientific and technological efforts such as pollution abatement and increased food production. Another way of quantifying international economic policy is to define it as "the sum total of actions by the nation-state intended to affect the economic environment beyond the national jurisdiction." It is a hybrid, combining general elements of foreign policy as well as economic policy in general.[1]

The mechanics and goals of U.S. international economic policy go beyond concern with cultivating a favorable international environment. They are greatly concerned with the need to respond to the domestic political pressures that demand a favorable, that is, prosperous, domestic economic environment. The external sector is an increasingly important determinant of this prosperity. In a sense international economic policy becomes a means to the end of both domestic and foreign political success. The need to pursue both ends creates the situation whereby domestic economic policy objectives and foreign policy priorities forever are meeting at the intersection of international economic policy. The latter is therefore intrinsically concerned with the nucleus of the other two policy areas. Like domestic economic policy, it is responsible for determining the allocation of scarce resources relative to insatiable demands, as well as influencing employment and price patterns. At the same time, this policy is concerned specifically with national security, that is, preservation of the state's physical integrity and political values. In general, it is concerned both with contributing to a more prosperous domestic economy and to a more harmonious prosperous global political environment.

This duality of character means that international economic policy can be coopted by states to promote either domestic priorities or international political and economic priorities. The problem is that both priorities normally cannot be successfully pursued simultaneously in international economic relations.

Depending on the subject matter and the exigencies of the moment, U.S. international economic relations may experience a range of government involvement from full-scale to none at all. The various forms of international economic relations are conducted by a number of different actors on a number of different levels—domestic business and foreign business, domestic business and U.S. government, domestic business and foreign government, U.S. government and foreign government, two governments and one business (for example, an expropriation dispute), or two industries and one government (for example, antidumping proceedings). Furthermore, when the government encounters the private sector, it by no means deals exclusively with businessmen. Workers, trade associations, legal counsel, and consumer groups are all part of the public participatory process.

International economic policy can be made to serve a variety of economic interests. Pursuit of liberal trade policies leads to a more rational allocation of resources and therefore to lower-cost production. This is in everyone's economic interest in the long run. But in the short run, politicians are responsive to the minority who perceive themselves to be hurt by market forces. The economics book is no guide to policy actions. Imposition of special tariffs or quotas usually benefits only a special-interest group. Transfer of resources to a developing country serves no domestic interest in the short run, but is in the economic interest of the recipients. A few actions, such as the export controls on soybeans, are inimical to everyone's economic interests and unsettling to foreign-policy considerations as well.

If a purely market-oriented model served as the basis of international economic relations, governmental involvement would be almost nonexistent. International economic policy per se also would be minimal. Since the trend of economic policy management is clearly in the opposite direction, that is, away from laissez faire, the scenario of a reduced governmental role in international economics is pie in the sky. The two major responsibilities of nation-states, the national defense and national prosperity, are close to being coequals in rank. Senior officials play close heed to both.

International economic policy straddles these two most important objectives of national sovereign nation-states—national security and economic well-being. Each is so important to every government that each has generated a large bureaucracy operating in two different worlds. International economic policy thereupon becomes a target of both camps. It is usually viewed by policy makers not as a separate or distinctive phenomenon, but rather as a subordinate tool to accomplish either international or domestic objectives. Indeed, international economic policy must serve two masters. It is not an independent phenomenon with exclusive ingredients. But it is more than the simple sum of its parts.

U.S. international economic policy is different in scope from those of other countries because the U.S. role in world affairs is extraordinary. There are three principal reasons for this. One is the simple quantitative involvement of the U.S. private sector in the world economy, via trade, finance, and investment. The second is the qualitative one devolving from possession of the world's reserve and transactions currency. The final factor is the U.S. role as political superpower, leader of the non-Communist world, and chief military guarantor against the proliferation of governments unfriendly to the free world. In other words it is the chief container of communism.

The international economic policies of most other countries can be based on a more straightforward concern with promoting exports, fostering the growth of favored domestic industries, minimizing unemployment, attracting foreign investment capital, ameliorating the greater excesses of multinational corporations, and placating the demands of countries who are principal suppliers of critical raw materials. The "Plowden Report" of 1964 surveyed the entire purpose and structure of the British diplomatic service and concluded:

> The survival of Britain, let alone her influence, depends on trade. The work
> of our representatives overseas must be increasingly dedicated to the support
> of British trade. Economic and political motives intertwine throughout our
> foreign policy and have always done so; but economic and commercial work
> has now assumed a position of fundamental importance. It must be regarded
> as a first charge on the resources of the overseas Services.[2]

The perspective of a country with the global objectives of the United States perforce must be broader. Policy reflects purposes. "Our purpose is not simply to defend but to construct, not simply to react to events in a world which others shape but to initiate so as ourselves to shape a world order in which we can live peaceably and prosper."[3]

U.S. international economic policy interests are all-encompassing and pervasive in terms of the world economy. But at times this policy relegates economics purely to a means to political ends. Our short-term commercial interests at times have been subordinated to the long-term salutary effects of a modest unilateral transfer of our wealth to struggling countries abroad. However, this country no longer is sufficiently insulated from foreign competition to do that with a minimum of domestic impact or debate. Our relative international economic strength has declined, just as our immediate postwar economic recovery policies in Japan and Western Europe were brought to a successful conclusion. The result is a profound change in the substance of our policy and in the method by which the United States formulates this policy. This government moved to a point in 1971 where it abdicated its world leadership role, at least momentarily, to protect domestic considerations.

## HISTORICAL OVERVIEW

There are two principal characteristics of the evolution of U.S. international economic policy. The first is that its historical life span is relatively brief. The second is that one major shift in policy priorities has occurred, and a new balancing effort is underway. An activist and a broadly based policy is essentially a post-World War II creature, one whose birth dates back only to the Bretton Woods Agreement of 1944. Prior to this time, the U.S. tradition in this area had a blend of economic isolation and economic nationalism. "Before the mid-1930s the United States paid little attention to international economic problems; on the occasions when it was forced to do so, it played a lone hand without much regard for the interests of other countries."[4] Abstinence was by no means total. For example, the United States was heavily involved in the financial aftermath of World War I: debt renegotiations and German reparations. But in the main, the executive branch did little more than articulate attitudes; there was little vigorous pursuit of specific policy objectives across the foreign economic spectrum.

A systematic, clearly articulated U.S. international economic policy did not begin until the emergence of the United States as a superpower and the structural shifts in the world economy following the Second World War. Prior to 1945, the dollar was not the linchpin of the international monetary system; the U.S. balance of payments experienced the same constraints as other countries. The poor countries were mainly colonies of European countries, and there was no U.S. foreign-aid program. The multinational corporation existed, but far from a magnitude that caused any meaningful repercussions or controversy.

Trade policy, at least prior to the New Deal era, ranged from primitive to nonexistent. The Congress established the U.S. tariff schedule mainly on the basis of placating particular constituents' demands. The latter were usually protectionist, and in the first 140 years of the Republic, U.S. tariffs were inflexible and protective. Since it had miniscule discretionary tariff-setting authority, the executive branch's duties in the trade sector mainly involved acting as a collector of customs duties. Trade promotion services were provided abroad by embassy personnel. Occasionally, statements were issued to criticize certain restrictive foreign practices to which the United States objected, for example, the British system of imperial preferences within the empire. For all intents and purposes, however, policy making was nonexistent, except during war years and international conferences such as the London Economic Conference of 1934.

The major breakthrough came in 1934 with the passage of the Reciprocal Trade Agreements Act. This landmark legislation represented the first transfer of tariff-setting authority from the legislative to the executive branch. The State Department thereupon set out to negotiate bilateral reciprocal tariff-cutting agreements within the limits authorized.

The short leash provided by Congress notwithstanding, the statute did represent the beginnings of a calculated operation by the executive branch to influence international economic relations in order to attain domestic economic and foreign-policy objectives. The guiding light behind the legislation, the then Secretary of State Cordell Hull, believed that a clear relationship existed between an open international economy and a peaceful world order. At the same time, however, the immediate objective of the Trade Agreements Program, at least as explained to Congress, was to augment other New Deal efforts. Its particular role was to stimulate the domestic economy out of the depression through an increase in exports. (A reduction in the price of imports and the stimulative effects on other countries were minor afterthoughts in the marketing of this bill.)

The next six years of U.S. international economic policy were devoted to bilateral tariff-cutting negotiations, and some 28 agreements were concluded. By 1940, the clouds of war reappeared. Economic-policy objectives were quickly subordinated to achieving victory: resources were to be denied to the enemy and provided to allies.

World War II irrevocably changed many things. One of the changes was the emergence of an activist, comprehensive U.S. international economic policy. Superpower status had been thrust upon this country initially because of our comparative economic strength. We fruitfully used it in the construction of the Bretton Woods Agreement, which effectively designed the rules and structures of the postwar international economy. In this case, the main impetus was the need to prepare for economic reconstruction and the desire to avoid repetition of the absurd beggar-thy-neighbor economic policies of the 1930s as manifested in exchange rate depreciations. Then came the advent of the cold war and the perceived need to urgently strengthen the free world and contain the spread of Communist aggression. The traditional isolationist posture of the United States was discarded. This country's course was clearly set: the bountiful productivity of its large, strong, and undamaged economy would be used in part to finance the establishment of a first line of defense in Western Europe and Japan.

For upwards of 15 years after the war, U.S. international economic policy was designed to maximize and accommodate its national security needs. Market conditions assured only a minimal threat from import competition. They also dictated a finite overseas market for U.S. exports owing to the war-ravaged world and the emergence from colonialism of desperately poor Asian and African countries. The U.S. economy was invulnerable to import competition, a veritable colossus. Even the acceptance of temporary European discrimination against U.S. goods and of depreciations by other countries relative to the dollar seemed a small price to pay to secure larger political benefits. This sense of magnanimity received a further boost in the form of a growing trade surplus.

Furthermore, in the U.S. Government's mode of thinking, its efforts to foster recovery abroad were fully compatible with assuring the long-term success of the economic institutions it helped to design in 1944. All were designed to promote a liberal international economic system and to discourage a repeat of the disastrous nationalistic economic policies of the 1930s. Financed principally by the United States, the International Monetary Fund (IMF) was created to prevent a resurrection of the beggar-thy-neighbor trade policies of the 1930s. The General Agreement on Tariffs and Trade (GATT) was formulated to provide an impetus to multilateral trade liberalizations. International economic policy, in short, served foreign policy.

Total U.S. hegemony and the very skewed balance of power were transitory phenomena and not a permanent state of affairs. Even with twenty-twenty hindsight, what was completely unexpected was the vigor and speed with which Western Europe and Japan recovered their economic strength and political vigor. The gold-buying spree at the expense of the U.S. Treasury, begun by President de Gaulle in the mid-1960s, signified the beginning of a new era in international economic relations. The real problem was that the system was ill-equipped to react to the structural changes that were at first imperceptible. By the time they had become clearly evident, for example, by the shrinking U.S. trade surplus, the United States was experiencing the reappearance of isolationist feelings, mainly because of the war in Vietnam. The burden of acting as the world's "policeman" had brought considerable disillusion about our role in world affairs and at the same time had further reduced our relative international competitiveness.

The international monetary system was being stretched to its breaking point by the chronic balance-of-payments surpluses of the European Community countries and Japan and the corresponding U.S. external deficits. The very success and dynamism of the international economic order, which the United States had sponsored and led, had done much to undermine it. In the words of a special report submitted to President Richard Nixon in 1971 by the first head of the Council on International Economic Policy (CIEP), Peter Peterson: "the international institutions created after World War II were simply not equipped to deal with these changes, and governments were either disinclined or thought themselves unable to cope effectively with the rapidly changing realities."[5]

For the United States, these "realities" were a trade account moving from the black into the red, increases in domestic consumption being accounted for by increased losses of export markets, and unemployment attributed to foreign competition. Slowly, but steadily, the suspicion spread that the existing international economic order was working against the United States, whose citizens perceived it as being no longer able to "hold its own" in global competition.

> The United States grappled with a stubborn inflation, a deteriorating position in foreign trade, high defense costs, and, beginning in 1969, serious unemployment. Its balance-of-payments deficit, chronic though reasonably stable for two decades, suddenly grew much larger and became subject to alarmist interpretations. Western Europe and Japan, on the other hand, were characterized by prosperity, continuing balance-of-payments surpluses, strong foreign trade positions, and comparatively low defense costs. . . . Did not this contrast between the United States and its once economically prostrate industrial partners mean that there was something "unfair" about the ground rules governing our foreign economic relations and something misguided about our foreign economic policy? Was the United States not overemphasizing the importance of foreign relations in foreign economic policy and thereby paying a heavy economic price?[6]

These questions were all answered in the affirmative when, on August 15, 1971, President Nixon announced the new economic policy. His administration's concern with domestic politics and economics, momentarily at least, had seized control of international economic policy. Concerns with national security were put aside as dollar-gold convertibility was terminated and a 10 percent import surcharge was initiated. Already gone on a de facto basis, the postwar monetary system was ended on a de jure basis. The trading system was given a severe jolt and was set up for a major new round of trade negotiations to deal with the full range of outstanding trade issues. The first historic shift in U.S. international economic policy had occurred with monumental effects.

The era of the foreign-policy imperative had ended. While John Connally, then secretary of the treasury, ran U.S. international economic policy for the rest of 1971, domestic economic considerations were completely dominant. A return to isolation, however, was out of the question. Connally's exclusive concern with domestic priorities was short-lived because serious foreign-policy strains were developing as domestic objectives overrode the needs and interests of U.S. allies.

From the chaos wrought by the fallout of the new economic policy, efforts began for longer-term reforms of the international monetary and trading system. The United States had destroyed the old "liberal" international system in order to save it. The international economy needed quick reconstruction and refinement to reflect the shifts in national economic strengths. For the United States, an entirely new approach to international economic policy was needed, one which meticulously balanced creative, progressive external policies with old-fashioned inward concern with domestic employment and price levels.

This new balancing act would have been different enough in its own right. But within a few months, unprecedented strains would be introduced to severely try the external economic policies of all countries. A simultaneous swing in the international business cycle produced first global inflation and then by late 1974, global deflation. Superimposed on these moves were the unprecedented economic pressures that resulted from the sharp increases in oil prices by the Organization of Petroleum Exporting Countries (OPEC). The problems and promises of international interdependence had reached a major new plateau.

## A SURVEY OF CONTEMPORARY AND FUTURE ISSUES

The overriding contemporary issue in international economic relations is to come to grips with the effects of one era ending and a new one beginning. The post-World War II international economy is over. The world has lost the virtues of a benevolent, hegemonic dictator (the United States) skillfully steering a course of global economic recovery. The system has also lost the luxury of inexpensive petroleum supplies. The emerging new international economic order is still of an uncertain nature. It threatens to be a period of unprecedented economic strains and opportunity alike, one where management, for better or worse, will be done by a committee system composed of many economically significant countries with dissimilar governments and societies.

The central question is whether postwar economic growth and the trend towards a liberal international economic order are aberrations that have reached a plateau, or whether they are the prelude to a new, higher degree of international economic cooperation. It may be that national governments will feel the need to restore protection for domestic groups from external competition. A change of this kind may be the legacy of the fading of the special circumstances existent in the 1945–70 period: rapid postwar economic recovery, cheap energy, the war years being a time that discouraged the opportunity or will to take advantage of international economies of scale, the bipolar international system based on U.S. and Soviet domination, and the benevolent U.S. dominance of the global economy. On the other hand, enlightened self-interest may be the precursor of new patterns of cooperation.

Before specific issues can be resolved, the basic orientation of the international economic order will have to be determined. A critical factor for all countries is that, in most respects, the international economic policy of the United States has been forced to become comparable to that of less powerful countries in many of its emphases and perspectives. The diminution of U.S. leadership in the global economy has not been offset by a rise in European or Japanese constructive leadership. Despite a lingering sense of "world-view" in U.S. policies, this country can block, but it can no longer unilaterally force or promote action. This country can no longer play the role of the "N-minus-one" member of international trade and financial systems, unilaterally accepting export discrimination and running an open-ended balance-of-payments deficit.

The end of the postwar order and the crisis of international economic leadership are reverse sides of the coins of change. Given the increased importance of international economic policy to all countries (see Chapter 2), the stakes are tremendously high. Compounding the problem is the dilemma of an international economic order characterized by the pursuit of conflicting objectives and by the absence of a clearly dominating national presence. An egalitarian decision-making process has appeared simultaneously with the elevation of international economics from "low policy" to "high policy" and with a disintegration of the old economic order. It is this central dilemma that U.S. international economic policy is confronting. The search for a new spirit of cooperation and adaptation is critical.

A number of specific tasks must be undertaken in the context of an untried international economic system. Considerable progress has been made in the direction of international monetary reform. A tacit understanding already has been reached that legitimizes both fixed and floating exchange rates. Similarly, agreements have been reached on enlarging the resources of the IMF and on limiting the monetary role of gold. More specific rules and obligations on exchange-rate management and balance-of-payments adjustment remain to be negotiated.

The multilateral trade negotiations (MTNs) underway in Geneva under the auspices of the GATT are a second set of economic talks with critical importance. On the technical side, the progress, or lack of it, in the so-called Tokyo Round will be a major determinant in shaping the international trading system for the 1980s. On the political side, this new forum of diplomacy provides a litmus test for the willingness of national governments to move up to a new level of interdependence.

The real significance of the Tokyo Round is that it is the first trade negotiation that must come to grips with the reality that the relatively simple task of reducing tariffs on industrial products is close to being completed. A new generation of more complex trade issues is at hand. Agreement on a series of codes is needed now to reduce or eliminate nontariff measures that distort trade flows. To move successfully in this direction, unprecedented infringements on national sovereignty are required. The ultimate issue at the negotiating table is the extent to which national governments are prepared to yield control over sensitive domestic economic practices and policies. This is an issue requiring extraordinary skill and patience by the participants. A further liberalization of trade presupposed that agricultural support programs, government procurement practices, and labeling, safety, and health standards will need to conform to multilateral codes so as not to affect the flow of international commerce. Managed interdependence at this advanced stage creates the need for a radically different approach to international economic policy.

Similarly, the newly emerging interrelated issues of export controls and guaranteed access to foreign supplies will tax the imagination of international economic diplomats. The simultaneous worldwide economic boom of 1973–74 introduced the wrinkle of soaring energy and raw materials prices to international economic relations. Added to the existing challenge of exported deflation (that is, domestic job protection) was the attempt to protect the domestic supply picture in times of excessive demands. Ironically, the United States was one of the major miscreants in this regard. As the world's major exporter of food, the United States in the years ahead probably will be confronted with the frequent dilemma of having to decide on what basis to parcel out relatively scarce food to a hungry, overpopulated world. The potential implications of food power are enormous for the U.S. role in the world.

The future operation of the trade and monetary systems, essentially the province of the industrialized countries, may be dramatically affected by their overall rate of economic growth in the years ahead. The basically liberal international economic order that has flourished in the postwar period is largely a reflection of unprecedented worldwide economic growth. The latter has reduced the overall domestic economic sting of trade and capital liberalization. Should the international secular rate of growth diminish, national concerns with domestic economic stability (mainly jobs) may rise to challenge seriously the international economic principles and guidelines that have been more often adhered to than ignored. In other words, increasing interdependence is a problem in a prosperous global situation. It may be an unbearable burden in a lingering period of economic stagnation and high energy costs.

While economic problems within the industrialized countries are a theoretical possibility, the wolf is already at the door where the developing countries are concerned. The central problem here is how to integrate the developing countries into the mainstream of an international economy that is dominated at present by the industrialized countries. The North-South dialogue is but in its infancy.

The need to materially assist the developing countries shifted from a long-term issue among development specialists to an immediate issue of sensitive proportions as a result of the collective action of the member-countries of OPEC beginning in 1973, in forcing major increases in oil prices. The demonstrated vulnerability of the industrialized world, first to the oil boycott of the Arab exporters and then to the price hikes, meant that the demands of the less developed countries (LDCs) had to be taken more seriously than ever before. The cry for a "new international economic order" has served to initiate an entirely new style of debate between the countries of the North and South.

Foreign aid is no longer enough. It has become necessary to investigate modifications in traditional international trading arrangements (commodity agreements), changes in international investment (easier terms for technology transfer, for example), changes in international finance (debt moratoria), and initiatives in the international monetary system (the special-drawing-rights link to development finance). The plight of the countries of the so-called fourth world, those having no natural resources of any consequence, adds a further complexity to this problem.

Policy in the international investment sector has trailed the trade, monetary, and development sectors in terms of governments coming to grips with the real issues. As host country of the majority of major multinational corporations, the United States will need to be the most responsive to the growing need for rules and institutions to delineate international investment rules of the road. A vacuum has existed for too long on an international consensus concerning the activities and effects of multinational corporations. An international laissez faire attitude cannot hold out against the growing sensitivities of sovereign countries towards foreign investments within their borders. Guidelines will need to be devised for acceptable behavior by host government, home government, and corporation alike, as well as for settlement of disputes. As Fred Bergsten has warned:

> Foreign direct investment and multinational enterprises have now replaced traditional, arms-length trade as the primary source of international economic exchange. . . . [H]ost countries are increasingly adopting explicit policies to tilt in their directions the benefits generated by those enterprises. The

impact of these efforts may turn out to be even greater than their trade predecessors of the 1930s, both because the economic interpenetration of nations is now more advanced than in the 1920s and because governments now pursue so many more policy targets.[7]

The agenda of international economic negotiations is growing rapidly. The issues are not only proliferating beyond pure economics to include cooperation in international energy distribution and development, the law of the sea, and research on population control; they are also proliferating in complexity and political sensitivity. Along with this trend has come a proliferation of international groups and quasi-organizations. In every case the challenge to the international economic policy of the United States and all other countries is clear. A responsive, substantial, and consistent position is necessary in each case. For these reasons, economic discussion is the principal thread of international relations today and will be for a long time to come.

## NOTES

1. Benjamin J. Cohen, *American Foreign Economic Policy* (New York: Harper & Row, 1968), p. 10.

2. *Report of the Committee on Representational Services Overseas* (London: Her Majesty's Stationery Office, 1972), p. 3.

3. Anthony M. Solomon, "Administration of a Multipurpose Economic Diplomacy, *Public Administration Review,* November–December 1969, p. 585.

4. Richard S. Gardner, *Sterling-Dollar Diplomacy* (New York: McGraw-Hill, 1969), p. 1.

5. Peter G. Peterson, *The United States in the Changing World Economy* (Washington, D.C.: U.S. Government Printing Office, 1971), p. iii.

6. Edward Fried, "Foreign Economic Policy: The Search for a Strategy," in *The Next Phase in Foreign Policy* (Washington, D.C.: Brookings Institution, 1973), p. 161.

7. C. Fred Bergsten, "Coming Investment Wars?" *Foreign Affairs*, October 1974, p. 149.

CHAPTER

# 2

## THE CONTEXT OF U.S.
## INTERNATIONAL ECONOMIC
## POLICY

Economic forces are in fact political forces. Economics can be treated neither as a minor accessory of history, nor as an independent science in the light of which history can be interpreted. . . . The science of economics presupposes a given political order, and cannot be profitably studied in isolation from politics.

E. H. Carr

International economic policy operates in a complex environment consisting of domestic as well as external economic and political forces. It does not exist independently. Its existence is a spin-off, a kind of subsidiary, of foreign policy and domestic economic objectives. But international economic policy is three-dimensional, not two-dimensional. It is also a separate, distinguishable policy mode. The balancing of components and the complex context in which this policy functions are the keys to understanding and appreciating its truly distinct nature.

## A DISTINCT PHENOMENON

As noted above, international economic policy is a distinct phenomenon. Neither by process nor substance is it merely the economic branch of foreign policy. Nor is it merely the external dimension of domestic economic policy management. International economic policy is a complex and constantly shifting blend of foreign-policy and domestic-policy considerations. By definition, it touches on the interests and activities of other countries. Depending on the time and the circumstances of a particular issue, concerns about this country's external security and diplomatic relations may be an overriding consideration.

But also by definition, it involves economic issues that touch on the interests and activities of domestic citizens and organizations (private and governmental). Again depending on the time and the circumstances, concerns about internal needs and demands will be the dominant consideration in the policy equation. International economic theory is relevant to a moderate degree, but as a determinant of actual policy, it plays a limited role.

If the quality of U.S. international economic policy is to be increased commensurate with its importance, it will have to be accepted as having a separate identity. The alternative is asymmetrical thinking and unbalanced policy. If there is inadequate appreciation for viewing international economic policy qua international economic policy, the United States will employ second-best organizational arrangements to produce third-best policy.

Unfortunately, international economic policy is seldom analyzed or promulgated on its own terms. Most scholarly treatments of the subject are confined to the economics chapter of a foreign-policy book or the external sector chapter of an economics book. Economic bureaucrat and scholar alike have been trained in a discipline emphasizing rational assessments of cost and benefits. Political scientists study imprecise human behavior, the art of the possible, compromise, and political considerations. International economic policy perforce is dealt with by each of these two schools in the course of larger duties. Each tends to approach the broad field of international economic policy with certain preexisting instincts, knowledge, and objectives, which collectively produce relative narrow-mindedness.

This failure to treat international economic policy as a separate entity increases the tendency for it to be subsumed by one of the dominating bureaucratic camps: foreign policy and domestic economic policy. Pursuit of policy excellence all too often falls victim to the uncertain outcomes of power struggles within the federal bureaucracy.

Two schools of thought on international economic policy are involved. The first views it as being primarily the economic aspect of the pursuit of a stable, secure, and prosperous international environment. Hence, economic considerations must be subordinate to the general objectives of U.S. relations with other nations. The clear implication of this viewpoint is that primary responsibility for formulating an international economic policy consistent with these general objectives must of necessity rest with the ministry of foreign affairs—that is, with the Department of State.

The second—and newer—school approaches it from the economist's point of view. This view maintains that it must be regarded primarily as the external dimension of the U.S. pursuit of a stable, growth-oriented, and fully employed domestic economy. Foreign-policy considerations should be judged in terms of domestic economic—and occasionally domestic political—priorities. Subordinating international economic policy to domestic economic needs and ideology means that primary responsibility for it should rest with the finance ministry—that is, with the Treasury Department.

The inclusion of State and Treasury interests in every major international economic issue is not coincidental. Both agencies usually agree that both the foreign-policy and the domestic economic points of view must be considered. The relative weighting of these two sets of interests is the point of contention. This substantive conflict is expressed in organizational terms as the issue of whether State should have primary jurisdiction and Treasury should have secondary authority, or vice versa. Given the nature both of the contemporary international economic system and of domestic economic and domestic political concerns, the appropriate weights to be assigned to each set of interests vary in all policy matters.

The art of creating optimal international economic policy is based on insuring the prompt collection of all relevant data, articulating goals in domestic and foreign policies, and the continued existence of an objective reconciling force to balance all of the conflicting pressures and reach a quick, coherent decision. The omnipresent need for trade-offs, for reconciling legitimate domestic and foreign needs, is what makes such policy a distinct entity. To approach its formulation by seeking least-common-denominator compromise is unsatisfactory since indecisive policy will result. To approach its formulation by giving one viewpoint dominance is unsatisfactory since skewed policy will likely emerge. Sensible international economic policy making forever must walk the proverbial tightrope. The only constant is the inexorable shifting of the relative importance and immediacy attached to each of its component parts, that is, domestic and international politics and economics. Ideally, international economic policy is the result of thorough, dispassionate analysis of the data and then of a balanced consideration of policy options. At its worst, *this* policy can damage the domestic economy while simultaneously straining U.S. relationships with other countries.

# THE EXTERNAL SECTOR'S IMPACT ON THE U.S. ECONOMY

The external sector has become a major concern of economic policy-making officials because of three major trends. The first and crucial one is the seemingly permanent wave of growing governmental intervention in the economy. The U.S. government has joined with its counterparts in bearing the responsibility for achieving a widening array of economic and social objectives. A major source of political popularity for any democratic government today is its ability to fulfill promises of fostering real economic growth, price stability, full employment, and an equitable distribution of income. The U.S. government, like most other governments, has added to this list concerns for regional economic development and social benefits (for example, food stamps and Medicare).

The extent to which the government has been encroaching on the U.S. economy since World War II can be measured in a number of ways. For example, total governmental expenditures as a percentage of GNP were 13.5 percent in 1950, but had climbed by more than one-half to 21.4 percent in 1974, according to data compiled by the president's Council of Economic Advisers (CEA). In addition, all levels of government currently employ more persons than the entire durable goods segment of manufacturing. Between 1960 and 1974, 17 new independent regulatory agencies were added to the federal bureaucracy, 11 in the last five of those years.[1] A rough estimate by the CEA places the cost burden of total regulatory activities on the U.S. private sector at more than $15 billion annually, about 1 percent of the U.S. GNP.[2]

In the demise of laissez faire policies, the United States has lagged behind other countries. But the series of wage and price controls that began in 1971, together with the rising sentiment in some quarters for increased economic planning, reflect the pervasive Washington interest in the functioning of the economy. Any variable that might upset or threaten the chosen economic policy course is a major concern to the policy maker in this area. The advance of global interdependence accounts for one of the more important of these variables. But on the other hand, external forces also offer additional policy instruments, often of very high value, for the achievement of economic policy objectives by governments that can harness them effectively. This situation produced a tendency for countries to welcome foreign transactions as long as they can assure that it points in desired directions.[3]

The potential of the external sector in providing assistance and hindrance to domestic objectives is reflected in the fact that economic intercourse has increased so rapidly in absolute terms and in relation to domestic economic growth. Perhaps the single most important statistic demonstrating this second major economic trend is the growth of world trade, shown by the following CIEP data:

| Year | World Trade |
|------|-------------|
| 1955 | $ 94 billion |
| 1965 | $188 billion |
| 1975 | $866 billion |

In contrast to this nearly tenfold increase (much of it admittedly induced by inflation and the oil price rise) is the less than sixfold increase in world domestic production, that is, the global GNP. International trade thus was growing more than 50 percent faster than total domestic economic growth. The result is that for the average country, an increase occurred in the proportion of GNP accounted for by foreign trade. For the United States, exports increased from $14 billion in 1955 to $107 billion in 1975, with imports increasing from $12 billion to $96 billion in the same time period. As a result, exports and imports as a percentage of GNP each increased from less than 4 percent to about 7 percent during this time.

The full external-impact story goes beyond exports. It is generally presumed that the value of the total annual overseas production by U.S. corporate subsidiaries and majority-controlled industries amounts to about four times the value of U.S. exports. This would put the annual output of U.S. overseas investment at a figure exceeding $400 billion—more than the GNP of all but the largest half-dozen countries. An estimated 22 percent of total U.S. corporate profits is now accounted for by foreign earnings.[4] The size and efficiency of movement of international funds can thwart the tight monetary policy of the United States (as it did in 1969). Foreign dollar holdings also can, and do, get invested in Treasury securities; this means that a significant portion of the federal debt is financed by foreigners buying liquid dollar assets.

The third trend accounting for a greater impact of the external sector on the U.S. economy, in many respects an amalgam of the two previously noted, involves the growth of intense domestic political lobbying efforts designed to influence external economic programs. U.S. international economic policy became politicized only in the 1960s. In the immediate postwar period, the U.S. economy was so internationally insulated and competitive that no special-interest group felt threatened. A liberal trade policy was politically acceptable across the political spectrum. But as interdependence increased and the bite of import competition was felt with greater severity in the 1960s, special-interest groups perceived their livelihood and interests being threatened. The activities of the AFL-CIO on behalf of the highly protectionist Burke-Hartke bill is the most noteworthy manifestation of this trend. Another is the vociferous dissatisfaction of the farm bloc with U.S. trade policies that developed in the wake of constricted export markets caused by the European Economic Community's (EEC's) common agricultural policy. In sum, the domestic economic departments have been hearing very clearly from their constituents that U.S. international economic policy must reflect the latter's growing vulnerability to the external sector.

## THE IMPACT OF ECONOMICS ON WORLD POLITICS

Economics has long been intertwined with politics in the international system. The prevailing international economic and political systems influence one another. What is different today is that on both the levels of process and of structure, international economic relations have become so important as to have shed their traditionally subordinate, technical function in the international order. The evolution of foreign affairs has ushered in a period when the priorities of sovereign governments and the policy means at their disposal for achieving these objectives have a very high economic content.

The daily relations between virtually all sovereign nation-states have come to be dominated by economic considerations. The threats of, or resort to, military force is an unthinkable consequence of disputes within the first world. Trade, financial, and investment issues dominate international relations in this case; a retaliatory tariff increase or quota is the normal indicator of state displeasure, not a military initiative.

Contemporary relations between the industrialized countries of the North and the developing countries of the South also are dominated by economics. Discussions on the transfer of resources through the pursuit of a new international economic order have displaced the priority of thwarting the spread of communism by winning hearts and minds and by providing splashy aid programs. Commercial relations between East and West, especially between the United States and the Soviet Union, are looked upon as a catalyst for the successful pursuit of political detente.

The pattern of world politics, and specifically U.S. foreign policy, has been altered structurally by the implications of increased global economic interdependence. The broad objectives of any country's foreign policy, in the short run, are survival and the promotion of an international environment most conducive to its immediate physical security. In the long run, the objective is a flourishing of its political and economic values. U.S. foreign policy since World War II has ultimately rested on military strength, conventional and nuclear. An increasingly important second pillar has been international economic policies. The latter can be extended in a positive, friendly manner, such as in the forms of aid and trade liberalization. These policies can also be brandished in a negative, hostile manner: boycotts, export controls, withholding of aid, freezing of assets, and so on.

Indeed, economic relations with other countries have become a principal means of pursuing medium-to-longer-term U.S. foreign-policy goals. Given the nuclear stalemate and the Vietnamese experience, U.S. military options have become circumscribed at the same time that the world is concentrating on improving living standards and the quality of life. These problems require multinational solutions and a commitment of economic resources. A new style of international relations is developing in response to the current reordering of global priorities. "There is no longer a single international system dominated by strategic concerns. Military security remains an important issue, but the new concerns of world trade, energy, food, raw materials, the world monetary system—each one with its own power hierarchy—have arisen."[5]

Influence and power in foreign relations increasingly are becoming functions of economic capabilities. The term "national security" needs to have its definition broadened to include economic strength and stability along with military strength and deterrence. The costs of a global foreign policy are enormous. A strong domestic economic base is therefore a critical prerequisite, at least for a democracy, for assuming superpower status. As the *Wall Street Journal* editorialized, the weaker the U.S. economy gets, the more the secretary of state "must deal from weakness, the less patience the public and Congress have in his free hand, the less regard U.S. allies have for his proposals, the less regard the Soviet Union has for the fundamental economic strength of the United States that should be backing him up but is not. When an economy contracts, its society turns inward, which is not the kind of milieu our Secretary of State can thrive on."[6]

Thanks mainly to the horrors of modern weapons technology and partly to the increased need for multilateral cooperation stemming from the growing economic obsolescence of the nation-state, the pursuit of international power is no longer characterized and measured primarily by resort to warfare.

Concerns with economic issues have expanded not only because of their inherent importance, but because the real margin for international maneuver is concentrated in this sector. Increased economic welfare for a country's citizens, status, and assuring the financial resources to maintain an extensive foreign presence are objectives best pursued by international economic policy. Instruments of economic warfare are being resorted to more frequently as a surrogate for military confrontation when the latter is impractical or too risky. The Arab embargo of oil sales to the United States and the Netherlands in 1973–74, and U.S. export controls vis-a-vis the Communist bloc countries are examples. Another was the effort by the State Department to have the Gulf Oil Corporation withhold royalty payments to the new Angolan government when the Congress prevented resort to traditional destabilizing tactics.

Another factor attracting economics to the conduct of traditional foreign relations is the frequency with which linkages are arising between these two phenomena. Concern with reducing its balance-of-payments deficit has affected U.S. foreign policy in several ways. The U.S. military presence in West Germany since the 1960s has been linked (until 1976) to special offset agreements to defray the foreign-exchange costs of this activity to the United States. The U.S. foreign-aid program was altered in the same period by tying loans to purchases of U.S. goods and services. For different reasons, the Nixon administration implicitly linked its willingness to revert Okinawa to Japanese control to Japanese willingness to accede to its demand for textile export restraints.

## INTERDEPENDENCE: HAS ANYTHING REALLY CHANGED?

The context in which U.S. international economic policy operates is dominated by two important trends. The first is the increased involvement of the U.S. government (as is the case for all other national governments) in the management and manipulation of the domestic economy. The degree of real change in this case can be viewed empirically and has been examined earlier in this chapter. While governments have never callously regarded price and employment levels, it can be argued that the progression, especially in the U.S. case, into micro policies and finely tuned efforts is a modern-day phenomenon. U.S. administrations prior to the 1960s spent little effort pondering the Phillips curve,* protecting the environment, or enforcing a broad range of consumer protection laws.

The second important trend, global economic interdependence, is more difficult to demonstrate as being radically different today than in an earlier period. A part of the problem rests with the development of the term "interdependence" into a popular cliche. Cliches seldom are vigorously defined or scrutinized. Rather than rely on popular conception, the critique of U.S. international economic policy making and proposals for reform should proceed from a firm hypothesis as to what interdependence is and what it implies for the national interest.

In the first place, interdependence per se is not of recent vintage. One measure of interdependence is the extent to which external events intrude into internal developments. Even for the relatively well insulated United States, this intrusion is many years old. In 1949, a government-sponsored study of governmental organization stated that "the traditional line of demarcation between domestic and foreign problems has completely disappeared, and the governmental organization must be shaped to formulate and execute national policies which have both domestic and foreign aspects."[7]

Reliance on foreign supplies is not new, either. Countries have traded with one another for centuries to obtain products not readily available domestically. Throughout the first century of the Unites States, inflows of capital borrowed abroad played a key role in economic development. The Marshall Plan and a deliberate balance-of-payments deficit were the major policy ingredients in the U.S. effort to hasten the recovery of Europe after World War II.

Interdependence, on the other hand, has taken on new importance in quantitative terms. Better means of transportation and communication, together with the demands of high-technology industries for economies of scale, have contributed to what is an unprecedented increase in world trade, both in absolute terms and as a percentage of domestic production, that is, GNP. The specific economic ramifications of these increases is less clear, however. While it might seem plausible to expect that an increased volume of international

---

*A means of graphically illustrating a fundamental dilemma: unemployment is reduced at the expense of increased inflation. This trade-off problem is commonly called the "Phillips curve" in honor of Mr. Phillips, who popularized it.

transactions would be associated with increased sensitivity of economic developments among countries, this link has not been proven conclusively.

Strictly speaking, economic interdependence should be measured by the sensitivity of economic transactions among countries to economic occurrences within those countries. Absolute amounts are less critical than the marginal propensity of change. A large volume of bilateral trade would not in itself constitute a significant level of interdependence unless the trade were sensitive to price, exchange-rate, and income developments in the two countries. Similarly, a low-volume, highly elastic trade flow could qualify as representing interdependence. Furthermore, interdependence presupposes two-way sensitivity; one-way sensitivity leads to a situation in which there is a dependent economy.[8]

Increasingly, world trade appears to be meeting this criterion. A growing sensitivity between increased world trade and increased income seems apparent, even if an increased price sensitivity is less obvious.

Merchandise trade is by no means the only sector of international economic relations experiencing a heightened degree of sensitivity. Increased interdependence also is being registered in international employment levels, primarily through increased labor mobility across national boundaries. International capital flows, for short- and long-term investment, probably represent the greatest actual increase in interdependency as measured on the sensitivity basis. The integration of the world's capital markets, as well as the increased sophistication and financial wherewithal of speculators and international money managers, enables billions of dollars to move daily in immediate response to interest-rate differentials and expectations of exchange-rate movements. Long-term direct investments across national boundaries (that is, multinational corporations) have spread dramatically, generally in response to expectations of greater earnings potential through cheaper labor costs, market-share protection, and so on.

Increased interdependence has been fostered by the increased mobility of capital, labor, and technology. The mobility syndrome directly challenges domestic policies whose successful pursuit presupposes fragmented national markets. As countries become increasingly interdependent, as capital and skilled labor become less exclusively national in their orientations, countries desiring to pursue tax or regulatory policies that deviate widely from these same policies in other countries will find themselves stimulating large inflows or outflows of funds, firms, or persons. These induced movements in turn will weaken the intended effects of the policies, or make them more costly.[9]

A presumed, or psychological, interdependence is the last, but an equally important, qualitative innovation here. The term has been discussed so extensively that there is a perceived degree of high interdependence that transcends any specific or measurable amount. Real or not, interdependence is causing a sense of controversy, discomfort, and cost in the minds of many national decision makers. The Arab oil embargo and problems of certain labor-intensive domestic industries arising from import competition are examples.

> Such controversies indicate that many countries are reaching an awareness that the risks inherent in the rapid growth of international transactions are now outweighing the expected gains. . . . Domestic politicians have recently been trying to insulate the more easily definable domestic political problems from the problems generated by the more dispersed impact of international economic costs and benefits. The result has been that, for the first time in the postwar era, domestic political considerations have been causing political leaders to place more new restrictions on international operations than they are removing or modifying.[10]

The implicit assumption of an advanced state of interdependence was voiced at the 1975 annual meeting of the IMF. Fresh in the minds of the world's officials were the synchronous boom and subsequent recession in the world economy. The duties of the larger countries to lead the rest of the world out of the trough of the business cycle through adoption of more expansionary domestic monetary and fiscal policies received blunt discussion. The IMF's managing director, not sounding like a polite international civil servant, said it was "necessary" to ask the United States, West Germany, and Japan "to conduct demand policies so as to take particular account of the international recession and of the serious constraints felt by many other countries in pursuing an expansionary course." In response, U.S. Treasury Secretary William Simon's address to the IMF acknowledged that his country's economic policies "bear heavily" upon other countries. However, to those advocating a more stimulative economic policy than the United States was pursuing, he replied that "we respectfully disagree." Concern with a rekindling of domestic inflation was said to be the dominant policy constraint.

Another manifestation of presumed interdependence is the extent to which the consensus world economic forecast for 1976 accepted the assumption that the recovery in this country could, and would, engender an export-led recovery in Western Europe. Although the technical weakness of this assumption was later demonstrated, it was widely voiced and never challenged in early 1975. And at the June 1976 ministerial meeting of the Organization for Economic Cooperation and Development (OECD), Treasury Secretary Simon argued that the United Kingdom needed to reduce its budgetary deficit if it expected a renewal of the $5.3 billion international support package obtained (mainly from the United States) to bolster the pounds's exchange rate.

A different way of viewing the interdependence issue is in the growing obsolescence of the nation-state as an entity capable of serving its people's economic needs. Military alliances have been necessary for centuries to augment shortcomings in the defense sector. Recourse to trade blocs and multilateral economic institutions, however, is mainly a twentieth century phenomenon, a kind of institutional interdependence. To reach certain economic objectives, an ever-growing number of multilateral discussions and joint decisions are needed. Examples of this range from creation of man-made liquidity (special drawing rights) to population-control and antipollution efforts. The feelings of interdependence surely are reinforced in policy makers today by the sheer volume of international conferences. New organizations now spring up regularly, such as the International Energy Agency (IEA) and the Conference on International Economic Cooperation (CIEC). All reflect the need to foster global cooperation, lest the international economic system be disrupted. Eventually, a new group probably will be convened on a regular basis at the finance-minister level to follow through on the cooperative spirit demonstrated at the first two economic summit meetings held in 1975 and 1976 at Rambouillet and Puerto Rico.

In many respects, what is really happening is that nation-states are experiencing a greater degree of mutual dependency. Individually, they are unable to do what can be accomplished multilaterally. Literally, interdependence indicates a higher degree of economic vulnerability to shifting economic events in other countries. Looked at from another angle, it pushes technically sovereign states to discuss and coordinate economic actions that previously would have been considered part of the domestic realm exclusively. The six heads of state, who participated at the economic summit at Rambouillet, epitomized the elevation of this coordinating dynamic to the very highest political level.

The need to sacrifice autonomy and sovereignty to achieve desired national goals has major implications for the conduct of foreign policy by the United States and all other countries. There will be increased participation in foreign issues by domestically oriented government departments. To quote Richard Cooper, "increased economic interdependence will result in more varied and more frequent official and semi-official contact between nations—far more than foreign ministries can handle in volume, scope, or technical detail. As a result, the relative importance of foreign ministries in relations among the western industrial countries will decline."[11]

The United States does not escape the forecast, valid for all other industrialized countries, that the perceived and real levels of interdependence in the world economy will increase. This country can be expected to witness a continuing growth in the percentage of domestically produced goods being exported and in the percentage of goods consumed being imported, increased foreign investment in the United States, a growing dependence on foreign supplies of raw materials and energy, and ever more tightly knit international financial markets. The result of this trend is twofold. First, the United States will periodically have to revise its working assumptions about the international economic order. Secondly, we and all other countries will have to conduct our international economic relations better than ever before.

# NOTES

1. Richard Erb, "National Security and Economic Policies: The Challenge to National Security Planning," mimeographed (American Enterprise Institute, Washington, D.C., June 1975), p. 9.

2. Quoted in *The Morgan Guaranty Survey,* March 1976, p. 11.

3. C. Fred Bergsten and Lawrence B. Krause, *World Politics and International Economics* (Washington, D.C.: Brookings Institution, 1975), p. 6.

4. Peggy Musgrave, *Direct Investment Abroad and the Multinationals: Effects on the United States Economy,* Senate Foreign Relations Committee print (Washington, D.C.: U.S. Government Printing Office, 1975), p. 16.

5. Stanley Hoffmann, "Toward a New World Order," New York *Times,* January 11, 1976.

6. "Mr. Kissinger's Problem," *Wall Street Journal,* March 7, 1975.

7. Harvey Bundy, "The Organization of the Government for the Conduct of Foreign Affairs," in *The Commission on Organization of the Executive Branch of the Government* (Washington, D.C.: U.S. Government Printing Office, 1949), Appendix H, p. 1.

8. Richard Cooper, "Economic Interdependence and Foreign Policy in the Seventies," *World Politics,* January 1972, p. 160.

9. Ibid., p. 166.

10. Gregory Schmid, "Interdependence Has Its Limits," *Foreign Policy,* Winter 1975, pp. 193, 195.

11. Cooper, op. cit., pp. 177–78.

CHAPTER

# 3

## THE IMPACT OF
## ORGANIZATION ON
## INTERNATIONAL ECONOMIC
## POLICY

The size and the performance of the existing administrative apparatus impose a certain inflexibility on the direction of policy. Large-scale organizations display a number of characteristics which reduce their responsiveness to political control: attachment to precedent and continuity, loyalty to the organization as such and to its clients, established routines for handling business and established views of the environment in which they operate. . . . Decisions once made must be followed through; where political objectives conflict with organizational habits or objectives, they are likely to gain ground only slowly.

William Wallace

The international economic policies of the United States are the outgrowth of four basic factors: the values, ideologies, and personalities of the president and his senior political-economic advisers; the sentiment of Congress; trends and events overseas; and the organization in the executive branch by which policy is constructed. The first two factors reflect the preferences of U.S. voters. The third is largely beyond the control of any one country. The final variable, organization, is the easiest to control and the subject of this book. It is therefore deserving of intensive analysis.

Organizational variants and bureaucratic behavior patterns are important, if not critical, variables in determining policy substance. U.S. international economic policy is frequently a reflection of organizational dynamics, namely the procedures for reconciling values and goals. Individuals articulate and defend these values and goals, but there is a high correlation between the positions taken by individuals and their bureaucratic affiliation. In effect, role playing becomes the first stage of policy formulation. The second stage is the

27

efficiency with which organizational processes reconcile competing intrabureaucratic concerns and perspectives.

## THE BUREAUCRATIC-POLITICS MODEL OF DECISION MAKING

The study of the U.S. foreign policy has undergone a major shift in
emphasis. No longer is policy attributed simply to the construction of a national interest-related, power-seeking response by a unitary, rational actor,
that is, the federal government. The bureaucratic-politics model dismisses
grand theories of policy, be they pragmatism or imperialism. The model doubts
that events in international politics consist essentially of deliberate, purposive
acts of unified national governments or that their behavior can be understood
as being analogous to the intelligent, coordinated acts of individual human
beings. Devil theories, conspiracies, and the gross incompetence of the bureaucracy are all discarded as determinants of policy.

What the bureaucratic-politics model does suggest is that, in most instances, government policy can best be understood in terms of the outcome of
bargaining among participants in various parts of the bureaucracy. Policy
emanates not from a centralized, objective decision maker, but from a con-
glomerate of large organizations and political actors with different missions,
different perceptions, and different priorities. Frequently disagreeing among
themselves about what their government should do on a particular issue,
bureaucracies compete against each other in attempting to determine both
governmental policies and actions.[1]

Bureaucratic units having jurisdiction in a policy sector negotiate among
themselves when considering the formulation of U.S. policy. Each unit has a
reasonably predictable visceral reaction to policy issues, which determines the
departmental position to be presented and defended in interagency groups.
These reactions are directly related to bureaucratic "essence"—the dominant
view held in each organization concerning its mission and needs. The actual
technique of bargaining is affected by existing organizational arrangements.
So, too, are the outcomes of the negotiations. In any event, the individual
positions of the bureaucratic players in international economic policy could
generally be predicted in specific instances if one knows merely how each
organization perceives its own overall self-interest. Bureaucratic officials seldom have an a priori vision of a common approach to an issue. They seldom
are venal or stupid. Rather, they are all searching, but from different angles.
In point of fact, few situations suggest a response or course of action that is
unambiguously, unequivocally correct and consonant with everyone's priorities and preferences. More often than not, policy is determined by a committee-
bred consensus that everyone can live with, that is, a line of least resistance,
not a font of dynamism.

Shared perceptions of broad principles held by all in the bureaucracy can render the normal bargaining process unnecessary. In the case of international economic relations, the desirability of promoting essentially free market-oriented trade and investment systems is universally accepted within the U.S. government as being good policy. It is thus a shared perception, as is the need in principle for the rich countries to financially assist the poorer countries. However, conflicting microactions and micropolicies can, and do, fall within the broad limits set by these perceptions. When the virtue of an action or policy is ambiguous and uncertain, as is generally the case, a quick consensus is rare, despite a few shared images.

At any given moment, divergent viewpoints can exist on the precise means of proceeding towards a stable, growing, and equitable market-oriented world economy. In studying international economic policy or foreign policy, it is insufficient to say that the United States seeks global prosperity in the former and seeks to protect and enhance its security in the latter policy area. Such generalizations afford very little predictive power concerning policy specifics. Similarly, they ignore the fact that if these two objectives prove to be mutually exclusive vis-a-vis a specific issue, priority weights will have to be apportioned on a case-by-case basis. If we are to explain and anticipate a nation's international economic policy decisions and actions, we must first identify the various participants of the bureaucracy, discover the sources of their particular perceptions of the national good, and seek to understand the process of interaction that yields decisions and actions. This process of identification would be of enormous value in determining how U.S. interests are measured and what resources could be utilized to pursue these interests.

Given the imprecision of the social sciences, the form of international economic policy is subjective in nature. To those who argue that "good policy is good policy," the question that must be asked is: Who is to determine exactly what is good policy at a given moment? In the case of U.S. international economic relations, the answer is that it must be a joint or group effort among dozens of executive branch departments, agencies, and offices. The system is not built to allow major decisions by one department in callous disregard for the views of others. Indirectly, this effort includes congressional preferences and the viewpoint of organized public opinion as expressed by corporations, trade associations, labor unions, and consumer and environmental groups.

The interaction of these groups is the raw material of U.S. international economic policy, just as it is in the case of traditional national security-related foreign policy. Certain principles of the bureaucratic politics model are applicable to economic-policy interaction: government officials will examine any policy proposal, at least in part, to determine whether it will increase the effectiveness with which the mission of their particular organization can be carried out. Their organizational responsibilities will help to define for these officials the nature of the issue as they see it.[2]

Policy officials' viewpoints (at least on the record) typically become identified closely with those of their agency, which is where their careers, reputations, and professional self-esteem are made or broken. In the course of his duties, the typical public servant seldom perceives any major conflicts either between his personal views and those of his organization, or between his organization's attitude and his view of the national welfare. In the first place, persons are not likely to be attracted to, or to flourish in, organizations whose missions are antithetical to their personal values. Few persons who are antagonistic to utilizing negotiations as a means of pursuing international harmony would be attracted to the foreign service. An antagonism towards big business would discourage career employment with the Commerce or Treasury Departments. Furthermore, barring crass hypocrisy, most bureaucrats who have developed a philosophic difference of opinion would seek transfer to another agency.

The image of the U.S. government employing a unitary strategy to march lockstep towards an international economic grand design is a chimera. Individual actions and policies are better understood—and are predictable—as the end products of ceaseless bureaucratic maneuvers, which only occasionally are dominated by the objective intellectual merits of the issue. In the abstract, countries do pursue broad national interests. But bureaucracies play politics. They pursue individual values and goals in a milieu of differing opinions. They seek to maximize these values by using their own resources and capabilities to determine what exactly is "good policy." Each bureaucracy is created to perform a specified function. Bureaucrats are paid to worry about a relatively narrow aspect of overall U.S. interests. "All organizations seek *influence;* many also have a specific *mission* to perform; and some organizations need to maintain expensive *capabilities* in order to perform their mission effectively."[3]

There are five key factors that influence a government organization's performance and motivations:

1. Essence—the view held by the dominant members of the organization as to what the main capabilities and primary mission of the organization should be.

2. Domain—where the operations of one organization end and those of another begin.

3. Autonomy—the desire of an organization to control its own resources so as to preserve what it views as its essence and to protect its domain against encroachment.

4. Morale—the means of preserving the loyalty of personnel, of assuring that they are motivated, and of fostering their belief that their jobs are important and worthwhile.

5. Budgets—which are protected and promoted to provide the resources necessary to accomplish the organization's mission and permit it to remain bureaucratically autonomous.[4]

## THE RELATIONSHIP OF THE ORGANIZATIONAL PROCESS
## TO POLICY SUBSTANCE

The organizational process by which international economic policy is formulated cannot erase the dynamics of bureaucratic politics, but it can control or distort them. An organization will pursue a certain viewpoint commensurate with its perceived mission and self-interests under any conventional arrangement. The success or failure of its drive to maximize certain values will be a function of the extent to which the government's decision-making process listens to and takes seriously the various bureaucratic inputs. An overall organization that is biased in favor of, or against, certain agencies probably will tilt policy initiatives in certain directions. Assuming the bureaucratic politics process is operating within an efficient overall process and in a democratic environment, a balanced policy is more probable than in a situation where the environment is controlled by a "benevolent despot" operating with a clear presidential mandate and an equally clear policy orientation. The policy-making process is a political process.

The impact of organization on the substance of policy cannot be described or predicted with precision. Furthermore, economics, being more an art than a science, would present limitations on policy prognosis under any type of organization. The reasons for the importance of government organization and procedures in general were well summarized by the Murphy Commission and are relevant here:

> Good organization does not insure successful policy. Nor does poor organization preclude successful policy. But steadily and powerfully, organizational patterns influence the effectiveness of government.
>
> Policymaking on any subject of importance requires adequate information, careful analysis of the implications of that information, consultation with the various parties legitimately concerned, and balanced assessment of the alternative courses of action. Once a decision is made, it must be clearly communicated to those responsible or affected by it, carefully monitored in its implementation, and evaluated for its actual effects. . . .
>
> But organization affects more than the efficiency of government; it can affect the outcome of decisions. Organizational patterns determine the probabilities that a decision will be taken at one level rather than another, or in one agency instead of another.[5]

The question of the impact of organization in this case should be divided into two reasonably distinct processes. The primary one is how the different goals, perspectives, self-interests, and ideas of the participating bureaucracies are to be introduced and assigned weights and priorities. The existence or nonexistence of particular departments and offices, the distribution of powers, procedures for concurrence or consultation, and staffing patterns are organizational arrangements that present advantages and disadvantages to competing interests. The key question in organizing, therefore, is, specifically: Which perspectives are introduced, when, and with what weights in the processes of decision and action? The key is to assure that before the government embraces a given policy, all important interests will be represented, and that the weights accorded to competing considerations will be appropriately balanced and reviewed in a timely fashion.

The struggle to maximize the impact of one's own values in the weighting process is the heart of bureaucratic politics. Energetic bureaucracies seek to do this by protecting their domain and autonomy and by enhancing their budget. Sheer size can be an effective tool in the bureaucratic struggle by assuring that a pool of talent is available first to provide an agency position and then to overwhelm competing agencies with a barrage of expertise and argumentation. An agency's having the chairman of an interagency working group can be turned to its advantage if it is possible to dominate the setting of the agenda or the selection of participating organizations. The control of communications from overseas embassies and delegations or of data reported by the private sector (for example, crop forecasts and harvests) are powers that, if used selectively, can affect the delicate balancing of the weighting process. Recourse can be made to the power and influence of constituents or allies in the private sector and in the Congress as an aid to the intrabureaucratic struggle.

Access to the president's Oval Office is another organizational means of affecting policy. This can be done by being the last official to talk with the president before he decides a delicate issue, or by being able to add a cover note commenting on the memoranda submitted by the responsible departments on a given matter; or, it may be the power to write the memorandum to the president on behalf of the departments and agencies involved in policy formulation; finally, it may be the method itself by which the bureaucracy makes policy recommendations to the president. President Eisenhower's wanting a unified recommendation from his advisers often led to a watered-down consensus being the standard procedure. In contrast, President Nixon's wanting to see all of the options allowed the extreme range of viewpoints to be brought before the president's attention. In one documented case (Nixon's renunciation of U.S. chemical and biological warfare capabilities), the difference in presidential memo styles affected the substance of policy by impelling the president to upset the long standing status quo.

The second and lesser process normally precedes the weighting process —it may be broadly categorized as the support function. Included here would be personnel training and practices; lines of communication and authority; liaison with groups outside the executive branch; and information—intelligence, analysis, and planning. In terms of the stages of policy making, this category would emphasize problem identification, data collection, and evaluation stages. The viewpoint weighting category would emphasize the enunciation of options and actual decision stages.

Organizational issues, in sum, are much more than academic ponderings as to where to move boxes on a chart. They involve struggles for position and power. By making it easier for some officials than for others to have access to the most senior ranks, by providing for the accumulation of one kind of information and not another, or by following procedures that let some problems rise to the top of the government's agenda before others, some organizational procedures facilitate certain kinds of policy while other procedures facilitate other kinds of policy.[6]

## THE BUREAUCRATIC POLITICS OF INTERNATIONAL ECONOMIC POLICY

There is no single answer to the question, What is the ultimate overriding objective of U.S. international economic policy? Is it to prevent international chaos and warfare? Is it to contribute to the domestic political base of the Democratic or Republican parties? Is it to increase the relative wealth and comfort of U.S. citizens? Is it to contribute to a better distribution of the world's income? Or is it to serve as an external outlet to increase the profits of those sectors of U.S. industry venturing into international business transactions. To resort to cliche, honorable people can differ. To use logic, the answer includes all of the above. There cannot be one answer for overall policy for any extended period of time. International economic policy on a day-to-day basis requires the constant reconciliation between ever-changing priorities in domestic politics and economics and overseas politics and economics. These competing interests cannot be quantified and assigned fixed weights over an extended time period.

As a consequence, there can be no unambiguous, self-apparent strategy or tactics in U.S. international economic policy on a permanent basis. Trade-offs are required in the policy formulation process. Strategy becomes a series of variations on a number of themes. Even when general agreement existed that national security concerns were dominant, there was no unanimity as to exactly which tactics would best serve national security priorities. The current coequal status of national security and domestic economic concerns serves to multiply the need to reconcile competing interests within the federal bureaucracy. Rather than a methodical process of determining what is in the overall national interest under such circumstances, inexact shortcuts are more likely to be used. The policy search seeks out the acceptable, not necessarily the excellent.

There are many instances when direct presidential intervention or perfectly shared perceptions in the bureaucracy have negated the effects of bureaucratic politics on international economic policy. An example of the first situation was the crude bullying of Japan between 1969 and 1971 by the Nixon

White House to restrict that country's textile exports to our market. Not only did this policy violate the basic U.S. preference for market forces over governmental intervention, it excluded any meaningful participation by the line departments. On the question of whether to limit new foreign direct investment abroad or within the United States, there is a bureaucratic consensus that the national interest requires an essentially "open-door" approach. Similarly, a consensus exists on the merits of flexible exchange rates over fixed ones.

The majority of efforts at international economic policy making, however, must follow from a basic dilemma: Is a strong, stable domestic economy the prerequisite for an effective, domestically popular U.S. involvement in the world order in general and in international economic relations in particular? Or is an accommodating, flexible international economic policy the means of assuring national security in a favorable world environment at the tolerable cost of occasional, limited financial losses to certain sectors of the domestic economy? International economic policy is simultaneously subtle and complex. This situation encourages bureaucratic participants to regularly argue different, predictable points of view.

The general principles of bureaucratic politics are similar in the cases of both national security and international economic policies. The presence of bureaucratic disagreement is assured in the latter area for three reasons: the larger number of bureaucratic participants involved; the pervasively unclear lines of jurisdiction, or domain; and the imprecision of economics, wherein economists continually differ on both technical analyses and policy prescriptions. On questions of defense and military operations, a pattern of shared responsibilities has developed between the National Security Council (NSC), the Pentagon, the State Department, and the Joint Chiefs of Staff. But a far messier, overlapping pattern exists in the international economic area. Not only does primary jurisdiction vary according to the sector involved (trade, investment, and so on), but even within the same sector, considerable confusion and overlap exist. This pattern of fragmentation unfortunately is repeated in the corresponding jurisdictions of the congressional committee system.

The jurisdictional arguments that arise frequently in international economic policy formulation are surrogates to a significant degree for deep-rooted cleavages of basic objectives, perspectives, and self-interests. Discussions of jurisdictional and coordinating problems often mask what are really conflicts over the priorities of the two fundamental approaches to the subject. International economic policy can be viewed as being *primarily* an extension of domestic economic policy management, or as *primarily* the economic aspect of foreign regulations. The resolutions of these conflicts indicate which bureaucratic players have the most power and influence in translating their objectives into actual policy. This is a very healthy exercise if reasonably controlled to prevent prolonged or excessive argumentation. It must be remembered that right answers are elusive, and by definition, a number of factors must be inserted into a valid calculation of the national interest in international economic relations.

Bureaucratic politics in this area reaches its zenith in the rivalry between the State and Treasury departments. This is no coincidence. The former is the most important department in the conduct of U.S. foreign policy; the latter is the most important department in the conduct of domestic economic policy. Each department has extensive interests and resources, and each has a very different perception of its mission. The key to most policy formulation is the reconciliation of their two missions, that is, pursuit of a harmonious world order versus pursuit of a stable, prosperous domestic economy. In matters of food policy, the U.S. Department of Agriculture (USDA) substitutes for Treasury, in name only, to pursue domestic values, sometimes against State's foreign priorities.

The power to influence economic policy formulation normally is concentrated in these three departments. Only in special circumstances, such as White House-run operations, budgetary matters, or clashes between economic theory and commercial policy, are other departments and agencies the primary actors.

A compromise or a common position between State and Treasury normally is tantamount to the establishment of U.S. international economic policy, except when extraordinary congressional pressures are applied. There are many instances when their perspectives and goals coincide, such as the need for a hard-line American attitude to the oil price increases by the OPEC cartel and a disinclination to impose quotas on specialty steel or footwear imports in response to escape-clause recommendations by the International Trade Commission in 1976. In other cases, there are only minor nuances in their policy recommendations. Disagreements stemming from their dissimilar missions, values, and internal structures are innumerable but not inevitable.

The Department of State has overall charge of the design and conduct of American foreign policy. Other things being equal, that organization's perspective will emphasize the needs and sensitivities of other countries as well as their responses to U.S. policies. The department will argue the need to prevent the isolation of the U.S. position on international issues, and it will defend the utility of give-and-take negotiations to promote agreement and international harmony. Given the role of world leadership assumed by the United States, the State Department is not happy when other countries are unhappy with U.S. indifference to their legitimate economic interests.

Although the attitudes and actions of other countries are legitimate, necessary factors in policy formulation, the perception of the State Department as a knee-jerk spokesman for foreigners has grown so extensively that it is more relevant than whatever is the real situation. This perception has weakened the department's credibility in the policy-making process, especially in Congress. State is also disadvantaged by having no natural domestic constituency (as do the Treasury, Commerce, Agriculture, and Labor Departments) from which to gain additional support from outside the bureaucratic system.

The State Department view is also affected by the existence of an extensive foreign-service subculture and by the fact that it is a career service set apart from the main-line civil service. The subculture syndrome includes the beliefs that the only experience relevant to the activities of the department is experience gained in the foreign service and that the really important aspects of the foreign affairs of the United States are the political ones, and a hostility toward management and planning. Once an idea is imbedded into the subculture, it tends to be taken for granted. The career-service syndrome "may encourage parochialism, undue self-satisfaction, a low estimate of the value of other agencies and groups, excessive caution, organizational rigidity, and an intolerance of change."[7]

Previously, both of these forces came together to produce an indifference towards the need for maximizing the department's competence in international economic matters. Prior to the belated discovery that economic issues were here to stay, and that the foreign service was losing clout because of its lack of economic expertise, an actual career disincentive existed for foreign-service officers specializing in economics rather than political affairs. Changes in recruiting and promotion techniques have eased this situation. Nevertheless, the hiring of senior economists on a lateral entry basis is all but unknown in the department at the present time. Overall, the approach of State to international economic policy today is still influenced by the inevitable priorities of bright, career-oriented people who are being paid to be responsive to a foreign viewpoint and who are usually looking ahead to their next overseas assignment.

The erasure of the demarcation line between foreign and domestic concerns means that the Treasury Department has demonstrated a continuing and significant leadership role in the international sphere since the 1950s. A profound effect on the policy-making process has resulted from the different values and missions that are associated with the Treasury. Whereas State has been active in the foreign arena since the founding of the Republic, Treasury's continuing involvement has been both relatively recent and sudden. It has relatively little tradition or experience, therefore, in dealing with and accommodating the policies of other sovereign countries. It judges friendly countries not so much on a military basis as in terms of their impact on the American economy. Whereas State's values are rooted in international political cooperation, Treasury's values are rooted in the pursuit of a healthy U.S. economy and preservation of such basic capitalistic principles as the market mechanism. This fosters an insular approach based on economic orthodoxy.

Just as businessmen look for profits, Treasury and Commerce look to the advancement of American domestic economic interests and values as the indicator of sound international policy. The implication of this is that the

Treasury tends to have a "nondifferentiated-adversary attitude" towards international relations. Allies deserve no special economic favors at the cost of the domestic economy. Unlike State, which primarily deals with and worries about foreign governments, and Defense, which worries about foreign military bases, the Treasury Department has relatively little dependency on the goodwill of other countries.

The Treasury Department as an organization has capitalized on the fact that the performance of the economy has become critically important to the fortunes of the incumbent president and his party. Aided by a succession of strong secretaries in the 1971-76 period, a large, influential organization has been built. No other line department has Treasury's number of professionally trained international economists. No other department has established such an extensive series of links with congressmen and business and financial leaders. These outsiders generally are more knowledgeable and have greater personal stakes in international economic relations than in foreign political questions. In general, their domestic orientation and emphasis on fiscal soundness coincide with the Treasury's approach.

It now takes a very strong secretary of state to neutralize the greater domestic political appeal and stronger alliances of the Treasury Department. An examination of the machinery to administer U.S. international economic policy will suggest just how departmental strengths are apportioned.

## NOTES

1. Graham Allison and Morton Halperin, *Bureaucratic Politics: A Paradigm and Some Policy Implications*, Reprint 246 (Washington, D.C.: Brookings Institution, 1972), p. 42.

2. Morton Halperin and Arnold Kanter, *Readings in American Foreign Policy* (Boston: Little, Brown, 1973), p. 10.

3. Ibid.

4. Ibid., pp. 10–11.

5. [Report of the] *Commission on the Organization of the Government for the Conduct of Foreign Policy* (Washington, D.C.: U.S. Government Printing Office, 1975), p. 21.

6. Roger Hilsman, *The Politics of Policy Making in Defense and Foreign Affairs* (New York: Harper and Row, 1971), p. 152.

7. Andrew M. Scott, "The Department of State: Formal Organization and Informal Culture," *International Studies Quarterly,* March 1969, pp. 3, 6.

PART

**II**

**PROCEDURE**

# 4

## WASHINGTON'S
## POLICY-MAKING
## MACHINERY

Form is substance. A properly organized decision-making process does not guarantee decisions of high quality, but you are certain to have uneven decisions without an orderly process.

Donald H. Rumsfeld

An examination of the formal structure of responsibility and jurisdiction in Washington provides less help in understanding the international economic policy process than it would in other industrialized countries. A skeletal appreciation of the means by which governmental bodies operate the data-gathering, option-enumerating, and decision-making processes is what emerges from a study of formal organization, that is, that which can be gleaned from published organizational charts and job descriptions. Incredibly casual organizational arrangements, the cult-of-personality syndrome, and the vagaries of international economics necessitate considerable attention to informal organization and process. But a full appreciation of this inner level of bodily activity—the nervous system and the personality—presupposes a familiarity with the bones and joints, of which there are many.

## HISTORICAL EVOLUTION OF ORGANIZATION

Organization and procedures to plan, formulate, implement, and manage a comprehensive U.S. international economic policy were not necessary until after World War II. Prior to 1934, Congress controlled tariff levels, and the commercial sector conducted international business on a relatively unfettered basis. Only warfare interrupted the nonexistence of formal executive branch policy making before that time. The passage of the Trade Agreements Program in that year necessitated both an increased trade negotiations capability in the State Department and a mechanism for consultations with the Agriculture and Commerce Departments prior to the signing of reciprocal trade agreements.

It was not until 1942 that international economic relations became big business in terms of governmental involvement. With the advent of U.S. involvement in the war came the need for radical new economic policies and programs. For a variety of reasons, bureaucratic, political, and philosophical, White House-centered operations (for example, the Board of Economic Warfare and later the Foreign Economic Administration) were initiated as the preferred alternative to having the State Department act as coordinator. With the advent of peace, the temporary wartime organizations were disbanded, and responsibility for administering America's new global economic role in the main was returned to the regular cabinet departments. The most notable exception involved creation of the Economic Cooperation Administration to administer the Marshall Plan.

Throughout the early 1950s, U.S. international economic policy followed two tracks. First, it was the servant of national security policy and therefore was not measured for the most part by commercial terms. Secondly, it was the reflection of the American fondness for international law and organization. International economic relations for the most part were neatly confined to the technicians and delegations participating in the international organizations (the IMF, the World Bank, and the GATT) sponsored by the United States and its allies to administer the postwar world economy. As long as the global political status quo was preserved and American hegemony was unchallenged, international economic policy assumed the characteristics of a slumbering giant. Structural changes in the international balance of economic power, however, caused an awakening that changed American attitudes and organization.

Two major organizational changes have occurred in the wake of external economic forces being elevated from "low" to "high" policy in the postwar era. Otherwise, the formal organization chart has not undergone significant changes. The first is the creation and proliferation of new offices having international economic responsibilities within the Executive Office of the President. The overall expansion of presidential power, and the increased need for a presidential view have made for a fertile ground for coordination and operational duties being incorporated into the White House's functions.

The second evolutionary phenomenon has been the wide array of domestic departments whose small international economic advisory staffs have expanded into full-scale bureaus. The blurring of the dividing line between domestic and international economic policy is directly proportional to sizable increases in the international staffs of Agriculture, Commerce, Labor, and so on. But change is nowhere more dramatic than at the Treasury Department. The outstanding change in modern U.S. international economic policy organization has been the relative ascendency of the Treasury Department's authority and influence.

The Treasury Department's natural strengths in economic policy and the internal weaknesses of the State Department have combined to cause a steady increase in the Treasury Department's size and power in this policy area. Today, it is the full equal of the State Department in being an organizational superpower where international economic policy is concerned. Being a departmental supervisor connotes presence in all sectors of international economic policy formulation and the ability to veto a final decision below the presidential level.

The battle to be primus inter pares continues to be waged by the two departments. A rapid increase in State's economics competence has slowed the steady erosion of its responsibilities and clout. But with the introduction of each new problem area, be it energy or commodity agreements, State must grapple with Treasury's unstinting quest for jurisdiction and predominance.

## THE SUPERPOWERS: STATE, TREASURY, AND THE WHITE HOUSE

For the first 150 years of American history, the State Department dominated the economic as well as the political aspects of this country's relations with other governments. The administrative linchpin of U.S. external economic policy making in the interwar period was the department's Division of Commercial Policy and Agreements, formed in 1934. In 1943, liaison functions with the special wartime economic agencies necessitated the evolution of the economic adviser's office (created in 1922) into the office of the assistant secretary for economic affairs. Today, the Bureau of Economic and Business Affairs consists of 120 professionals, almost all of whom are foreign-service officers with an economics background. One of State's most important functional bureaus, it is the heart of the department's economic-policy activities. As seen in Figure 1, the bureau is headed by an assistant secretary. After numerous reorganizations, he currently has four deputy assistant secretaries working immediately under him. Corresponding to specific policy sectors, the deputy assistant secretaries each oversee a number of offices handling trade; finance and development; resources and food; and transportation, telecommunications, and commercial affairs.

The relatively neat organizational table within the Bureau of Economic and Business Affairs masks three organizational complications. The first is that the erosion of State's power in international economic policy making means that only a relatively few of the 14 offices within the bureau take the lead, that is, have prime responsibility, for the issues they deal with. On most trade, finance, and development issues, the leadership has gravitated to the Treasury

FIGURE 1

Bureau of Economic and Business Affairs

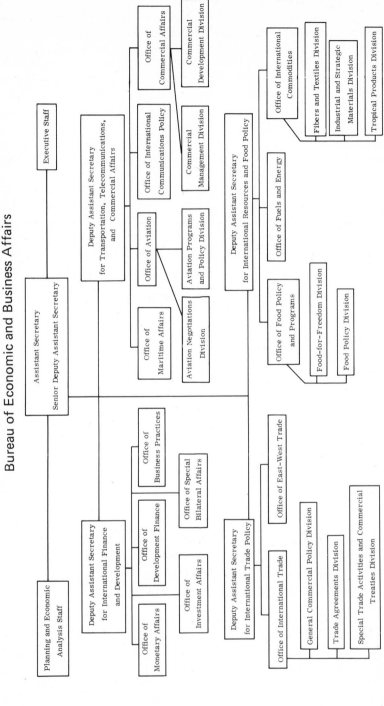

*Source:* U.S. Department of State.

44

or Agriculture departments or to White House offices. State retains leadership in some bilateral trade matters and in transportation, communications, and scientific issues.

Nevertheless, the State Department participates in the overall field of noncrisis international economic policy formulation as extensively as any other department. The secretary of state is the president's chief foreign-policy adviser. Additionally, the department is charged with the overall conduct of American foreign policy and construction of an international grand design. International economic policy by definition involves relations with other countries. For a country playing a world leadership role, it is generally recognized that State's unique worldwide perspective and the ability to assess foreign reactions to U.S. policies are needed for any aspect of international economic relations that has a modicum of political implications. The department also provides most of the economic reporting from U.S. embassies abroad. Although some Treasury, Agriculture, and Commerce economic officers are assigned to the larger embassies, State officials head the economics sections and control communications between Washington and overseas U.S. missions. In most international economic organizations and conferences, the State Department is at least the titular head of the American delegation.

But to return to the bottom line, the State Department in the mid-1970s had become more of a participant than a leader in this area. Avoiding program management and not previously taking economics seriously, the department inflicted much of this decline on itself. State cannot match the technical expertise and national political bases of the domestically oriented agencies. Furthermore, it has yet to overcome its stigma as being predisposed to accommodating the foreigners' positions. Whenever the United States feels the need to show resolve, it is the State Department's position that suffers. The disenchantment with the department had clearly surfaced during World War II when new White House units were created to coordinate international economic policy. In 1957, the Trade Policy Committee was established, with the secretary of commerce as chairman to dilute State's control over the operations of the Trade Agreements Program. This pattern accelerated in the 1960s.

The organizational chart of the Bureau of Economic and Business Affairs also hides a major administrative quirk with respect to its relationship to the Seventh Floor, the collective term for the senior State Department hierarchy. The permanent post of undersecretary of state for economic affairs was created in 1972 to increase the department's representative clout in interagency deliberations. However, except for a miniscule personal staff, this official has no one reporting to him. The Bureau of Economic and Business Affairs reports to the secretary. The undersecretary's control has been essentially a function of the personal relationship between him and the assistant secretary for economic and business affairs.

A third organizational issue is the bureau's relationship with the geographic bureaus within the department. A kind of internal bureaucratic politics model operates between the worldwide view of the technocrats of the Bureau of Economic and Business Affairs on the one hand, and the relatively more parochial political officers assigned to enhance U.S. relations with specific geographical regions. A noticeable shift in the internal balance of power has occurred in the bureau's favor. It reflects the overall tougher posture assumed by this country in international economic relations, the increasing domestic politicization of U.S. international economic policy, and the belated discovery by the State Department of just how important economics had become to the conduct of foreign policy. What was once a backwater of the department has become a growing and active glamour spot. Where there had once been a career disincentive to join the economics hierarchy, economics-oriented foreign-service officers are moving up the ranks at least as quickly as their political colleagues. Ultimate equality is just now beginning to appear: Foreign-service economics specialists are being elevated to the ambassadorial ranks.

The Treasury Department is the enfant terrible of U.S. international economic policy making. Its ascendency to power, the outstanding organizational feature of U.S. international economic policy since the end of World War II, is the result of at least three larger forces: the relative international decline of U.S. economic strength, as measured in the deterioration of the U.S. balance of payments and two subsequent dollar devaluations; the increased impact of the external sector on domestic economic policy management; and the increased interest of Washington in achieving a broad range of economic-policy goals.

The bulk of Treasury's international economic activities is concentrated in the Office of the Assistant Secretary for International Affairs (OASIA). The assistant secretary who heads this office in turn reports to the undersecretary for monetary affairs, who has become the chief operations officer for Treasury's international economic policy. From the relatively obscure Office of International Finance, which in the early 1960s numbered well under 50 professionals, a bureaucratic colossus has developed. With a staff today of well over 200 professional economists and access to economists in other Treasury bureaus, OASIA has the resources to weigh in on any governmental excercise involving international economics. Not only does this staff represent the largest single government body of international economic expertise (with the possible exception of the Central Intelligence Agency [CIA]), but the quality of its work is respected within the bureaucracy.

OASIA has undergone repeated internal reorganizations and facelifts in the 1970s, including one inspired by an expensive management-consultant study. It was carved in half in 1974, and in early 1976 was reincorporated; in both cases, the moves were to accommodate the preference of a senior aide to the then Secretary Simon—an aide who later became OASIA'S head. The current organization chart, reproduced in Figure 2, provides insight into OASIA's reach, but not its power. Responsibilities for policy making in virtually all aspects of U.S. international economic policy are to be found in one of the 20 offices operating under five deputy assistant secretaries, all of whom have an extensive economics background. The diversity of OASIA responsibilities and the repeated reorganizations have created some awkward internal organizational arrangements; for example, East-West trade, commodities agreements, and oceans policy are jointly pursued in one of the five divisions, and investment and energy policy jointly in another. Treasury's oversight of international financial and monetary policies is more neatly portrayed in the International Monetary Affairs and the Research divisions. The Office of Developing Nations is concerned with managing multilateral foreign aid and the financial aspects of the new-international-economic-order issue.

Treasury offices outside OASIA handle legal and technical aspects of international economic relations. The Office of Tariff Administration performs certain investigations concerning foreign-trade practices in accordance with the terms of U.S. trade legislation. Federal laws exist to neutralize unfair foreign-trade competition, namely, the dumping of goods in this market (sales at less than fair value) and the existence of foreign-government bounties or grants bestowed on the manufacture of foreign goods sold in this market (countervailing duties). For the laws to be triggered, the existence of the illegal foreign practices must be verified. Although this office impartially enforces specific legislation, there is sufficient flexibility in its techniques to have enabled it in the past to project a soft or hard trade-policy line vis-a-vis U.S. trade partners. The office also administers this nation's customs laws.

The special assistant to the secretary for national security advises that secretary on the international financial aspects of national defense policy and serves as a conduit to the intelligence community. The Office of International Tax Counsel handles the arcane subject of double-taxation treaties and other foreign-taxation issues (for example, withholding taxes on foreign-held securities and domestic-international sales corporations).

In addition to the three broad trends mentioned above, Treasury's presence and power were fueled by more immediate considerations. For most of the postwar period, the secretary of the treasury has been treated by the president as the senior economic-policy official in the U.S. government. This has been especially true with three secretaries: John Connally, George Shultz, and William Simon. Empirical evidence of the effects of this bond include Connally's total control of American international economic policy in late 1971, and the naming of Shultz and Simon to chair the major White House economic-policy-coordinating forums.

A second fillip was the high priority accorded in the 1960s to the ending of the persistent American balance-of-payments deficits. Closing the dollar gap

# FIGURE 2

## Organization of the Office of the Assistant Secretary for International Affairs

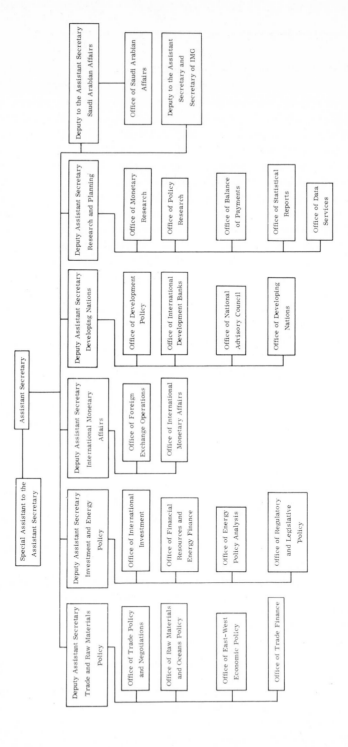

*Source:* U.S. Treasury Department.

became a metaphor for the government's resolve and the ability to put its international economic house in order. As a consequence, the external deficit was attacked by a host of foreign expenditure-plugging programs, which grew in number with the persistent appearance of new holes in the dollar dike. Every dollar spent overseas by the U.S. government, and by U.S. business and tourists became fair game for Treasury perusal. Every aspect of U.S. international economic policy required a Treasury presence to see if the balance-of-payments implications received proper deference. Once people began looking at the era after the deficit ended, reform of the entire international monetary system became a major item on the world economic agenda. By 1971, the correlation between the shrinking U.S. trade surplus and the overall strength of the dollar became fully apparent. Trade policy immediately was added to full-time Treasury preoccupations.

A third factor has been Congress's extension of Treasury leadership through new economic legislation. The Bretton Woods Agreements Act placed the secretary of the treasury in charge of U.S. participation in the IMF and the World Bank. U.S. participation in the regional multilateral development banks (Inter-American and Asian Development banks, for example) similarly was placed under the overall guidance of the treasury secretary. The U.S. executive director in the IMF and the governors in the banks come from the Treasury Department.

The international authority and responsibilities of the Treasury grew not by conscious design, but by circumstance. They grew within a rapidly widening field, not at the immediate expense of other bureaucratic actors. It should not be viewed as a zero sum game, where one gains only at the expense of others, but rather as Treasury's ability to assume (along with the White House) an expanding share of a growing area of U.S. government responsibility. The net effect is Treasury dominance in these traditional policy sectors: overall U.S. balance-of-payments policy, international capital flows, gold, international monetary reform, multilateral foreign aid, and discussions of international coordination of domestic economic policies. Treasury's dominant role in domestic economic policy management has been used as leverage to assure itself of participation equal to any other department on any new issue that can be construed to have a domestic economic impact—energy, resource transfers to LDCs, access to foreign-produced raw materials, the multinational corporation, and so on.

The State Department is the only other department actively involved in all international economic issues. The foreign-oriented viewpoint is accepted as a necessity in all but the most technical, and therefore apolitical, matters. The State Department, like the Treasury, is sufficiently powerful and ubiquitous to be in a position to veto intragovernmental agreement on virtually any international economic issue. The existence of a vehement opposition by either requires a moving of the bureaucratic debate up the line of seniority, even onto the president's desk if necessary. Initiatives are still taken by the department; it is still given the lead role in international negotiations. The real difference is that it has taken the richness of State's historical legacy in this field and all of Henry Kissinger's energy and presidential links to slow the Treasury Department's clearly evident initiative, which began during World War II and gained momentum in the 1960s.

The inability of the State Department to retain its pre-1950 share of international economic-policy dominance is also a reflection of the rise of White House supercoordinators and of the Office of the Special Representative for Trade Negotiations. An obvious administrative solution to the problems presented by a number of line departments and agencies bringing a specialized, relatively narrow point of view to the broad subject of global economic relations is to establish neutral coordinating groups in the White House. The main task of these professionals is twofold. First, they must be prepared to provide the president with an independent, complete, and wholly objective analysis of an international economic problem, one prepared with the chief executive's interests in mind. Secondly, they must exercise gentle persuasion to cause the line departments to focus for the long term on certain issues and to reconcile in the short term their differing points of view. Ideally, a president's man takes a noninterventionist approach in which he emphasizes his credibility, not his muscle. Ideally, White House coordinating groups divorce themselves from the advocacy process, contenting themselves with encouraging a constructive dialogue among those bureaucratic actors possessing policy management responsibilities. This is done by assuring that all legitimate views enter high-level policy debates and by fostering a consensus.

Proximity to the chief executive and control of interagency deliberations efforts affords great potential for the president's men to influence the outcome of policy. But the actual degree of clout is uncertain, being the derivative of a complex equation incorporating presidential workstyles, cabinet-level personalities, and the standing of international economic-policy issues in the administration's priorities at a given moment.

The NSC is the oldest of the White House coordinators that have become involved in U.S. external economic relations. It was established by the National Security Act of 1947 for the purpose of advising the president with respect to "the integration of domestic, foreign, and military policies relating to the national security so as to enable the . . . agencies of the Government to cooperate more effectively in matters involving the national security." The president is its chairman, and the other members are the vice president and the secretaries of state and defense. Depending on the existence of White House coordinators especially designed for economic policy, the NSC can be intimately involved in international economic policy or it can be narrowly involved, only where economics intrudes directly into the national security sphere.

The Council on Foreign Economic Policy (CFEP) in the 1950s and the CIEP and the Economic Policy Board (EPB) in the 1970s represent the concept that high-level coordination should be applied to the operating units of the bureaucracy (from the White House) rather than by them. This concept, traceable to the exigencies of World War II, is discussed at length in the next chapter. Suffice it to say at this point that the modern organizational structure of U.S. international economic policy has been characterized by repeated attempts to charge members of the president's office with the responsibilities of coordinating the workings of the policy-making system.

The function of the president's special representative for trade negotiations lies midway between that of a line official with operational responsibilities and that of a coordinator. The distinctive feature of this position is that it is a creation of Congress. Misgivings on Capitol Hill and in the private sector about the State Department's ability to drive a hard bargain and bring home the most advantageous trade agreement in the then impending Kennedy Round inspired the Congress to create the position in the Trade Expansion Act of 1962. (The supporting office was created the next year by an executive order.) After considerable debate, it was thought that a White House location would afford the chief trade negotiator maximum objectivity and prestige. The statute charges the chief negotiator with two main functions. He is to be the "chief representative" of the United States in all trade agreements negotiations (synonymous with multilateral efforts to reduce trade barriers) and "such others" that the president assigns to him. Secondly, he is to be the chairman of an interagency organization, which "the President will establish to assist the implementation of his trade agreements, tariff adjustment and orderly marketing agreement functions under the Act." In practice, it has also been the chief trade negotiator who is responsible for securing congressional support and the necessary supplemental legislation for trade agreements entered into by the executive branch.

The history of the negotiator's office has been written for the most part in the Kennedy Round and in the current Tokyo Round of trade negotiations. But the office's small staff (usually 20 to 30 professionals) mandates the active participation of the State, Agriculture, Commerce, and Treasury Departments, among others, in the U.S. delegations to major trade talks. The office provides leadership, while the line departments (and the International Trade Commission [ITC]) provide supporting personnel and data resources. The office's coordinating function is also manifested in its leadership of the trade policy coordinating committees established first under the Trade Expansion Act and then under the Trade Act of 1974. The office's officials currently chair the cabinet-level Trade Policy Committee (terminated in 1963, but resurrected in 1975), the subcabinet Trade Policy Review Group, and the Trade Policy Staff Committee. These groups are responsible for formulating all administration actions emanating from the 1974 act, including trade restrictive actions recommended under the escape clause by the International Trade Commission. The 1974 Act gave a further boost to the negotiator's office by elevating the position to cabinet status and giving it a legislative life. These actions represented Congress's displeasure with efforts by the CIEP in 1972–73 to absorb the office, its rival within the White House for senior trade-policy responsibility.

Three other units within the Executive Office of the President perform specialized tasks that have a bearing on international economic policy. The International Affairs Division of the Office of Management and Budget (OMB) intrudes into the policy-making process via its influence on budgetary decisions and its presence whenever the expenditure of government funds is involved. This responsibility is most evident in deliberations on the annual question of how much money to request of Congress for foreign aid. Other instances include a longstanding controversy within the bureaucracy concerning what is the proper magnitude of governmental export promotion efforts and the cost of U.S. participation in commodity price stabilization schemes (see Chapter 7).

The three-member CEA was created by the Full Employment Act of 1946 to provide an overall assessment and interpretation of developments in the U.S. economy, and to advise the president on policies necessary to promote growth and stability. The recognized impact of the external sector has led to one of three members of the CEA being assigned international responsibilities, with the support of at least one senior staff economist. The lack of personnel means that CEA involvement in international economic policy management is mainly on a pick-and-choose basis, where potentially serious domestic economic consequences, that is, those that threaten economic growth, price stability, or full employment, are perceived. The CEA's chairman heads the U.S. delegation to the Economic Policy Committee of the OECD and is the vice chairman of that committee. A CEA member is also part of the delegations to other specialized economic committees in the OECD, most notably Working Party Three, where multilateral surveillance of the industrialized economies originated.

The CIA, seldom identified as being in the Executive Office of the President, has channeled increased resources to international economic intelligence in response to demands of its customers (policy makers) and to the overall thawing of the cold war. The CIA is the chief supplier of covert economic intelligence and is developing a sophisticated analytical capacity on international economic relations in general. It is the source of the week-to-week international energy data most widely used in the federal government today, and it provides daily economic intelligence briefings to senior policy makers.

## THE SPECIALISTS: DEPARTMENTS AND AGENCIES

Ubiquity in the international economic policy-making process and possession of de facto veto power are the distinguishing characteristics of the Treasury and State Departments, and, to an extent, the Executive Office of the President. While other departments and agencies have important roles to play in the formulation and administration processes, their presence and impact are limited to certain specialized sectors touching on their domestic missions. The list of participants is theoretically endless. Almost every department and large agency has at least one international program or policy concern. The Transportation Department participates in conferences pertaining to international transportation issues; the Justice Department applies U.S. antitrust legislation both to U.S.-owned companies abroad and to foreign-owned companies in this country; the Civil Aviation Board provides advice when international air routes are being negotiated; the Energy Research and Development Administration has responsibilities in the export control field. What follows is a brief discussion of the operations of the relatively more important bureaucratic actors influencing the major issues of U.S. international economic policy.

The critical role played by U.S. agricultural food abundance in feeding the world and the fact that annual agricultural exports of more than $22 billion make the United States the world's premier food exporter mean that the USDA is mightily concerned with international agricultural trends and policies. As the Treasury worries about the external sector in terms of its impact on its prime constituent, the American economy, so too does Agriculture view the external sector impact on its prime constituent, the American farmer.

The USDA provides the bulk of technical expertise, data collection, foreign economic reporting, and export promotion of farm commodities. In any period of a tight worldwide food supply situation, such an input assumes major importance. The USDA has also provided a major voice in formulating U.S. trade policy in this sector, especially vis-a-vis agricultural import barriers maintained by the European community and Japan and the occasionally heavy buying demands of the Soviet Union.

Operating under the assistant secretary for international affairs and commodity programs are two agencies dealing with the overseas function. The first is the Foreign Agricultural Service (FAS). Through its representatives serving in some 60 U.S. embassies abroad, the FAS pursues its overall mission of expanding agricultural exports by such activities as formal presentations to foreign governments; reporting on foreign agricultural production, trade, and policies; communicating overseas marketing opportunities to the U.S. private sector; and analyzing foreign competition in terms of prices and marketing techniques. The FAS coordinates the USDA's participation in international organizations and conferences such as the 1974 World Food Conference and in the current efforts to establish an international food stockpile.

The FAS also administers the foreign sales functions of a second unit, the Commodity Credit Corporation (CCC). The latter is a wholly owned U.S. government corporation begun in 1948 to stabilize and protect farm income and prices and to help maintain balanced and adequate supplies and distribution of agricultural goods. Foreign operations conducted through the CCC by the FAS include the Export Credit Sales Program and concessional sales of agricultural commodities under Public Law (PL) 480. The amount and terms of such sales represent a major effort in the U.S. aid program. USDA chairs the Interagency Staff Committee, which approves the sales and emergency donations carried out under PL 480. Finally, the USDA has responsibility for administering the import quotas maintained by this country on agricultural commodities, a responsibility which includes the setting of annual bilateral allocations for exporting countries.

The relatively weak position of the Department of Commerce in the economic policy-making councils of the federal government is the great anomaly of the organizational machinery. Of all major trading countries, the United States has the weakest commercial ministry. The reasons for this situation are rooted in the traditional arm's length distance between bureaucrats and the business sector that is preferred by both sides. It reflects the abhorrence to planning in general and the absence of a national industrial development policy. For whatever reason, the industrial sector remains perfectly content to employ a decentralized system of contacts in the executive branch and in Congress in lieu of a powerful ministry to represent it directly. As a consequence, the Commerce Department must content itself with more of an operational than a policy-making role. And the international economic policy machinery must adjust to the absence of a strong commercial ministry. Whereas the Commerce Department can assume a leadership role in certain trade issues when the secretary receives a presidential nod (for example, Maurice Stans with the Japanese textile negotiations and Peter Peterson with East-West trade), its normal role is to be a junior participant, not a leader, in interagency councils.

International economic responsibilities on the operational level are discharged by the Domestic and International Business Administration (DIBA), headed by an assistant secretary. In congressional testimony in 1975, DIBA's overall mission was described as strengthening the U.S. economy by learning as much as possible about the U.S. and foreign economies and then going to the U.S. business community to help them sell more effectively in the domestic and foreign markets. Policy input comes from the Bureau of International Economic Policy and Research, which in mid-1976 was removed from DIBA and placed under the supervision of the newly created post of assistant secretary for policy. It provides the personnel for participation in interagency policy discussions, concentrating mainly in the trade and investment sectors.

Since the Commerce Department has the main responsibility for the promotion of U.S. nonagricultural exports, the Bureau of International Commerce operates numerous promotional efforts designed to make domestic industry more export conscious. It disseminates trade data—foreign market analyses and trade opportunities—and provides export and counseling to specific companies on an ad hoc basis. To make potential foreign buyers more aware of U.S. products and suppliers, the bureau sponsors overseas trade fairs shows, and missions.

The Bureau of East-West Trade has two principal functions. The first is the promotion of trade (that is, U.S. exports) with the Communist bloc countries through specialized marketing research data explaining the trade laws and practices of those countries. In support of this function, the bureau also provides support services for the joint commercial commissions established at the ministerial level since 1972 to serve as the primary vehicles for official trade consultations between this country and the Soviet Union, Poland, and Romania.

The bureau's second major function is to administer all U.S. export controls, as authorized by the Export Administration Act. The Office of Export Administration at one time did little more than restrict the sales of strategic goods to Communist bloc countries. Since the act was amended in 1969, however, the office now is authorized, after appropriate interagency clearance, to restrict exports of goods in short supply (to protect shortages and minimize inflationary pressures), and to support U.S. foreign-policy objectives. (Controls on soybeans in 1973 and the still existing export controls on petroleum products are administered by this office.)

The Bureau of Resources and Trade Assistance is responsible for administering adjustment assistance (in the form of financial and technical assistance) to domestic companies that can demonstrate the appropriate degree of injury from import competition, as spelled out in the Trade Act of 1974. Finally, mention should be made of Commerce's responsibility to collect foreign-trade and foreign-investment data; the Treasury collects data only on international capital flows.

The Labor Department has no specific international economic policy-making responsibilities and only two major operational duties: administering adjustment assistance to qualified workers whose job loss can be attributed to import competition, and participating in international labor conferences. Nevertheless, organized labor, particularly the AFL-CIO, has undertaken intensive lobbying efforts to restrict imports and curb the overseas activities of U.S. multinational corporations. The new thrust of import competition, experienced only since the mid-1960s, has necessitated a greater concern for the worker's interests in international economic policy formulation. The staff of the deputy undersecretary for international labor affairs, therefore, attempts to ensure that the interests of American workers are taken into account in the formulation of international trade and investment policies.

In strictly budgetary terms, the Agency for International Development (AID) is the largest bureaucratic actor in the international economic policy machinery. The successor to a long line of postwar aid-dispensing agencies, AID performs its functions under an administrator who reports to the secretary of state. Simply stated, the agency plans and administers the bilateral U.S.

economic assistance program from its Washington headquarters and its field offices in recipient countries. The organization of the U.S. aid agencies has changed consistently through the years because the objectives and scope of the U.S. aid program have been changed frequently by the executive and legislative branches. AID at present is acting in accordance with the congressional initiative of 1973. In place of capital-intensive development loans, AID channels most of its budgetary and personnel resources into providing resources and know-how in four sectors: food and nutrition, population planning and health, education and human resources development, and rural development. In addition, AID dispenses a significant portion of its funds in the form of security-supporting assistance. The latter consists of grants extended to poorer countries deemed to be especially critical to U.S. foreign policy, which in the late 1960s meant Indo-China and in the mid-1970s, meant the Middle East. AID also participates in interagency debates on other forms of bilateral aid, for example, PL 480 and debt relief.

The Export-Import Bank of the United States (Eximbank) is an independent governmental corporation established in 1934 "to aid in financing and to facilitate exports and imports." The bank has no policy functions. Its sole responsibility is to encourage U.S. exports by providing supplementary services to the commercial banking sector: direct loans, guarantees, insurance of repayment, and a rediscount facility for export loans held by private banks.

This discussion of agencies concludes with the International Trade Commission (ITC) and the Federal Reserve System. Because of their statutory bases, they are technically outside of the administration's control. The ITC is the renamed Tariff Commission, whose existence traces back to 1916. A once obscure independent fact-finding and research organization, the commission was given not only a new name by the Trade Act of 1974, but a new significance as well. Acting neither as part of the administration nor under control by Congress, the six commissioners of the ITC are charged with making recommendations to the president after an impartial, nonpartisan investigation based on the merits of petitions for import relief filed by domestic workers or companies.

The trade legislation of the United States stipulates conditions and procedures under which imports can be restricted if they are injuring, or threaten to injure, domestic industries through the escape-clause mechanism, or in cases of illegal foreign-trade practices (dumping, patent infringement, and so on). The ITC determines whether injury exists in accordance with legislative guidelines. The Trade Act of 1974 considerably eased the previously strict eligibility criteria for approval of escape-clause petitions, and it reduced the president's ability to ignore an ITC recommendation of increased import barriers to assuage domestic injury. A spate of escape-clause petitions quickly followed passage of the act, no doubt encouraged by the brighter prospects for governmental import relief. Suddenly, the dispassionate findings of the ITC loomed large in the relations of this country with its major trading partners and in the calculated efforts of the administration to encourage the successful pursuit of trade liberalization in the Tokyo Round. A case involving dumping allegations against foreign manufacturers of automobiles, subsequently dropped, involved imports valued at $7 billion. The significance of the ITC goes beyond its being a direct link between assessment of domestic economic health and import programs. The ITC's professional staff expertise on technical trade issues is unique. This fact and ITC's lack of any proprietary concern with existing policies have served to produce a number of highly respected research efforts on trade issues by the ITC's economists.

In order to separate the management of monetary policy from the political process, the Federal Reserve System is also independent of both the executive and legislative branches. As with the other agencies with specialized economic policy concerns, its interests and responsibilities in the international economic sphere are outgrowths of its domestic concerns: money and credit aggregates, the banking system, and the capital markets. These concerns, together with a high-quality professional staff, afford the Fed a respected, but unofficial voice in administration international policy deliberations.

Through its Board of Governors in Washington, the Federal Reserve System is the junior partner of the Treasury Department in determining exchange-rate policies for the dollar. The principal instrument used to influence exchange-rate management is a complex array of foreign exchange market operations performed by the Federal Reserve Bank of New York under guidelines established in Washington. The board's Division of International Finance has provided an input in U.S. policies concerning international monetary reform, and has been active on various international financial issues, such as administering the Voluntary Credit Restraint Program during its existence (1965–74). Sooner or later, legislation will be passed to extend the Fed's bank regulatory function to include the operations of the growing number of foreign-owned banks in this country.

## THE CONGRESS

The principal source of the legislative branch's authority in the foreign commerce of the United States is Article 1, Section 8 of the Constitution, which specifically empowers Congress to "lay and collect Taxes, Duties, Imports and Excises" and to "regulate commerce with foreign Nations." Congress's specific duties include approving the budgets of the makers and managers of international economic policy, passing supplementary legislation (dealing with changes in the par value of the dollar, U.S. membership in international organizations, international taxation, and so on), and approval in the Senate of international economic treaties and political appointees.

The depth of Congress's imprint on American international economic relations has varied historically. Prior to 1934, it was very deep indeed; the executive branch was more administrator than policy formulator. But the growing volume of international trade and the growing burden of constituent pressures for tariff protection gave birth in 1934 to a transitory phase in which control over international economic policy began moving to the administration. By the early 1960s, Congress was doing the president's bidding. The complexity of the balance-of-payments problem and the paucity of grassroots interest channeled the average congressman's interest elsewhere. The politicization of international economics later in that decade marked the beginning of Congress's effort to redress the imbalance of influence. The overall post-Vietnam and post-Watergate reassertiveness marked the maturity of this effort. The Trade Act of 1974 is its first major offshoot.

No other national legislative body more extensively creates, revises, and offers critiques on a nation's international economic policy than does the Congress of the United States. To fulfill the duties of a separate and equal branch of government, it has an elaborate organizational structure to prepare legislation, challenge and reject administration proposals, evaluate existing policies, and suggest new ideas and approaches. The general reassertiveness of the Congress and specific statutory controls combine to assure that the legislative branch has become an active member of the policy-making process. That the executive branch must seriously consider congressional sentiment, the possibility of a congressional override of a trade action, means that an application of the bureaucratic politics model to international economic policy decision making may be specious if it concerns itself only with the clash of executive branch viewpoints and perspectives. Perhaps this is only a temporary situation. Nevertheless, at the present time, for specific policy decisions, the president may be forced to swallow hard—to the extent even of ignoring a State-Treasury Department consensus—and adapt U.S. policy to meet congressional demands.

At the heart of the congressional machinery are the committees. They are the vehicles for preparing legislation, confirming treaties, receiving briefings by executive branch policy makers, and exercising the oversight function. Relatively unknown outside of Washington, oversight hearings begin where the legislative function ends. A fact-finding process from which new legislative proposals may result, oversight hearings normally are held for one of four purposes: "(1) to review and control unacceptable forms of bureaucratic behavior; (2) to ensure that the bureaucracy implements the policy objectives of the Congress; (3) to determine the effectiveness of legislative programs and policies; and (4) to analyze . . . problems requiring Federal action."[1] International economic legislation has begun to mandate tighter congressional scrutiny of policy. This fact, along with strengthened professional staff support for all committees, and increased scheduling of oversight hearings are the main manifestations of the new era of interest in international economics on Capitol Hill. Another symptom is the unofficial consultations that are becoming increasingly common on a personalized basis between international economic policy leaders in the two branches.

There are two striking features of the congressional committee structure in the international economic policy sphere: the large number of committees involved and the overlapping committee jurisdictions. The situation is, from an administrative point of view, strikingly similar to that which prevails in the executive branch. A major difference is the absence of any real attempts at coordination in Congress.

A reasonably complete, albeit nondefinitive, breakdown of committee responsibilities in international economic policy demonstrates that six legislative committees and one joint committee have jurisdictions involving the international economic relations of the United States:

| Committee | Function |
| --- | --- |
| House Ways and Means, Senate Finance committees | Basic trade legislation and tariffs; international taxation |
| Banking committees | Export controls (Senate only); Export-Import Bank; exchange-rate and gold policy; international financial and monetary institutions (House only) |
| Foreign Relations, International Relations committees | General international economic policy; bilateral foreign aid; international financial institutions (Senate only); export controls (House only); multinational corporations |
| Commerce committees | Export promotion; foreign direct investment in the United States |
| Agriculture committees | Agricultural exports; international food stockpiles and food aid |
| Appropriations, Budget committees | Departmental, representational, and program budgets |
| Joint Economic Committee | Oversight on general international economic policy, especially in the international monetary and finance sectors |

On hot and complex issues, such as energy, international commodity agreements, and the multinational corporation, jurisdiction is fragmented ad nauseam. Aspects of the issues usually are parceled out on a narrow basis in response to initiatives and demands by several committees.

Most of the technical expertise is provided to members of Congress by the professional staffs retained by each committee. Since 1970, a rapid expansion of those staffs has taken place. Although the previously minuscule number of international economists working on Capitol Hill has increased geometrically, their numbers are still a small fraction of those employed in the executive branch. Additional expertise is provided on request by specialists in the Congressional Research Service, which is a part of the Library of Congress. The congressionally controlled General Accounting Office (GAO) undertakes investigations and evaluations of policies, practices, and programs maintained by the executive branch. The Congressional Budget Office, which provides analytic and research support for the budget committees who manage the Congress's newly adopted (1975) budget procedures, has the mandate, resources and influence to make it a further source of congressional ideas on international economic policy.

A final example of Congress's expanding involvement in this area has been the increased number of invitations by the executive branch to have congressional members serve as unofficial members of U.S. delegations to international economic conferences and negotiations.

## THE PRIVATE SECTOR

No discussion of American international economic policy machinery would be complete without mention of the means by which the views of the private sector are transmitted to the official sector. Traditional foreign policy may be dominated by a small elite, and it may attract the active participation of only a few specialized public groups. But international economic policy, mainly in the trade sector, is a multibillion dollar pocketbook issue touching on every American consumer and a large percentage of the workers and businesses in the industrial and agricultural sectors. Washington representatives, trade associations, specialized legal counsel, educational groups, and lobbyists are today the backbone of a multimillion dollar program to influence governmental policy, as well as public opinion in this area. On a nonpartisan basis, respected research institutions, most notably the Brookings Institution, produce international economic policy papers, which receive attention both in the executive and legislative branches. Selected academic economists serve as consultants and also provide a source of ideas and advice to both branches. The larger industrial, financial, and labor groups, having an international perspective and views similar to those of their counterparts in other countries,

have become important transnational actors. They transcend national boundaries and communicate with executive and legislative leaders throughout the
world.

Through a prolific number of personal visits and letters to officials' offices,
congressional testimony, publications, expense account lunches, and so-called
Georgetown dinner parties, the private sector's problems and demands are
transmitted directly to Washington's policy makers. Virtually every industry,
company, or union with any stake in international transactions are conveying
a point of view—freer trade or protectionist—or explaining in detail unfair
trade practices abroad. The most influential private domestic forces in determining U.S. trade policy are currently U.S. multinational corporations. Their
interests in a healthy export environment and a liberal international investment order are eloquently specified in key policy-making centers. These views
have been instrumental in keeping the thrust of this country's policy in the
freer trade direction. This situation and the export dynamism of the U.S.
agricultural community have meant that the executive and legislative branches
have been under no pressure from the business community to implement
arbitrary, across-the-board protectionist policies since the exchange-rate realignment of December 1971.

The private sector is also a key part of the bureaucratic politics equation
in the international economic policy process. They are the respective constituents for whom both executive departments and congressional committees
concentrate their concern. Agriculture and organized labor have specific
spokesmen for their interests in both branches. The banking sector and the
foreign viewpoints also have specified forums in both branches of the U.S.
government. Industry, having no clear-cut governmental counterpart, must
touch a number of key power centers, for example, the White House and
Treasury Department, and the Senate Finance and House Ways and Means
committees. The unorganized voice of the consumer is the least franchised of
all the constituencies that must be taken into account by the interplay of
bureaucratic forces.

The idea-and-data transmission process operated by the private sector in
the U.S. international economic policy sector can be very effective for three
main reasons. The first is the relative openness of U.S. policy in this area,
especially the trade sector. Secrecy is limited for the basic reason that policy
is designed to serve the private sector: consumers, workers, and businesses.
There are few national security issues involved. For the initiated outsider, it
is not difficult to monitor closely the policy-making process. The trend towards
more openness in government has also helped, such as the decision of some
congressional committees to allow the public to view legislative mark-up (bill-
drafting) sessions.

Secondly, those who form the "shadow cabinet" of international economic policy are talented, bright, and well organized. Many of the senior

people have held high-ranking administration positions; many have an in-depth technical expertise on specialized issues that is tapped by bureaucrats. Internal communications have been honed to a razor-sharp level. The Trade Action Coordinating Committee is an informal group of more than 100 liberal trade-oriented consumer, agricultural, and business representatives that meets weekly to exchange information and organize lobbying efforts.

A third factor is the importance of Congress in the policy process. In sharp contrast to career civil servants' job security, all members of Congress face reelection. The economic health of their constituents is a matter of great import. At times their self-interests require congressmen to play the role of ombudsman to assure that the executive branch policy does not become insufficiently responsive to the needs and demands of key groups within the domestic sector. It was for this reason that the Congress mandated a complex series of private sector advisory committees in the Trade Act of 1974. Presumably, continuing consultations between business, labor, and government would preclude the U.S. delegation at the Tokyo Round talks from becoming unmindful of domestic needs.

The transmission of ideas and data is one thing. The degree of their actual impact is quite another. The U.S. government may or may not be relatively less sympathetic and responsive to business demands, but this question transcends a study of organization and procedures.

## NOTE

1. *Committee Reform Amendments of 1974: Report of the House Select Committee on Committees* (Washington D.C.: U.S. Government Printing Office, 1974), p. 267.

# 5

## THE COORDINATION OF
## INTERNATIONAL ECONOMIC
## POLICY

It is time to end the intellectual and bureaucratic separation of economic issues one from another, with parts of each specific issue scattered throughout the government machinery without any sense of overall purpose and general guidance from the top.

Senators Russell Long and Abraham Ribicoff

The preceding analysis of U.S. international economic policy making demonstrates a central organizational need: coordination. A large number of bureaucratic entities have a valid and necessary viewpoint to infuse into the decision-making process. Domination by a single point of view must be avoided. A decentralized series of interagency groups can easily be assembled on the working level to cope with the plethora of international economic issues confronting the government at any given time. The real dilemma is posed by the manner in which the various microissues are to be coordinated at the senior policy levels in an effort to assure good macropolicies.

## THE NEED FOR AND NATURE OF COORDINATION

Being an administrative "buzz-word," coordination needs to be defined with some precision as it relates to international economic policy. Two separate, but related activities are involved. The first consists of resolving the basic disagreements and the subtle differences in nuances that are inevitable when so many bureaucratic players, with such varied missions, are trying to influence policy. The test of good coordination in this case is threefold.

1. Does the conflict get resolved in a reasonable length of time?
2. Is the resolution effected with a reasonable expenditure of effort, particularly at senior levels?
3. Is the resolution reasonably satisfactory to the disputants?[1]

On the second level, coordination strives to integrate the various actions and agreed-upon policies into a balanced, consistent, and coherent program designed to best attain U.S. objectives while serving the overall national interest. Within both of these levels, the coordination process itself may be pursued with varying shades of formality. A series of breakfast or luncheon meetings may be involved, or simply a series of phone calls among contemporaries in various agencies. Informal consultation between agency officials is a frequently used and valuable tool in harmonizing efforts and keeping agency positions reasonably compatible. Alternatively, coordination may utulize a formal group assembled to negotiate a government-wide policy platform.

It has been noted by one scholar that the quest for coordination "is in many respects the twentieth century equivalent of the medieval search for the philosopher's stone."[2] If only the right coordination formula could be found, the U.S. government could harmonize competing and wholly divergent interests, overcome irrationalities in our government structures, and make hard policy decisions on which no one will dissent.

Such a formula is unrealistic. It is unattainable because the real problem comes from the opposite direction. In international economic policy, especially, coordination problems are the result, not the cause, of the national inability to agree on specific tactics and strategy, as well as of the official refusal to move decisively to correct basic organizational shortcomings.

Indeed, the formulation of international economic policy in the United States cries out for coordination. In the absence of an omnipotent, brilliantly organized Department of International Economic Policy, it always will. There simply are too many bureaucratic participants possessing different priorities, pursuing different values, possessing fragmented and overlapping jurisdictions, and examining dozens of major issues in several policy sectors to obviate the premium on coordination. Even on the purely technical side, there are questions of method (grants versus technical assistance, for example), differences of philosophy (for example, free market and commercial sector emphasis versus government involvement), and conflicting economic theories. Most importantly, international economic policy is ultimately the coordination of other priorities: domestic and international politics and economics. The urgency for coordination in this area is exceeded only by the sheer volume of work involved and the difficulty of assuring effective coordination. Without a centralized system of coordination, the strongest departments resort to the law of the jungle; policy would reflect the interests of the dominant bureaucratic actor.

The traits and effectiveness of interagency coordination in this policy area are not unique to governmental decision making. It can be said, however, that all of the problems, foibles, and weaknesses of the interagency coordination process can be found in international economic policy. The coordinating groups in this area reinforce Harold Seidman's description of interagency committees as being "crab grass" in the garden of government institutions. "Nobody wants them, but everyone has them. Committees seem to thrive on scorn and ridicule, and multiply so rapidly that attempts to weed them out appear futile."[3] Issue for issue, and bureaucrat for bureaucrat, the proliferation of working-level coordinating groups to resolve disputes in international economic policy surely would match any other issue area.

## EARLY ATTEMPTS AT HIGH-LEVEL COORDINATION

Coordination efforts, like international economic policy itself, blossomed in the post-World War II period. The only major example of prewar commercial policy, operation of the Trade Agreements Program, was itself coordinated through the State Department-chaired Committee on Trade Agreements (with the Departments of Commerce and Agriculture the other major participants). During the war years, a number of high-level groups existed temporarily in connection either with economic warfare or planning for the postwar period. As early as 1940, an Interdepartmental Group on Post-War International Economic Problems and Policies was formed. It was followed by the Committee on Post-War Foreign Economic Policy (1943) and the Executive Committee on Economic Foreign Policy (1944), both of which were chaired by the State Department.

Since that Department was dominant in international economic affairs, the only major struggle for bureaucratic control was waged between it and the White House staff. Symbolic of this struggle was the creation in 1941 of the Economic Defense Board (later renamed the Board of Economic Warfare). Its duties were to advise the president on the entire range of international economic and communications fields, coordinate the work of the various departments in these fields, and develop integrated plans for the war years and postwar period (while leaving policy administration and implementation to the line departments). Chaired by Vice President Henry Wallace, the board quickly became a power to be reckoned with:

> While the franchise of the board seemed to absorb all international aspects of economic policy and action, an old inhabitant of the bureaucratic jungle like Mr. [Cordell] Hull knew that Cabinet boards and committees were paper tigers. They made a fine show in a parade but soon dissolved in the rain. Cabinet officers are too busy and too suspicious of one another to join a raid against a colleague. . . .

> Henry Wallace soon confounded all expectations about the board by a
> gross departure from the rules of bureaucratic warfare. He introduced into
> a harmless committee of busy men an executive director in the person of one
> of the most able, adroit, and energetic administrators whom the war had
> brought to Washington. . . .[4]

The board died a sudden death in mid-1943, when President Roosevelt lost his patience with jurisdictional quibbling among the members. The Foreign Economic Administration was created under White House control in September of that year as a replacement. The Foreign Economic Administration "was the last battle in the civil war within the Roosevelt Administration over the control of economic policy and operations abroad."[5] The Foreign Economic Administration was liquidated at war's end; its duties were disbursed to the civilian departments.

Still another wartime coordinating group was the Executive Committee on Economic Foreign Policy created in April 1944. Chaired by the State Department, the group's other members were the Departments of Treasury, Agriculture, Commerce, and Labor, as well as the Tariff Commission and the Foreign Economic Administration. The committee's principal function was to examine the full range of problems and developments affecting the economic foreign policy of the United States and to formulate policy recommendations in this area for either the president or the secretary of state.

In some respects, this was the last hurrah in terms of State's being assigned the chairman's role in international economic policy coordination. Subsequent groups were chaired by Treasury, Commerce, and the office of the Special Representative for Trade Negotiations. In 1948, the Economic Cooperation Administration was established. Reporting directly to the president, the administration's purpose was to coordinate the most important program of immediate postwar U.S. international economic policy: the $13 billion Marshall Plan, designed to restore the war-torn economies of Western Europe to their prewar vigor. Organizationally, it represented an unwillingness to entrust the State Department with the management of a top-priority foreign-policy program.

The growing involvement of the executive branch in commercially oriented international economic relations was highlighted by the establishment in 1954 of the CFEP in the Executive Office of the President. The CFEP was created pursuant to a letter by President Eisenhower appointing a special assistant for foreign economic policy (Joseph Dodge). He was given the role of assisting and advising the president "in accomplishing an orderly development of foreign economic policies and programs and to assure the effective coordination of foreign economic matters of concern to the several departments and agencies of the Executive Branch." His responsibilities included anticipating problems and issues, analyzing information for the purpose of clarifying and defining issues, and taking other steps necessary to produce a coordinated position. The relation of international economic policy to domestic economic policy was specifically included within the purview of the special assistant. He was also expected to establish appropriate relations with the NSC and the National Advisory Council on International Monetary and Financial Policies, the major coordinating groups in international economics at that time. In 1956, the special assistant's role was broadened to include advising the president on the development of international economic policies and programs to meet the special problems created by Communist economic activities in LDCs.

As indicated by the foregoing, the position of special assistant for foreign economic policy and the CFEP were created because of the belief that the executive branch lacked an adequate organizational means for the development and coordination of international economic policy. There was dissatisfaction, for example, with the NSC machinery in dealing with major foreign economic-national security problems, particularly when those problems required the reconciliation of foreign and domestic considerations with a scope exceeding that of the NSC's regular membership.

In order to provide for formal participation of the affected agencies in carrying out this role, the special assistant was authorized to establish and serve as chairman of the CFEP. The basic membership in the CFEP consisted of the secretaries of state, the treasury, commerce, and agriculture. (Alternates were at the undersecretary and assistant secretary level.) There were also three ex officio members: the president's special assistants for economic affairs and for national security affairs, and a member of the CEA. Other agencies were invited regularly to participate: Defense, Interior, Labor, the Bureau of the Budget, and the CIA.

The operations of the CFEP were described in detail in a 1961 Bureau of the Budget study:

> Subjects for consideration by the Council are generally suggested by member agencies, although they may also come from the President, the Chairman, the NSC, and others. The range of subject matter considered by the CFEP has been very broad, as illustrated by the following topics: East-West trade, economic defense, international commodity agreements, disposal of agricultural surpluses, trade agreements policy and legislation, expansion of private home ownership in less developed countries, programs to stimulate U.S. exports, and supplemental stockpile policy.
>
> Despite the broadly stated scope of the role of the Special Assistant and the CFEP, the Council has tended to deal with specific subjects and issues as they arise, with the line between broad policy matters and other concerns frequently blurred ... decisions must of necessity result from agreement or a "sense of the meeting," or no decision is forthcoming, unless the issue is referred to the President. Many difficult problems frequently are not brought to the attention of or are not resolved in the CFEP, but rather by officials in their individual and separate capacities.[6]

The CFEP in retrospect has to be judged a failure in terms of its primary objective of providing overall policy coordination among the many policy threads and contributing to a systematic, coherent international economic policy. The definitive post mortem of the CFEP's failure was contained in this same Budget Bureau study, written one year after the former's demise. The following passage is of special significance since it is also an *ex ante* analysis of the failures of the CFEP's successor body, the Council on International Economic Policy:

> Although the range of subject matter considered by the CFEP has been very broad, including almost every possible area of foreign economic affairs, it cannot be considered the principal interagency forum for any area. Foreign assistance matters are considered and coordinated elsewhere. The NAC is the dominant forum for international monetary and financial policy, as is the NSC in national security policy. . . . Preparations for trade negotiations are considered primarily by the Trade Agreements Committee. . . . The CFEP is used to a large extent as a forum for information exchange. Despite the broad charter of the Council, it has tended to deal with specific subjects and issues as they arise, with the line between broad policy matters and other concerns frequently blurred. Because the Chairman has no command authority, decisions must of necessity result from agreement or a "sense of the meeting" or no decision is forthcoming, unless the matter is referred to the President. Frequently, it appears that decisions reached elsewhere are merely ratified in the CFEP.[7]

The major reasons why the CFEP failed included the lack of cooperation by the major line departments and the continuation of specialized independent coordinating groups in every policy sector. Another reason was that it failed to live up to its advance billing as being designed as a parallel to the NSC in the economics area. The CFEP could not achieve comparable strength and influence because the president chaired only the NSC. With insufficient command leadership from its chairman, the CFEP became more of a consultative body than an action-forcing body and more of a specific issue resolver in special circumstances than an integrator of overall policy substance. The next White House-based international economics council would follow this exact route in the 1970s.

The NSC is primarily designed for national security policy coordination, yet it became the central international economic policy coordinating mechanism in the Kennedy-Johnson years (1961–68). President Kennedy terminated the CFEP structure and replaced it with a special deputy to the assistant to the president for national security affairs. Specializing in international economic affairs, the deputy operated as a senior NSC official and had a very small staff, never exceeding two or three persons. Auxiliary staff support existed in the form of close working relationships with senior international economic affairs specialists in other White House offices such as the CEA, the office of the Special Representative for Trade Negotiations, and OMB. At no time, however, did the NSC approximate a central economics coordinating body. The deputy served strictly as personal staff to the president. International economic policy coordination during this period was as highly decentralized as it was informal. White House officials whose primary responsibilities lay outside of this sphere became increasingly active and involved as they saw fit. In the closing months of the Johnson administration, the deputy's position was abolished; the job was divided between two men, one taking responsibility for foreign aid, the other for international trade and monetary affairs.

The Nixon administration for two years retained the same kind of senior international economic policy coordination mechanism it inherited from Johnson: no formal group and no single official charged with responsibility for coordination of international economic policy and having direct access to the president. To the extent there was White House coordination by a president's man during this period, it was handled by C. Fred Bergsten, a middle-level staff member of the NSC. As he wrote, after his departure, however, he had scant access to Kissinger, the NSC's staff director, and even less to the president.

The existence of such loose coordinating machinery existing in the Nixon White House was paradoxical. The latter directly and pervasively set about to consolidate within itself control over the government's policy-making machinery. The apparent explanation is the simplest one: international economic relations received a very low priority and suffered a very low level of understanding. While the NSC was the titular source of coordination, Kissinger did not pay much attention to economics. Detente with the Soviet Union and China, as well as the secret peace negotiations with the North Vietnamese, were in the offing. The NSC at this time simply was overwhelmed with traditional national security matters. Kissinger would not discover the impact of economics on his grand design for a couple more years. The net result of this situation was to underline the limits to using the NSC as a coordinating instrument for international economic policy. Whenever it is devoting its attention to strictly national security policy or its executive head is uninterested in economics, the NSC abdicates its role as international economics coordinator. This was precisely the situation in the 1969–70 period. But just as nature abhors a vacuum, so too did the Nixon White House when it discovered an obvious gap in its authority over major policy issues.

## THE RISE AND DEMISE OF THE CIEP

Into this bureaucratic void eventually stepped the president's Advisory Council on Executive Organization—the so-called Ash Council. The report it submitted to the president in August 1970 recommended the establishment of a new professionally staffed Office of International Economic Policy in the Executive Office of the President. In addition, the cabinet-level CIEP was suggested. In order to avoid creating new units, the Ash Council suggested the Office of the Special Representative for Trade Negotiations be expanded to form the new Office of International Economic Policy. The head of this office, which also would provide the professional staff to the new CIEP, would become the assistant to the president for international economic policy and would retain the legislatively established title of special representative for trade negotiations.

In January 1971, President Nixon ordered the creation of the CIEP and the post of presidential assistant for international economic affairs. But no Office of International Economic Policy was created, and the Special Representative for Trade Negotiations was left untouched. Unlike the Ash Council's recommendation, the president was adding to the White House bureaucracy, not building on the existing machinery. In other words, another power center was introduced into the already numerous White House units having international economic responsibilities. The office of the Special Representative for Trade Negotiations and CIEP inevitably would become rivals in the trade sector.

The White House memorandum announcing the initiation of the CIEP noted that its purpose would be to provide a "clear top-level focus" for all international economic issues, to "achieve consistency between domestic and foreign economic policy," and to "maintain close coordination with basic foreign-policy objectives." The president was to be its chairman, and the other members would be the secretaries of state, the treasury, agriculture, commerce, and labor (the secretaries of defense and transportation were added later), the director of the OMB, the chairman of the CEA, the special representative for trade negotiations, and the executive director of the CIEP, who would be in charge of its small professional staff.

From the beginning, formal meetings of the CIEP were rare; the president attended only a couple of sessions. Most of the work was performed by the cabinet-level Executive Committee (headed by then Treasury Secretary George Shultz); the Senior Review Group, headed by the CIEP's executive director; and the Operations Group, chaired by the undersecretary of state for economic affairs.

Nevertheless, the creation of the CIEP was roundly cheered. In terms of reorganization, it seemed to be an idea whose time had come. Students of organization had, in the early months of the Nixon administration, cited repeatedly the problem of coordinating the 50-odd departments, agencies, and interagency working groups having operational responsibilities in international economic relations. "Gaping voids" had existed in the organization, Roy Ash later testified to a House committee. "There was simply no entity of government, except the President himself, that could examine the whole complex of foreign economic policy issues for consistency and for harmony with

United States interests abroad and with programs at home."[8] The Report of the President's Commission on International Trade and Investment Policy, released in July 1971, hailed the CIEP as "a significant step in providing a unified perspective on international economic policy." It further recommended the CIEP be given permanent legislative status and its own budget, instead of continuing to have it financed with general White House funds and staffed by personnel seconded from other departments and agencies. Congress eventually agreed to this in 1972 in the first of several short-term bills giving a statutory existence to the CIEP. According to the International Economic Policy Act of 1972, Congress bade the CIEP to "provide for closer Federal interagency coordination in the development of a more rational and orderly international economic policy."

The CIEP would never successfully perform such a task. The lack of presidential guidance and utilization of the CIEP; the jealousies of top State and Treasury Department officials, despite their influence and presidential access; internal weaknesses; and the approval by Congress of a seemingly innocuous executive branch amendment in the CIEP's 1973 renewal legislation—all had the collective effect of committing intellectual infanticide on the budding CIEP.

Indeed, the CIEP's failure to achieve its missions was preordained by the uncertain and uninspired attitude towards it by the president. It was launched with the usual high-blown Nixon rhetoric, but the concept was supported by a minimum of specific notions on how it was to function and exactly what tasks it should undertake. A study of the CIEP prepared for the Murphy Commission put it this way:

> The fundamental factor responsible for CIEP's failure to carry out its mission is the nature of that mission, its unrealistic scope and great complexity.... The mission statement is more an exercise of rhetoric and hyperbole than a realistic statement of purpose. It was impractical to expect any interagency coordinating mechanism to perform such a role, under the existing circumstances.
>
> CIEP was assigned, in vague terms, the difficult and delicate task of coordinating policy and of orchestrating the inputs of numerous, often squabbling, agencies whose relative power varied both with the specific issue at hand and with the particular agency principals involved at the time the issue arose.
>
> In international economic policy, real and ultimate power lies elsewhere. CIEP was instructed to recede in favor of NSC in cases of overlap. Two of its members—State and Treasury—are more equal than the others and, when they felt their interests threatened, they moved to exercise their power.[9]

The refusal or inability of President Nixon, like other presidents, to give priority, commitment, and leadership in international economics that would be comparable to what is accorded to national security considerations or domestic economic issues, is a critical matter transcending the immediate CIEP issue. Suffice it to say that the coup de grace to CIEP's hopes to become a comprehensive coordinator of international economic policy was delivered by a seemingly innocuous administration-sponsored amendment to the October 1973 bill that extended the CIEP's life to mid-1977. The amendment eliminated presidential membership, providing that the chairman would be selected from one of the remaining members. The formal loss of the presidential imprimatur meant that from then on, the CIEP was relegated to being an occasional coordinator of mainly secondary issues.

While it is true that the CIEP still exists according to statute, budget, and annual report, in operational terms it is defunct. Ostensibly, it serves as the international arm of the EPB, to be discussed below. Nevertheless, even by the most charitable standards, it is not performing at anywhere near the level originally envisioned for it. It has regrettably joined that long list of bureaucratic entities whose disuse and obsolescence are totally unrelated to its longevity. Was the CIEP to be a cabinet committee, a White House-centered forum for subcabinet officials, a professional secretariat on the president's personal staff, or all of the above? What precise issues was it to coordinate?

If the CIEP as a top-level-coordinator concept died in 1973, the official retention of it necessitated its finding a different role. In fact, it developed two. The first was as a "last resort" coordinator on specific issues when a neutral, government-wide coordinating unit appealed either to the president's economic czar (then Shultz), when subcabinet officials at both the Treasury and State welcomed such a vehicle, when the NSC did not claim authority over a national security issue, or when the CIEP staff itself took the leadership on a newly emerging policy question of noncritical importance, for example, foreign investment in the United States. The second life it assumed was that of an additional, marginal bureaucratic actor. A careful survey of interagency working groups will find numerous instances of the CIEP's joining the traditional cabinet departments and older White House offices (OMB, the office of the Special Representative for Trade Negotiations, CEA, and so on) as a committee member. In effect, the CIEP had been assimilated, like a line agency, into the ranks of the specialized, ad hoc coordinators. Whether a cause or a reflection of CIEP's inevitable demise, no reduction or streamlining of existing interagency working groups was seriously considered in the wake of the CIEP's creation. Indeed, the number of such groups continues to proliferate.

Regarding the leadership of the CIEP, none of the executive directors enjoyed a particularly close professional relationship with the president. And none met the other exacting requirements of being knowledgeable in the field of international economics and about the workings of the federal bureaucracy. Another internal shortcoming has been the uneven nature of the professional staff. Always adequate in absolute terms, its dynamism seldom has glittered in comparison with some other White House groups, notably the Kissinger-led NSC staff.

A final organizational factor in the demise of the CIEP involves the attitudes of the international economic superpower departments, State and Treasury. For a White House-based coordinating group to function success-fully, these departments either need to be ordered to use it, or they must themselves ascertain that it is in their mutual interest to use it. The occasional successes enjoyed by the CIEP usually can be traced to the infrequent material-ization of one of these contingencies.

All things considered, the need for a White House-based coordination is valid. The CIEP in theory was, and is, a good idea. But on an operational level, it fails a basic test of achievement: it never provided a consistent and substan-tial net injection of new effectiveness or efficiency into the coordination pro-cess. The absence of the CIEP from the scene would have done little, if anything, to have adversely affected the course of international economic policy formulation or coordination. What CIEP's demise suggests is that, however valid may be the concept of White House-based coordination, certain bureaucratic and organizational factors must be present to assure effectiveness.


## THE ECONOMIC POLICY BOARD

The pressing contemporary need for a White House-centered coordinat-ing mechanism for international economic policy has suggested that if the CIEP is not a fully operational coordinator, a surrogate must be invented and given a different name. The exodus of the president from the CIEP was facilitated by the creation in December 1972 of the Council on Economic Policy (CEP). Its creation marked the formal elevation of Shultz to a position of economic czar. In addition to being secretary of the treasury, he would be, by the end of 1973, chairman of the all-inclusive CEP, the CIEP, and the East-West Trade Policy Committee. The CIEP, in effect, was subsumed in the CEP, whose purpose was described by Shultz at a December 1, 1972 press conference:

> I think that the primary reason is to provide an identified, explicitly identi-
> fied, coordinating group and person responsible to the President for the
> overall relating of different aspects of economic policy.... It cuts across
> domestic and international spheres and, of course, within the international
> sphere there are many elements to this.

Although Shultz was no czar in ruling on the final substance of policy, he did command the process by which the bureaucracy approached all eco-nomic issues. He was a unique individual: a consummate public servant whose intelligence and integrity far surpassed his ego. International economic policy during the Shultz stewardship, not surprisingly, was unusually good. Not only did he have easy access to, and the trust of, the president, but he was extremely knowledgeable about economics. Last, but far from least, he was a genuinely impartial coordinator, seeking the best overall policy. No formal accusations were ever hurled at him that he abused his position by imposing the Treasury Department's position (which he occasionally overruled in his capacity as the president's man) on other departments. And it was Shultz who mandated what became the CIEP's finest achievement, the coordination of the interagency deliberations that produced the administration's Trade Reform Act proposal. The existence of a man with extraordinary position and personality traits, and of compliant State Department leadership, provided empirical evidence of just how good policy coordination can be under the right conditions. However, the departure of both Nixon and Shultz brought to the scene a new set of presidential preferences and cabinet personalities.

A new chapter in coordinating international economic policy at the senior level began in September 1974, when President Ford created the EPB. The White House said that the purpose of the new forum was to provide advice to the president concerning all aspects of national and international economic policy; to oversee the formulation, coordination, and implementation of all U.S. economic policy; and to serve as the focal point for economic policy decision making. Following in the tradition of the CEP, the secretary of the treasury was designated as chairman, and the membership again included most of the cabinet (only the secretary of defense and the attorney general are not members), and the heads of the economics offices within the White House. Like the CEP before it, the EPB absorbed the CIEP. At the heart of what overall has evolved into a relatively successful operation is the EPB's Executive Committee. Also headed by the treasury secretary, it meets almost every morning in the White House for an informal exchange of views and to set the stage for agreement on U.S. government positions.

If the EPB has had problems, they have been in the international sector. The State Department initially chose not to become actively involved. The reasons for this lay, first, in its being regarded as a Treasury-dominated enterprise and, secondly, in the preference of former Secretary of State Kissinger for using what was then his other post as the president's adviser for national security affairs to provide direct channels to the Oval Office. This is a situation analogous to the shoving aside of international economic issues by the NSC in the 1969–70 period. It reinforces the central thesis of this book, that unless international economic policy is treated by a senior coordinating group as an exclusive, top-priority responsibility and a phenomenon in its own right, such policy faces the clear and present danger of being ignored or downgraded. The belated addition of the secretary of state to the EPB's Executive Committee in July 1975, and the loss of Kissinger's NSC role have increased State Department participation in the EPB. An intellectual cease-fire temporarily prevails.

Nevertheless, the State Department still feels more comfortable in dealing with the more politically sensitive NSC. The Treasury Department remains very content in dealing with the domestic policy-oriented EPB. Both coordinating groups remain active in the international economic policy-making process. To use one at the exclusion of the other would be perceived as tilting this policy either in the foreign-policy or domestic economic policy direction. The upshot of the two-track approach to White House international economic policy coordination has been the creation of joint EPB-NSC working groups, as well as jointly written memoranda to the president. The tension between economic and foreign-policy concerns in international economic policy thus is still carried into the Executive Office of the President. Jurisdiction in the White House among the economists and the foreign-policy specialists is shared on a case-by-case basis in lieu of a precise delineation. The outcome of this situation is important: there is still no universally acknowledged coordinator in the U.S. government dealing primarily with U.S. international economic relations.

## THE SPECIALIZED COORDINATING GROUPS

The U.S. government surely is the world's leader when it comes to the number of interagency groups in general and in international economic policy in particular. Some of the latter are important, some obscure, some forgotten, some useful; and some are moribund. A number of basic organizational factors are involved. First, interagency groups, committees, and task forces spring up to handle almost all new types of problems because no single department has exclusive jurisdiction in any issue sufficiently complex and pressing to be dubbed important. Secondly, no one knows exactly how many groups there are. The groups and their subcommittees are so numerous and ephemeral, and occasionally deal with such obscure technical matters, that a definitive census of them would involve a major effort (no doubt conducted by an interagency working group). For example, in response to a Murphy Commission inquiry, the Treasury Department listed a total of 58 interagency groups in which its staff participated in 1975. The small Office of the Special Representative for Trade Negotiations responded to the same inquiry with a total of 16 groups.* Thirdly, there is no preconceived pattern or order to these groups. They spring

---

*The proliferation of these groups is further illustrated in the 1975 annual report of the ITC, which notes that the ITC participates in a number of interdepartmental committees, including the Technical Committee on Standard Industrial Classification, Federal Committee on International Statistics, Interagency Committee to Identify and Classify Cheeses and Other Dairy Products Offered for Importation, and the Interagency Advisory Committee on Customs Cooperation Council Matters.

up on an ad hoc basis as thorny new issues or legislation spring up. The resulting chaos seems to bother no one. Overpopulation, fragmentation, and jurisdictional overlaps are not concerns of the bureaucracy.

Fourth, the problem of proliferation is in part compounded by the fact that many of the interagency groups meet at two to three distinct levels corresponding to seniority—office director, assistant secretary, and under-secretary or secretary.

Fifth, many interagency groups never die, although they may very slowly fade away. No machinery exists to sweep away groups whose power has shifted elsewhere, or whose job has been displaced by subsequent legislation or executive orders. Trade groups emanating from the Trade Expansion Act of 1962 were still on the books in 1975.

Virtually every written discussion of organization still pays homage to the National Advisory Council on International Monetary and Financial Policies (NAC). Its title and history mask its steady move downhill in importance. Tracing back to the Bretton Woods Agreements Act of 1945, the NAC for many years carried out its original mandate of coordinating the policies and operations of the U.S. government pertaining to the World Bank and the IMF, as well as the policies and operations of all governmental agencies which extended foreign loans or engaged in external financial, foreign exchange, or monetary transactions. The responsibilities of the NAC have withered to the point where today its major continuing function is to routinely extend staff-level interagency approval of proposed loans in the multilateral development banks in which the United States participates and to extend formal approval of individual Eximbank loans. Although it does submit a lengthy annual report to the Congress and occasionally engages in special interagency studies, the NAC engages in routine procedural chores and is outside of the policy-making stream.

The recourse to numerous interagency groups cannot be used as evidence that the quality of senior policy coordination is good. Their proliferation can only demonstrate that working-level coordination is extensive. Perhaps it is excessive, even allowing for a large volume of work. Occasionally slowing down the decision-making process, interagency groups remain as the price to be paid for a democratic system of allowing the viewpoints of all involved ministries to be heard and for the inability of the U.S. government to look at policy objectives and strategy with a unitary viewpoint.

Every major sector of the international economic policy garden grows "crab grass." A partial list of the more important interagency committees will provide some appreciation for the systematic (profuse may be the more applicable adjective) means by which international economic policy is formulated through formal coordinating groups. Beyond the EPB, CIEP, and NSC machinery is the following representative list:

Trade:

 Trade Policy Committee (Under this Cabinet level group established subsequent to the Trade Act of 1974 are the more junior Trade Policy Review Group and the Trade Policy Staff Committee.)

 East-West Foreign Trade Board

 Textile Trade Policy Group

 Adjustment Assistance Coordinating Committee

 Export Administration Review Board

Monetary:

 International Monetary Group

Investment:

 CIEP Interagency Coordinating Group on Expropriation

 CIEP Interagency Committee on Transnational Enterprises

 Committee on Foreign Direct Investment in the United States

Aid and Resources:

 Energy Resources Council

 International Energy Review Group

 Commodities Policy Coordinating Committee

 Agricultural Policy Committee

 Agricultural Policy Working Group

 Development Coordinating Committee

 National Advisory Council on International Monetary and Financial Policies

 Development Loan Committee

 Interagency Staff Committee (PL480)

 OMB Senior Review Group (food aid policy)

## NOTES

1. U.S. Department of Commerce, Bureau of the Budget, "Organization and Coordination of Foreign Economic Activities," vol. 1, mimeographed (Washington, D.C., 1961), p. IV–2.

2. Harold Seidman, *Politics, Position, and Power* (New York: Oxford University Press, 1970), p. 164.

3. Ibid., p. 171.

4. Dean Acheson, *Present at the Creation* (New York: Signet Books, 1970), p. 70.

5. Ibid., p. 78.

6. U.S. Department of Commerce, Bureau of the Budget, op. cit., vol. 2, pp. C53–54.

7. Ibid., vol. 1, p. II–9.

8. Statement of Roy L. Ash, *To Extend and Amend the International Economic Policy Act of 1972,* Hearing of the House Committee on Banking and Currency, May 16, 1973 (Washington, D.C.: U.S. Government Printing Office, 1973), p. 28.

9. Dominic Del Guidice, "Creation and Evolution of the Council on International Economic Policy," in *Appendices* (to the [Report of the] Commission on the Organization of the Government for the Conduct of Foreign Policy), vol. 6 (Washington, D.C.: U.S. Government Printing Office, 1976), p. 123.

# CHAPTER

# 6

## THE DECISION-MAKING
## PROCESS AT WORK

Bureaucratic battles are not won by size, they are won by the ability of the people at the top.

British Treasury official

An empirical examination of the workings of the modern U.S. international economic policy-making process is an essential part of this study. Organization is the relatively static element of the system. Decision-making is the dynamic element. The two interact on an uncertain course. A survey of the organizational factors associated with important contemporary decisions is the basis for attempting to construct theories on how the system functions. There are two principal techniques for presenting such a survey: case studies and model building. Since each technique has certain drawbacks and because of space constraints in this chapter, an eclectic approach has been selected. For a number of reasons, relevance being the most important, the analysis that follows examines policies and actions developed since 1970.

## OBSTACLES TO CONSTRUCTING A UNIFIED THEORY OF
## INTERNATIONAL ECONOMIC POLICY MAKING

One of the inherent drawbacks of a scholarly study of how U.S. international economic policy is formulated and implemented is that the process is fluid, disparate, ad hoc, inconsistent, and just plain messy. The basic premises, priorities, perceptions, and personalities from which policy emanates are all dynamic. The only constant is the overall objective and near cliche of promoting a prosperous, growing world economy based as much as possible on the market mechanism. (This is of course on a level of generality just below suggesting that the goal of U.S. foreign policy is peace and freedom.)

The case study approach to explaining how the system functions has severe limitations in constructing any overall understanding or pattern. Some of these limitations would be obviated if literally dozens of separate decisions and operations were to be examined on a comprehensive basis and then meticulously cross-referenced according to very specific criteria. Even so, a relatively brief time frame would need to be chosen in order to examine a system reflecting similar presidential styles and prevailing global realities. A random sample of ten to 15 events is likely to produce interesting and illustrative anecdotes, but could not be extrapolated on any scientific basis to produce a systemic diagnosis. A carefully preselected sample of decisions, however, could be employed to support arbitrarily any number of hypotheses.

Recurring patterns in decision making do exist. However, they are far from being sufficiently significant statistically to lead to categorical theories or assertions. For example, the 11 case studies in international economic policy decision making written for the Commission on the Organization of the Government for the Conduct of Foreign Policy (and published in Volume 2 in the *Appendices* to its report) were vivid and expensive evidence of the fallacy of trying to capture the essence of universal truths about the organizational system from a small random sample. Collectively the case studies provide no means to either diagnose the system or to predict future actions.

The heart of the matter is that key U.S. international economic policy decisions and actions have been made on a highly idiosyncratic basis. Some were quickly devised in crisis situations; others grew by inertia. Furthermore, the dynamics of decision making in one sector, in one year, are not necessarily representative of those in other sectors (for example, the dynamics of decision making in international monetary reform compared to those in resource transfers to LDCs).

The problem with attempting to construct a model of international economic decision making is that no single construct appears to be valid. The shared-perceptions, bureaucratic-politics, presidential-fiat, and multiple-advocacy models applied to the foreign policy decision-making process have all been demonstrated, both in pure form and in variations, in international economic relations. At this time, it is not possible to predict a priori exactly which model will be relevant for any given issue. Nor is the interrelationship among these models fully understood. In an effort to remain scholarly, while simultaneously straddling the inherent problems of the simple case study approach and of the all-inclusive theory approach, the remainder of this chapter will make two separate attempts at examining the plurality of the system. The first is an examination of how different decision-making exercises can be categorized into various models of the policy-making process. The second

3 1303 00060 4026

examines organizational dynamics associated with generic issues areas, in each of which several specific policies may have been made at different times and in different ways.

## SIX MODES OF INTERNATIONAL ECONOMIC DECISION MAKING

Policy can be formulated, decided, and acted on through a variety of methods. The weights accorded to competing goals and objectives may vary accordingly, as might the timing and quality of decisions. Different circumstances make certain modes, or models, of decision making more appropriate than others. It is a strength of the U.S. policy system that it is sufficiently diverse to provide a number of options in so far as decisions are concerned. It is the system's weakness that the method of decision making normally materializes on the inconsistent, unplanned, catch-as-catch-can basis.

### Presidential Fiat

Decisions under the presidential-fiat model reflect the direct intervention and clear dictation of the president. The latter's personality, his operating style, and the attitude of his senior advisers represent in this case the critical determinants of decision making. In theory, all U.S. international economic policy could be made by such a highly centralized mode in the White House. In practice, very few such decisions have been made this way. The primary reason is that presidents only infrequently have elevated foreign economic relations to sufficiently high levels as to warrant their active and continuing leadership. In this model, the White House participates and dominates from the early formulation of policy through the effort to achieve the objectives selected. Such continuity differentiates this model from instances when the president is drawn into an issue merely to ratify a bureaucratic consensus or to arbitrate at the last minute a dispute among the line departments.

Ironically, the stamp of presidential pressure is relatively seldom found in trade policy. Although the bureaucracy can handle all routine issues, trade is, in dollar terms, the most important component of international economic policy and the sector having most direct impact on domestic and foreign industry, jobs, and consumers' pocketbooks. The main exception to this rule was President Nixon's demand in 1969 that Japan and other textile-exporting countries "voluntarily" restrict their shipments of man-made textile fibers to the U.S. market. The economics of the issue were all but entirely subordinated to the political imperative of fulfilling a campaign pledge designed to obtain political support, not redress actual economic dislocations. For almost three years, the clarity and emphasis of the U.S. position were perfectly clear. However, the absence of flexibility and input by a foreign-policy point of view caused a costly and unjustified trauma in U.S.-Japanese relations completely out of proportion to either the degree of import penetration or the benefits eventually obtained. Ironically, the results of the eventual export restraints agreement were soon dissipated as Japan began losing its competitiveness in international textile trade. From beginning to end, U.S. policy never wavered. It attained its objective, even if it never made sense in economic terms.

Presidents have participated actively in the international economic policy formulation process in selected crises associated with the chronic U.S. balance-of-payments deficits. The classic example was President Nixon's 1971 decision to terminate dollar-gold convertibility and to impose a 10 percent import surcharge as part of the overall new economic policy. This drastic, abrupt shift in economic policy was constructed by the president and a handful of senior advisers during a single fateful August weekend at Camp David. The parallels with the textile dispute are striking. U.S. policy was formulated quickly and enunciated at the highest level. Objectives were then pursued ruthlessly and unequivocally by the president's men with relatively little regard for foreign political sensitivities or foreign-policy considerations. Once again, the United States extracted maximum concessions from other countries while yielding relatively little. This country successfully attained its international economic objectives, but at a foreign-policy cost. Offsetting the responsiveness of the bureaucracy to presidential direction was the obvious drawback of not having an effective senior-level mechanism to analyze and integrate the political and economic dimensions of an international issue.

## Bureaucratic-Politics Model

Most decisions of U.S. international economic policy are the outgrowth of the far more mundane process described in Chapter 3: bureaucratic politics. This model of decision making includes all of those policies which are the end products of bargaining and consensus building by bureaucratic entities possessing different perceptions, goals, constituencies, and vested interests. Many international economic policy actions can be attributed to this model because of the differentiated bureaucratic actors involved, as well as the perennial need to reconcile economics with politics. In other words, much policy is understandably devised to be that which both State and the domestic agencies (principally Treasury) can live with. The decisions made in accordance with this model can usually be identified as involving sensitive, complex issues between governments and not directly involving the commercial sector.

A contemporary issue occupying a good deal of the bureaucracy's time involves U.S. reaction to the economic demands of the LDCs collectively known as "the new international economic order." It is a classic case of bureaucratic politics at work. Predictably, the Treasury Department assumed an orthodox free market approach, decrying suggestions that government intervention and budgetary funds be used to rig the international economic system to favor the LDCs. Sensitive to the political implications of an angry group of nations capable of disrupting the international order, the State Department is anxious to develop a serious dialogue wherever and whenever possible. With regard to some of the more extreme LDC proposals (for example, indexing of commodity prices according to the price trends of industrial goods and a generalized debt moratorium), there never has been a major State-Treasury dispute. The search for a common bureaucratic meeting ground was successful on a number of the aid proposals floated because of common perceptions. In general, U.S. policy has emphasized the use of official and private capital flows in lieu of price-fixing proposals. No U.S. agency prefers to emphasize antimarket forces to foster the development process.

An unusual number of organizational strains and innovations are associated with this new, complex discussion of how to alter the North-South status quo. They include the inherent difficulties of constructing a policy where a minimum number of precedents exist, where the technical questions associated with some of the proposals are very complex, where a clear mix of economic and political factors exist, where jurisdictional lines are blurred, where differences of opinion between departments escalate into a public, no-holds-barred rivalry, and where no arbitration mechanism is readily available to hammer out a harmonized policy.

From the official birth of the new-international-economic-order concept in the spring of 1974 at the Sixth Special Session of the United Nations General Assembly, until May 1975, the United States had assumed a hostile attitude, opposing the general view that structural changes were necessary to reduce the international economic system's alleged bias against the poor countries. The session produced a document entitled "Declaration on the Establishment of a New International Economic Order"; a subsequent document approved by the General Assembly, entitled the "Chapter of Economic Rights and Duties of States," contained a long shopping list of demands to redress the imbalance of world economic wealth. International commodity agreements to raise and fix commodity prices, unilateral reductions in industrial country barriers to exports of LDCs, elimination of all restraints on the expropriation of foreign direct investments including the requirement of full and prompt compensation, a general debt moratorium, transfer of technology on easier terms, and a generally increased voice for LDCs in international economic organizations—these were among the demands written in harsh, uncompromising terms.

Initial U.S. policy was negative for a number of reasons—the United States was still a leader of and a firm believer in a market-oriented international economy. There was a widely held, lingering hope that the OPEC would disintegrate, and thus a hard line—not appeasement—was necessary to prevent further cartels from being formed. In addition, the United States had a relatively minor dependence on developing countries for critical raw materials, exclusive of oil. This country is able therefore to risk more antipathy by the developing countries than could the far more resource-dependent Europeans and Japanese.

A major turning point in the heretofore unified U.S. position took place in the wake of the failure of the April 1975 preparatory meeting that was to set the stage for an international conference between producers and consumers of energy. The talks collapsed when an irreconcilable split developed between industrial and developing countries on the question of whether the agenda for the energy conference should be broadened to include discussion of other raw materials and the rest of the South's economic demands. Plans for an international energy conference between producers and consumers were postponed indefinitely; in short, a dead end had been reached. The time had come for an initiative. It would shortly be Kissinger who took it.

Separate studies by the State and Treasury departments of the international-commodity-agreement issue had begun in 1974, but were merged into an interagency task force on international commodity agreements in February, 1975. This group in turn reported to two other review groups, the EPB and the NSC, the former having a spiritual and intellectual affinity with Treasury, the latter with State. Thus, while a more efficient cooperative effort resulted, neither State nor Treasury yielded any control over the options-exploration process. Some consensus emerged, nonetheless. The principal conclusion reached by the task force was that the United States should be prepared to discuss commodity price and supply arrangements on an individual basis, and should avoid a single grand approach to commodity arrangements.[1]

In late April, Secretary of State Kissinger was reviewing the text of a speech concerning food policy, which he was scheduled to deliver on May 13 in Kansas City, Missouri. He thought the speech both boring and unresponsive to the existing issues. He thereupon ordered his staff to include language proclaiming a new U.S. flexibility on the North-South dialogue. By the time the rewritten text had been approved within State, there was time only for a perfunctory, eleventh-hour clearance at the very top levels of the Treasury Department. Despite the fact that technically there was an approval by Treasury, the last-minute, hasty clearance process permitted no opportunity for any real input by other departments. And so Kissinger announced that the United States was prepared to discuss "new arrangements in individual commodities on a case-by-case basis as circumstances warrant." He also stated that this country was anxious to attend a new preparatory meeting for a North-South dialogue. His talk began an unprecedented process of forcing U.S. new-international-economic-order policy by speech making. A major policy decision had been forged by Kissinger's last-minute command to his senior staff, to allow him to enunciate publicly a new U.S. posture on commodities. Interagency deliberations had at best been perfunctory.

A close analysis of Kissinger's speech would reveal a carefully hedged, least-common-denominator approach, which committed this country to very little in the way of specifics. Nevertheless, the speech triggered a savage bureaucratic counterattack at Treasury. The latter, whose legal jurisdiction in the issue of international commodity agreements is somewhat unclear, issued the first of what would be many broadsides against State, suggesting that U.S. policy had not really changed in this case. In a late May 1975 White House meeting, Treasury Secretary Simon attempted to impress upon the president that nothing Kissinger had said, or would say, would bind this country to anything specific. Assistant Treasury Secretary Gerald Parsky told a press interviewer shortly afterwards that "no decision has been made to make a change in the basic thrust of this country's policy in the commodities area, which is to maintain to the maximum extent the free functioning of the marketplace." What Kissinger said is settled U.S. policy; what it means is not yet settled policy, an official of the special trade representative's office was quoted as saying.[2]

The very subtle shift in attitude and the nonshift in actual policy notwithstanding, the commodity-cartel question assumed a life far out of proportion to its actual merits and importance. It became a symbol of the larger and oversimplified ideological question as to the need to occasionally circumvent the market mechanism with negotiated price fixing as a means of assuaging the economic demands of the poorer countries.

The approach of the U.N. Seventh Special Session, in September of 1975, meant another speech and the opportunity for another U.S. initiative. Not wishing to repeat the coordination fiasco associated with the May speech, the State Department initiated an ad hoc series of consultations, primarily with the Treasury and Agriculture departments. Once it was decided to have Secretary Kissinger's speech include a major series of resource-transfer proposals, each one was negotiated and cleared at all levels of the other agencies. An August meeting at the cabinet level went over each of the proposals for which technical agreement had been reached at the working level. In a few cases, the president had to resolve basic points on which no consensus could be reached. In each case he took the side of Kissinger against opposition from one or more top officials, their opposition largely stemming from budgetary concerns. Contact was also maintained with interested members of Congress who generally encouraged a responsive U.S. approach.

The Kissinger speech delivered to the United Nations on September 1, 1975 contained more than 40 proposals, some old, some new, some borrowed, and some misconstrued. They emphasized new or expanded financing facilities in the IMF and the World Bank. The scope and positivism of the U.S. program caused the speech to be extremely favorably received by everyone. The U.S.

bureaucracy, too, was happy. The executive branch had agreed to support a number of new financial facilities to transfer resources to LDCs, to demand guaranteed access of supply, as well as to oppose some of the South's more extreme economic proposals, such as indexing of commodity prices according to the price trends of industrial goods. After a concerted effort at interagency coordination, only one major difference remained in the wide range of aid policies.

Only the vexatious question of commodity agreements was not laid to rest by the second great policy-by-speech initiative. The policy-by-speech syndrome took another turn when Assistant Treasury Secretary Parsky told a San Francisco audience in January 1976 that "there appears to be a growing willingness to sacrifice economic principles for the sake of political gains. If, for political reasons, we agree now . . . with demands for a new economic system, it will be impossible to justify on economic grounds our desire to preserve our system later." He also announced that the United States would not sign the then pending international cocoa agreement.

None of this speech had been cleared with a horrified State Department. The latter had been hoping to push positively for a revision of the cocoa agreement's proposed language, not opt for a public declaration of opposition. Parsky's equivocal written clarification of U.S. commodity-agreements policy to the press on the next day did nothing to clarify U.S. policy. Despite the statement's reiteration of the principle of case-by-case approach for commodity agreements, he allegedly told the assembled reporters verbally that U.S. policy in principle opposed the concept of such agreements. The degree to which the relevant officials in the State and Treasury departments pursued bureaucratic politics exacerbated a unique characteristic of the American way of disagreeing: a propensity to air the disagreement in public, for all to see.

And so the U.S. government's posture towards a major element of the new international economic order has festered on an open-ended basis. The Treasury has assumed the role of protector of the market mechanism, while the State Department argues for a pragmatic posture to allow price stabilization discussions (as opposed to commitment) on any commodity. In the meantime, an interagency Commodities Policy Coordinating Committee, reporting to both the EPB and the NSC, has been formed to continue intragovernmental discussions on this subject.

It should be noted that this committee is the latest in a line of special groups coping with the international commodity question and related issues. During 1974, internal commodity working groups existed within both State and Treasury. When it was decided in early 1975 to unify these efforts into a single interagency task force, the Treasury found itself arguing for an EPB group, while State argued for an NSC group. As a compromise, preparations for the Seventh Special Session of the General Assembly were undertaken in a joint EPB-NSC group. (At the same time, food issues included in the new-international-economic-order debate were being discussed in three different groups—the State Department-chaired International Food Review Group, the joint EPB-NSC Food Committee, and the Food Deputies Group of the EPB, chaired by a member of the CEA.)

Following the U.S. initiative at the United Nations in the fall of 1975, the State Department proposed to terminate interagency commodity deliberations. This proposal was firmly opposed by the economic agencies, and thereupon the Commodities Policy Coordinating Committee was initiated. To assuage the bureaucratic rivalry, joint State-Treasury chairmanship was adopted. In addition, special groups were established in late 1975 to formulate the U.S. position in the raw materials working group of the multilateral Conference on International Economic Cooperation. Still another group was formed to manage U.S. policies at the meeting of the United Nations Conference on Trade and Development (UNCTAD) held in the spring of 1976. This procession of interagency groups had one thing in common: the continuing struggle of State, Treasury, and Agriculture to exert their special perspectives and personal objectives on the international food and commodity policy debates.

Bureaucratic politics dominate the formulation of a U.S. position on an international food policy. The USDA replaces the Treasury Department in this case as protector of domestic economic interests and the free market mechanism against State's desire to produce a system of maximum use of the world marketplace. The bureaucratic constant underlying Agriculture Department policies is the need to promote the welfare of the American farmer. To predict exactly how it pursues this mission, one must first analyze the ever-changing economic forces prevalent in the agricultural sector. Prior to 1973, U.S. international food policy was concerned with disposal of agricultural surpluses. In the resulting buyers' market, the interests of farmers required programs to develop new markets. Soaring worldwide demand erased this situation, thereby introducing concern in the USDA to maintain prices, while other departments were beginning to worry about domestic inflation, how to increase food production, and the increased costs to the U.S. government to acquire food for use as aid. Extraordinary supply pressures in that year led to the unprecedented imposition of export controls on soybeans despite Agriculture's opposition.

The formulation of the U.S. position on how much of a food aid commitment it should announce in 1974 illustrated differing emphases on a short-term attack on world hunger, domestic agricultural policies, and domestic prices and budgetary restraints. The bureaucracy debated the aid issue inconclusively for months while awaiting the final forecasts of the fall crop to determine availabilities. But a decision had to be made prior to the president's scheduled address to the General Assembly on September 18, 1974, when he would have to discuss U.S. food aid policy. Agreeing with Secretary Kissinger that the United States should raise substantially the value of its food aid, President Ford selected an increase to about $1.5 billion.

> The theme of the [president's] speech was victory for Kissinger, but every-thing else was a compromise. On the level of increase, the difference was roughly split between Kissinger, who wanted about $1.8 billion as the new total, and [OMB and CEA heads] Ash and Greenspan, who argued for holding the level at $900 million. In the middle, ranging from those advocat-ing less aid to more, were the CIEP, Treasury, and Agriculture. And the $1.5 billion figure was more a general target than a firm decision. Indeed, a month later there was still disagreement about what Ford had decided.[3]

When the U.S. government set about in 1975 to flesh out details of the second major component of its international food policy—an international grain reserve system—this pattern of bureaucratic politics repeated itself. The basic issue was the technical question of how flexible should the formula be by which reserves would be released from the stockpile. The State Department focused primarily on the specter of world malnutrition and hunger. It therefore opted for a system with specific rules of conduct, a large physical stockpile of 30–35 million metric tons of food grains, use of prices as the trigger for releasing reserves, and the use of sanctions (that is, export controls) during shortage periods against countries who weren't participants in the multilateral arrangement.

The Agriculture Department opted for a system run as loosely as possible (that is, with a minimum of specific, permanent rules); a stockpile only two-thirds the size proposed by State; a set of release triggers based on the quantity of available food (mainly as a means of discouraging any use of the stockpile as an indirect means of commodity price fixing); and a prohibition of export controls—that is, no special access to the reserve stockpile would be guaran-teed to participating countries.

The International Food Review Group, under whose auspices interagency discussions on this issue were taking place, could not reconcile these differ-ences. Established to follow through on U.S. policy towards the initiatives that grew out of the World Food Conference of November 1974, the group met at the cabinet and assistant secretary levels. The State Department chaired the group, with Agriculture as vice chairman. The other members, Treasury, OMB, CEA, the special trade representative's office, and the executive direc-tors of the EPB and CIEP, were only supporting actors in the State-Agricul-ture dispute. The special trade representative's office had originally suggested that the reserves negotiations be shifted from the International Wheat Council in London to the multilateral trade negotiations in Geneva, in which the office had direction of U.S. policy. Rebuffed by State and Agriculture on this juris-dictional issue, the office receded to an observer status.

The ending of the dispute began in early June 1975, when several members of the EPB openly voiced their dissatisfaction with the lack of progress. This new pressure, together with the impending fall speech by Kissinger to the United Nations, forced a State-Agriculture compromise to be hammered out. The U.S. position that was explained to a September 29 meeting of the International Wheat Council had all of the earmarks of something designed by a committee wracked by basic differences of opinion. The United States proposed a coordinated system of nationally held reserves totaling 30 million tons that would be accumulated on the basis of imprecise quantitative rather than price targets. Reserves from the food stockpile would be released in two stages. The first stage would come into being when a potential shortage existed, and would require consultations among participants as to what future action was necessary. Once an actual shortage materialized (it would be defined in advance), participating countries would be required to release a minimum quantity of wheat or rice, the exact amount being in accordance with each country's domestic food situation. Participating countries were assured access to supplies at market prices, but position of nonparticipants remained unclear.[4]

Another example of pure bureaucratic politics involves the question of export promotion. Among the many basic questions involved here are these: Is it necessary and proper for the government to provide support services to help the private sector increase its sales and profits?; if so, are present techniques cost effective and efficient?; and finally, how much priority should be placed on export promotion per se? The ensuing policy debate was, and is, one of those rare occasions when neither the State nor Treasury Department is involved as a primary actor; neither department has any mission or constituency directly involved.

Two specific aspects of the longstanding export promotion issue are of special relevance to this section. The first involves techniques of export finance. In the case of the U.S. government, this issue is synonymous with the operations of the Eximbank. Some of the recent presidents of that institution sought eagerly to expand U.S. exports through massive loans and guarantees on the most favorable terms possible, for example, at interest rates lower than comparable commercial rates. The rationale is ostensibly that the world marketplace is highly competitive, other countries are providing generous export financing, and that increased U.S. exports create more jobs and help our balance of payments. The Commerce Department, with its business orientation and its own program of export promotion, heartily endorses an active and generous Eximbank program of export financing.

In the early 1970s, the OMB and the Federal Reserve Board increased their existing opposition to the scope of Eximbank's operations. They argued that U.S. budgetary funds (the source of Eximbank loan capital) were being used inefficiently, and that any subsidization of the export sector violated a basic tenet of free market economic theory. Their opposition continued for some time without significant effect until the Treasury Department provided lukewarm support for their position. The latter's turnaround came largely as a result of technical balance-of-payment factors, whereby it was realized that exports sold on a cash basis provided more immediate external account benefits than exports that were financed on a long-term basis by Eximbank. One immediate result was a decision taken by a special working group of the interagency NAC to increase Eximbank's interest rates and thereby move them closer to prevailing commercial rates. Sensing this new environment, Eximbank took other unilateral measures, such as reducing the percentage of its own participation in individual loan transactions and thereby increasing the share of commercial bank participation in export loans.

A second major decision occurred in early 1975, when the OMB recommended a sizable cut in Commerce's budget for export promotion services (data collection, trade fairs, and so on). OMB argued that such funds never had produced any measurable benefits and were rendered even more unnecessary by the advent of flexible exchange rates (which tend to set exchange rates at equilibrium levels). The Commerce Department countered with an extraordinary attack on OMB reasoning, openly taking its views to Capitol Hill and to the business community. A major elimination of a services function in a department that already had been stripped of significant influence in policy making was something that Commerce could not live with. The rest of the bureaucracy (exclusive of Ex-Im) was generally apathetic to the debate, neither disapproving Commerce's services in this area nor having any great confidence that these efforts significantly aided the U.S. export performance. In any event, none of their own missions or perspectives was affected directly. Eventually, most of the funds were restored by a generous Congress that was apparently impressed with Commerce's protestations that for every dollar's reduction in export promotion, a multiple of U.S. exports, and therefore sales and jobs, would be lost.

A final example of a relatively pure application of the bureaucratic-politics model occurred when the Ford administration reached its decision in April 1976 as to what would be its reaction to the ITC's recommendation that the U.S. footwear industry be granted relief from import competition. Rather than invoke the escape clause to impose higher tariffs or quotas, President Ford accepted the narrow (one-vote) majority recommendation of his cabinet-level Trade Policy Committee, that funds for adjustment assistance be made available to the industry. In addition to the predictable votes of the foreign-trade-related departments who are members of the committee (State on the liberal side, and Commerce and Labor on the protectionist side), the Department of Defense's vote was exactly the one that conformed to its interests and mission. Two of the major shoe-exporting countries to this market are Spain and Italy. Since the former is the site of important military bases and the latter is a NATO ally facing serious economic difficulties and an increasingly powerful

Communist party, and since domestic suppliers of footwear to the American military were secure from foreign competition, the Defense Department cast its crucial vote against a resort to protectionist measures. As another indirect participant in U.S. trade policy, the Justice Department also is prone to see its mission and values enhanced by the liberal trade approach. A minimum of trade barriers increases competition, while a protectionist policy is an anathema to the enforcers of antitrust laws.

## Shared Images and Perceptions

Many international economic policies of the United States are routinely handled by a bureaucracy hampered by no real differences of opinion. In most cases, U.S. policy concerning international investment issues smoothly emanates from several shared assumptions. The dominant one is that the market mechanism should be allowed to function: a liberal investment system should exist side by side with a liberal trading system. No agency wishes to drastically alter the tax treatment of overseas corporate income (the tax deferral and tax credit) on a punitive basis, as advocated by the AFL-CIO in the Burke-Hartke bill. No agency had problems with U.S. participation in the OECD exercise to produce a voluntary code of conduct for multinational enterprises. And, no agency has opted for any shift in the essentially open-door policy that exists in this country for foreign direct investors.

Bureaucratic politics can, however, dominate certain sensitive international investment issues. For example, the State Department takes a relatively more relaxed approach to the question of foreign expropriations of U.S. direct investments; their position emphasizes quiet diplomacy and a low-profile approach. The Treasury Department's approach to the subject is a more hardline one that stridently defends the rights of U.S. corporations to receive prompt and just compensation, and also argues in general for the need to promote an attractive atomosphere for private capital formation in LDCs.

An example of the shared-perceptions model joining with bureaucratic politics occurred in early 1976, on the international business question of U.S. corporations' response to Arab boycott demands. Fearful of disrupting foreign policy and overseas U.S. business ventures, the international economic policy leaders, State, Treasury, and Commerce, opted for a very low government profile. The Justice Department's lonely determination to enforce the letter of U.S. law found itself completely isolated in one of its infrequent ventures into international economic policy.

The lack of any major dissension and the absence of any priority departmental interests in most international investment issues have resulted in a very loose, decentralized decision-making apparatus. This lack of bureaucratic fervor was responsible for the CIEP's being given significant coordination responsibilities in the past and for the virtual absence today of a formalized pattern of jurisdiction or decision-making in the international investment sector.

A second example of shared perceptions, often bordering on "group-think," has occurred repeatedly in this country's attempted formulation of an international energy policy. With the exception of the explosive State-Treasury feud on the infamous concept of a guaranteed floor price for oil, no continuing, serious differences of opinion are evident. The State and Treasury departments, the Federal Energy Administration (FEA), and the concerned White House offices have not disagreed on the need for certain basic policies: reduced dependence on oil imports, reduced vulnerability to future embargo threats through stockpiling and international sharing arrangements, increased cooperation by oil consumers to develop alternative energy sources and conservation techniques, and the need to develop a permanent multilateral dialogue between oil-producing and -consuming countries. Nor was there any disagreement on the fact that the high price of oil was at the root of energy-induced problems; that OPEC was imposing a political, nonmarket price for oil on the world; that divisiveness in OPEC should be encouraged, that international financial recycling measures could, and should, be put into effect, and that special financial facilities should be established in the IMF and in the proposed Financial Support Fund to be managed by the OECD to provide extra balance-of-payments financing for oil-importing countries.

In each case, formal organizational factors were irrelevant. What mattered was that State, Treasury, and the FEA met together in a variety of informal and formal groups (EPB and the Energy Resources Council) to consolidate a unified position. When the disagreement on the guarenteed-oil-floor-price proposal could not be reconciled at the cabinet level, President Ford made a clear-cut formal decision to approve Kissinger's positive recommendation over Treasury's opposition (based mainly on its inconsistency with the market mechanism). The major bureaucratic squabble on international energy policy was thereupon ended.

It is unfortunate and/or axiomatic that bureaucratic consensus on such a complex and vital issue is an outgrowth of a more fundamental dilemma. The ultimate reality, it can be argued, is that none of these elements of the policy begins to achieve the principal U.S. objective: a clear and present reduction, or at least a stabilization, in the quantity of U.S. oil imports. No international energy policy based on independence can be successful without imposing certain vigorous domestic measures reducing demand for oil or increasing domestic energy production.

To the extent that the bureaucracy believes that it can devise an effective international energy policy in the absence of a domestic energy policy that increases supply and decreases demand, it is suffering from delusional group thinking. Since no domestic decreases in consumption or short-term increases in the supply of energy have yet to be induced, only posturing and tinkering are possible on the foreign level. Perhaps an instinctive sensing of this dilemma has discouraged the presidential-leadership or bureaucratic-politics model—as well as an effective policy—from emerging.

## Multiple-Advocacy Model

Decisions taken under the multiple-advocacy model involve the forceful management of the competitive bureaucratic viewpoints by a dispassionate, neutral adherent to a presidential perspective. Power brokering is removed from representatives of line departments. Normally a White House official, the coordination manager has the responsibility to ensure an equitable distribution of power, information, staff resources, and access to the president among the participating bureaucratic actors. Ideally, the president participates from the beginning of the debate.[5]

The closest example of what might be posited as potentially the ideal means of decision making was the interagency deliberations in 1972–73 that produced a proposal for major trade legislation. The latter was submitted to Congress in April 1973, and eventually became the Trade Act of 1974. The process by which the trade bill was drafted reflected two principal realities. First, U.S. trade policy, then in the period subsequent to that of the new economic policy, was at a major historical crossroads. Intellectually, the questions of where and how to proceed legislatively were exceedingly complex. Even the basic question of the wisdom of submitting a comprehensive trade bill to the Hill had to be thrashed out. Secondly, the number of bureaucratic entities in 1972 with an overall or specific interest in major trade legislation was enormous. More than a dozen departments and agencies regularly participated in the interagency drafting sessions. Others attended occasionally. About 25 persons reportedly attended a typical meeting.

The so-called Trade Legislative Committee, the interagency group that handled the statute-drafting chore, was established formally in the CIEP machinery by George Shultz's acting in his informal capacity as "economic czar" and in his formal capacity as head of the CEP (the predecessor to the EPB and a body senior to the CIEP). The committee was chaired by the deputy executive director of the CIEP and reported to the cabinet-level Executive Committee of the CIEP. This committee was headed by Shultz by virtue of his also being chairman of the CIEP.

The starting-off point for the interagency discussions was provided by a nonbureaucratic source: the report submitted in 1971 by the president's Commission on International Trade and Investment Policy. It had been formed in 1971 by President Nixon to study independently and exhaustively all of the options open to the United States on all international commercial issues during the decade of the 1970s. The dozens of specific policy recommendations contained in the report were methodically sifted by the trade legislative group as its initial exercise in debating the issues.

By late 1972, work began in earnest to finalize the language of the bill. This effort also was under the overall supervision of Shultz, the president's man. Although he was the treasury secretary, Shultz's personal traits and style permitted him to play the role of the neutral custodian of the presidential perspective. His demeanor in this exercise was usually soft-spoken, at times enigmatic, and always pointed in the direction of building a consensus. His firm commitment to producing the best possible trade bill was reflected in his occasional opposition to Treasury positions.

Differences in goals and viewpoints abounded in the continuing interagency deliberations. State and the office of the Special Representative for Trade Negotiations shared a preference for a very liberal bill with a maximum of negotiating authority. The Treasury and Commerce departments were anxious to protect and promote the balance of payments and the business sector, respectively. The Agriculture Department was anxious to rectify what was presumed to be an insufficient agricultural liberalization package produced in the Kennedy Round. All of these viewpoints were valid inputs in a major governmental debate on trade strategy. Although these disagreements slowed down the drafting process, they forced an exacting and thorough debate on the issues and eventually produced a bill with broad support in the administration.

The reason that the bureaucratic-politics model is not an accurate description of the work of the Trade Legislative Committee is based not only on the means of supervision, but on the means of making final decisions as well. When an immediate consensus was not forthcoming on a relatively minor issue, the committee's chairman, Deane Hinton, deputy executive director of the CIEP, would make a ruling, in effect on behalf of the president. Substantive disagreements and appeals immediately would be sent up to the CIEP's Executive Committee for a decision. If no consensus developed there, the president's economic chief, Shultz, personally would make the final decision or request a presidential decision.

## Democratic-Politics Model

The policy-making process in the democratic-politics model is broader than it is in the previous model. The decision-making process is expanded to involve not only the White House and the agencies with operational responsibilities, but also the Congress and interested groups in the public sector. International economic policy made here is a function of persuasion, of working towards the broadest possible consensus inside and outside of the executive branch. One example of this model was the bipartisan support for the establishment of the Marshall Plan.

A second example was the process that began in the aftermath of the administration's submission of the Trade Reform Act Proposal to Congress in April 1973. The legislative process by which the Congress modified and then approved the bill reflected congressional-executive branch relations at their best. Despite the latent protectionist attitudes on Capitol Hill and despite the emerging Watergate-induced sentiment against any new extensions of power to the executive branch, the resulting Trade Act of 1974 bestowed an ample amount of authority on the president to negotiate reductions in trade barriers, and contained a minimal amount of trade-restrictive language. A very close working relationship was developed by William Eberle, the president's special representative for trade negotiations and his deputies, Harald Malmgren and William Pearce, with the two committees that drafted the statute. They often were allowed to attend the actual mark-up of the bill, providing last-minute data or arguments.

The final passage of the bill was delayed until January 1975, mainly because of a noneconomic issue; in fact, it passed on the last day of the 93d Congress. The extension of nondiscriminatory (most-favored-nation) tariff treatment to Communist bloc countries had been tied by the Jackson-Vanik amendment to their maintenance of a liberal emigration policy. Secretary of State Kissinger reacted by initiating a complex series of negotiations on this politically volatile point (which touched directly on detente) with both the Russians and Senator Henry Jackson, the de facto leader of the domestic forces arguing for this link. Meanwhile, the leadership of the special trade representative's office had extended its lobbying efforts and genteel powers of persuasion to the private sector. By the end of the year, every concerned special-interest group and business sector was advocating passage of the bill.The AFL-CIO in the end was its only major opponent.

The most interesting bureaucratic debate occurred later. Kissinger's foreign-policy concerns led him unsuccessfully to urge the president to veto the newly passed bill when the Russians suddenly denounced the emigration requirements, an action which rendered inoperative the nondiscriminatory tariff provision. The economic agencies argued otherwise. They wanted a trade bill immediately.

One factor behind this popular support was the specifically legislated dictum added to the trade bill by Congress. Section 135 directs the executive branch to consult formally with the private sector regarding "negotiating objectives and bargaining positions before entering into a trade agreement." A wide range of government public forums has been created to meet this requirement. At the top of this list is the president's advisory Committee on Trade Negotiations, whose 45 members run the gamut of the public-interest spectrum and are responsible for developing the broad policy overview. The industrial sector consults with trade policy officials (mainly the special trade representative's office and Commerce) through the 500-plus business people who are members of the Industry Policy Advisory Committee and its 27 industry sector advisory committees. The farm bloc consults with the special trade representative's office and the Agriculture Department through the Agricultural Policy Advisory Committee and its eight agricultural technical advisory committees. Finally, the Labor Policy Advisory Committee and six labor sector advisory Committees present workers' points of view to the trade negotiators. The latter consult among themselves on the U.S. position in the Tokyo Round by using the 11-member Trade Policy Committee, a cabinet-level group chaired by the special trade representative's office. The latter also chairs the sub-cabinet Trade Policy Review Group and the working-level Trade Policy Staff Committee.

That the Trade Policy Committee is cognizant of external bureaucratic variables was demonstrated by its formulating the president's response in March 1976 to the ITC's recommendation that through the escape clause, import quotas be imposed for five years to relieve injury alleged to have been suffered by the domestic specialty steel industry. The resulting decision to opt for a voluntary export restraint very clearly reflected the increased role stipulated for the Congress in escape-clause cases. Normal bureaucratic politics would have dictated a united stand (exclusive perhaps of Commerce and Labor) against the quota recommendation. At best, dubious economic analysis was used to demonstrate import-induced injury suffered by the U.S. specialty steel industry at a time that major trade liberalization negotiations were in progress in Geneva. Shared bureaucratic interests and attitudes had to be subordinated to the fact that the Trade Act of 1974 stipulates that Congress can override a presidential rejection of a majority ITC escape-clause recommendation by a simple majority of members voting in both houses. There were in fact indications that such an override would have resulted if the bureaucracy's (State's and Treasury's) instinct for a liberal trade approach had been chosen. The administration's course, therefore, was molded by the practical need to respect the private sector's ability to convince elected representatives in Washington of the domestic political need for import protection. Congressional influence had offset the normal guideline that a State-Treasury consensus presupposes the making of U.S. policy.

## The Personality Factor

Strong personalities being in the right place at the right time can force decisions and short-circuit the established operational decision-making organization. When the cult of personality successfully intervenes, all bets are off. Personalities can and do substitute for established organizational patterns.

Illustrative of this model was the intervention by senior officials who, operating on their own, encouraged President Nixon to order a shift in U.S.

policy on exchange-rate realignment in late 1971. In the aftermath of the new economic policy, foreign exchange rates were floating in response to free market forces. This was a highly unsettling experience to the financial authorities of almost every other free world country. John Connally, the then secretary of the treasury, personally dominated U.S. international economic policy during the latter third of 1971 as the result of his extraordinary relationship with the president and of his hard-driving personality. His strategy was to press hard on other industrial countries to revalue their currencies and reduce their barriers to U.S. exports, all the while refusing to be specific on the administration's terms for a negotiated settlement on exchange rates. The United States was relatively insulated from the prolonged international monetary chaos, and Connally was playing his strong hand for all it was worth .

Had the State Department enjoyed strong leadership and influence with the president at this time, a classic confrontation of bureaucratic politics would have developed. Economic initiatives were causing political problems of great concern to foreign-policy priorities. As weeks stretched into months, the economic strains were increasingly likely to spill over into the political-national security sectors. The timing was particularly inopportune for creating disarray in the Atlantic alliance, since presidential summit meetings with China and the Soviet Union loomed on the horizon.

A very informal alliance to alter U.S. policy began to develop between Kissinger, in his role as the president's national security advisor, and Arthur Burns, chairman of the independent Federal Reserve Board. Peterson, head of the CIEP, and Robert Hormats, Kissinger's assistant for economic affairs, played supportive roles by raising questions within the White House noting that the U.S. demands on the Europeans and Japanese were unreasonable, unattainable, and damaging to overall U.S. foreign-policy objectives. The immediate problem was tactical: the sheer force of Secretary Connally's personality and his close relationship with the president suggested the folly of a frontal attack that would force the president to choose between sides. In addition, the State Department as an institution was not in the picture to lend support.

Both Kissinger and Burns made informal, personal presentations to the president concerning the dangers of prolonging agreement on a monetary settlement. The former emphasized the political ramifications, while Burns reportedly emphasized the growing dangers of foreign retaliation, a move which could lead to global economic chaos.

> By mid-November [1971] the voices of Kissinger, Burns and the President's own friends on Wall Street began to make an impression on Mr. Nixon. They tried to convince him that to continue to follow the Connally policy could have disastrous consequences, that the United States could no longer keep the world on tenterhooks and had to make it clear that it was ready to devalue the dollar in terms of gold and agree to a new set of exchange rates. The President listened and gradually . . . decided to end the waiting game.[6]

Technically, the presidential model of decision making was operational. But it was bent by the force of two senior personalities.

## SELECTED CASE STUDIES OF POLICY MAKING

Not all means of organizational decision making in U.S. international economic policy conform to one or even a combination of the six modes described above. Other decisions and positions spring from the idiosyncratic and unique factors operating in specific issue areas. Any typology of decision-making techniques in U.S. international economic relations must be open ended to some extent. The very imprecision of the system precludes a narrow approach. A sample of the prominent examples of extraordinary policy formulation follows. These case studies discuss international monetary relations as representative of one-agency domination; agricultural trade blunders as the result of organizational failure; East-West trade policy as decentralized chaos; and a number of topics representing nonrecurring or routine issues.

The most important example of single-agency control is the Treasury Department's dominance of U.S. international monetary policy. The latter includes the balance of payments, exchange-rate adjustments, use of monetary reserves, voting in the IMF, and the monetary role of gold. These issues are exceedingly arcane in nature. They also are divorced from domestic politics and public concern, inasmuch as they do not affect the public in a direct or measurable manner. Outside of Treasury, only the State Department and the CEA in the administration have even a limited interest and expertise. Only the Federal Reserve Board, which formally is independent of the executive branch, shares with Treasury a major interest, expertise, and, through the Federal Reserve Bank of New York, operational responsibilities. In the public sector, a select handful of academics and Wall Street types maintain an active interest and sought-after opinions.

The normal pattern of international monetary policy decision making is for proposals and positions to be developed within Treasury by its relatively large complement of financial economists, all of whom report to the undersecretary for monetary affairs. The main vehicle for interagency consultation is the International Monetary Group, which achieved prominence as the Volcker Group when Paul Volcker was the Treasury's undersecretary for monetary affairs in the early 1970s. In terms of efficiency and effectiveness, it has proven to be one of the best of all coordinating groups in international economic policy. It has several factors working in its favor; for example, it is a small, tight group of technicians with similar analytical approaches, all of whom acknowledge and respect Treasury's dominance. The group has also successfully prevented the relatively conservative posture of the Fed (part of the central bankers' mentality syndrome) from charting the course of U.S. international monetary policy.

Extraordinary monetary developments such as the dollar devaluations have required presidential involvement. Important initiatives, such as the 1972 endorsement of flexible exchange rates, required consultation with cabinet-level economic officials. But on a day-to-day basis, the Treasury position is cleared neatly by the subcabinet International Monetary Group and thereupon becomes U.S. policy. Certain technical decisions on exchange-rate flexibility during the Rambouillet meeting in November 1975 were relegated to the finance ministries of just two countries, France and the United States. With only a few points preventing final agreement on a monetary reform package, the finance ministers of the other countries participating in the economic summit charged the financial officials of those two countries to reconcile the few remaining differences. The feeling was that whatever final language was agreed upon by the two delegations, it would be one that all of them could live with. Indeed, so much in command of the monetary reform exercise were the finance ministers, that they were in a position to select a two-nation subcommittee to reach a final understanding affecting the whole world.

A few other highly specialized, noncontroversial economic issues are handled by a single agency. Interagency clearance is little more than a pro forma courtesy in such matters as the double taxation treaties negotiated by the Treasury Department, and routine GATT business is attended to by the special trade representative's office.

A second set of policies and decisions can be looked at in terms of organizational shortcomings brought about by the failure of the system to foresee and quickly react to unforeseen and unsettling events. One example of this phenomenon was the federal government's being caught flatfooted by the massive Soviet grain purchases in 1972. The belated realization of the magnitude of Soviet buying, it is generally agreed, increased domestic prices because of resulting reserve shortages, and wasted millions of tax dollars in unnecessary wheat subsidies. In its haste to unload what were then major grain surpluses, the Agriculture Department ignored reports by its own attache in Moscow (and perhaps forecasts by the CIA as well) concerning the major shortfall in the Russian harvest. Because it did not collect data on the magnitude of the sales contracts handled by private grain exporters, the U.S. government had no way of foreseeing the depletion on reserves or the strain on transportation facilities. Nor was there any mechanism to guarantee that wheat subsidies were terminated as soon as it became obvious that only the U.S. had exportable quantities of wheat in 1975 and therefore was fully capable of establishing the world price. "At virtually every step . . . the grain sales were ineptly managed," concluded the Senate's Permanent Subcommittee on Investigations.[7]

A systematic reporting system was instituted, requiring that all U.S. grain trading companies promptly notify the Agriculture Department of all major export orders received. Using this data and keeping lines of communication open with the appropriate offices in the Soviet government, the USDA has increased its ability to forecast the size of harvests in, and demand for, U.S. agricultural commodities by the Soviet Union and other key importing countries. The changed situation was demonstrated by the meticulous management of grain exports to the Russians by an inflation-conscious Ford administration in 1974 and 1975. An informal set of export controls in 1974, and a temporary suspension of grain sales to the Soviets announced in August 1975, invoked the wrath of a farm bloc desirous of unfettered sales and higher prices.

Whereas the wheat deal demonstrated shortcomings of single-department organization, the soybean export embargo in 1973 demonstrated the limits of ad hoc interagency organizational arrangements designed to meet an unforeseen shift in U.S. trade policy. Branding the United States as an undependable supplier in foreign eyes, the embargo made suspect U.S. claims that foreign agricultural trade barriers were an unnecessary, but important detriment to U.S. exports.

The soybean decision was mainly the result of a limited soybean crop to begin with, a growing foreign demand, and President Nixon's food price freeze imposed on June 13, 1973. Exports were not subject to these price controls, and the government immediately established a reporting system for exporters of agricultural commodities. Everyone realized that soybeans were the most likely candidate for export restrictions because of the tight supply situation.

The monitoring facility in retrospect amounted to a self-fulfilling prophecy. Private soybean export contracts soared in anticipation of formal export controls. An Interagency Task Force on Food Export Controls, chaired by the CIEP, was established by the CEP at the working level on June 16, to study the situation and the government's options. The group's initial interpretation of the soybean supply and demand situation suggested an imminent exhaustion of that commodity, and they recommended to the White House that export controls be adopted. They were imposed on June 27.

The key to the recommendation for export controls was the ad hoc task force's inability to interpret accurately the data on export contracts collected for the export monitoring system by the Commerce Department. Despite soaring prices, a physical shortage of soybeans was never really a serious threat. Unfortunately, the interagency group lacked the expertise to recognize the immense padding of reported export contracts written as a hedge against later controls. The tremendous volume of double counting inherent in the contract totals was not appreciated at that time because only experts could have disregarded what in fact were a large number of "phantom" contracts. The actual amount of export contracts on the books as of June 13, 1973 later proved to have been almost double the amount of export business actually conducted.

A case study of the soybean decision written for the Murphy Commission noted that many of the government officials later interviewed insisted that if a more accurate and better researched set of data had been available in mid-

1973, the decision would not have been made as it was. The study concluded that even without the export controls, foreign buyers would have received the same amounts of soybeans that they received under the export control system. "Therefore, the American consumer was left with the same amount of soybeans that he would have had without an export control system. The decision . . . hardly achieved any of the U.S. objectives for an export control system."[8] In the main, the decision reflected government ignorance of commercial operations.

A third type of organizational case study involves the means by which the U.S. government formulates East-West trade policy and conducts operations in support of those policies. The potential for widespread, overlapping, and transitory organization is so richly displayed here that it could conceivably have been treated as a separate model of decision making, one perhaps facetiously dubbed the "multifaceted-duplicative model." The maze of bureaucratic entities and apparent managerial inefficiency reflects this country's inability to categorize trade relations with Russia, China, and other Communist countries as being primarily political, strategic, or commercial in nature.

Most of the models of decision making discussed previously could be applied to certain aspects of the U.S. East-West trade policy during different periods of time. President Nixon at one point became involved personally because of links with detente. Former Secretary of Commerce Peterson assumed a dominant role momentarily for his department mainly because of his personal interest in the subject and his relationship with the president. Bureaucratic politics are involved because of the political-strategic-commercial triangle in routine issues. Democratic politics were responsible for the Congress's linking of most-favored-nation tariff treatment to liberal Soviet emigration policies.

Top-level decision-making authority concerning trade relations with Communist countries today is nominally invested in the cabinet-level East-West Foreign Trade Board, created by the Trade Act of 1974. Despite the principal roles played in this area by State and Commerce, an historical fluke (Shultz's chairmanship of a predecessor group) led President Ford to select Treasury Secretary William Simon as chairman. Other board members include all the major economic departments and agencies. It is, consequently, virtually indistinguishable from the EPB, whose membership is in turn almost identical to that of the CIEP. The East-West Foreign Trade Board was established to formulate policy; monitor trade, credits, and technology transfers; and submit quarterly reports to Congress regarding U.S. trade with nonmarket economies. Its working group meets regularly to coordinate the development and implementation of U.S. trade policies with the second-world countries, referring important issues to the board for approval.

As the new coordinating group in East-West trade, the board has had to share jurisdiction with existing White House-level coordinators, namely, the NSC and EPB. This situation was described in a critique by the GAO:

East-West trade issues have been handled in many different ways, with no consistent pattern of study, analysis, and decisionmaking. Generally, issues have been reviewed by (1) ad hoc interagency groups under the Policy Committee, (2) task forces directed by a single department, or (3) interagency task forces operating under CIEP or NSC.

The decisions to delay and renegotiate the October 1974 Russian grain purchases were made within the Economic Policy Board's Committee on Food, composed of its Executive Committee supplemented by State and Agriculture representatives. An interagency Deputies Group on Food prepared the basic staff analyses and option papers for higher level review and decisionmaking.[9]

A fourth set of decisions is made through an organizational plan that is especially devised because of the extraordinary nature of the policy being developed or pursued. For example, the multiphased negotiating apparatus established to secure the Japanese voluntary textile export restraints demanded by President Nixon was unique and occasionally bizarre. Negotiations were pursued through front channels, secret back channels, and quasi-legal public-congressional channels. Secretary of Commerce Stans, who failed at the first crack at negotiations, eventually was replaced by presidential aide Peter Flanigan. He in turn was succeeded by special ambassador David Kennedy. Intermingled with these official negotiations were discussions involving Kissinger on the back channel, and unofficial talks with the Japanese by Congressman Wilbur Mills (the then chairman of the Ways and Means Committee) and by business leader and presidential friend Donald Kendall. Noticeably absent among the plethora of active U.S. government officials were representatives of the State and Treasury Departments and the president's special representative for trade negotiations.

An earlier effort at voluntary export restraints, this one involving steel, was quietly and quickly conducted on harmonious terms with the European and Japanese industries in 1968. Antitrust and other legal considerations dictated that the restraints appear to spring unilaterally from the respective national steel industries. The State Department acted as a quiet intermediary and provided its good offices to bring together the foreign companies offering to participate in an unofficial arrangement and the domestic steel industry. The need for restraints stemmed from the latter's pressuring Congress for import protection on national security grounds. The State Department's role was lowkeyed, but not enough to prevent the officials involved from being named as defendants in a suit filed by a consumer group in 1971 against senior State Department officials, as well as individual U.S., Japanese, and European steel companies. The suit charged them with conspiring to restrain trade in violation of U.S. antitrust laws and with circumventing the established escape-clause procedures of the Trade Expansion Act used to determine if import injury in fact existed. "Law-abiding" bureaucrats are not likely to opt for this procedure in the future.

Finally, some actions sail by without notice and fanfare through the efforts of established senior intergovernmental coordinating machinery. A case in point is the rubber-stamping in the EPB of the revised meat quota levels proposed for 1976 by the Agriculture Department in the beginning of that year. Despite its marginal effects on domestic prices and on relations with major meat-exporting countries, no agency had any problems with the modestly revised import quota.

## NOTES

1. "U.S. Takes First Hesitant Steps Toward Shift in Commodities Policy," *National Journal,* June 21, 1975, p. 915.

2. Ibid., pp. 915–16.

3. Leslie Gelb and Anthony Lake, "Washington Dateline: Less Food, More Politics," *Foreign Policy,* Winter 1974–75, pp. 183–84.

4. "Export Controls Possible Under U.S. Grain Reserve Plan," *Nation Journal,* October 11, 1975, p. 1427.

5. Alexander George, "The Case for Multiple Advocacy in Making Foreign Policy," *American Political Science Review,* September 1972, p. 751ff.

6. Harry Brandon, *The Retreat of American Power* (New York: Delta, 1973), p. 236.

7. U.S. Senate, Committee on Government Operations, *Russian Grain Transactions,* 93rd Cong., July 1974, p. 55.

8. Griffenhagen Kroeger, Inc., "Cases on a Decade of United States Foreign Economic Policy: 1965–74," vol. 1, mimeographed (November 1974), pp. 62, 64.

9. General Accounting Office, "The Government's Role in East-West Trade—Problems and Issues," mimeographed (Washington, D.C., 1976), pp. 4–5.

# 7

## A CRITIQUE OF
## EXISTING ORGANIZATION

Foreign economic policy in the United States is shaped not systematically, but almost by accident. It is a least common denominator, worked out, as some have so aptly put it, by a kind of guerilla warfare among the Departments of State, Treasury, Agriculture, the Federal Reserve Board, and a whole host of other Executive Branch agencies.

Senator Lloyd Bentsen

The society of the United States is hopelessly pluralistic. Government in general and international economic policy making in particular reflect this situation. As a consequence the strengths and weaknesses of American society and government can be found here. In a democracy with a population whose interests are as diverse as ours are, there is a degree of virtue and logic in providing each of several constituencies a designated pipeline to the decision-making process. The resulting pluralism is manifested in a large, decentralized, shifting, and overlapping organization. Despite this untidiness, the process at times can work efficiently, blending contrasting views into a consensus that serves the national interest and attracts broad support. But when the system is working poorly, policy usually is delayed, deficient, or both.

## PROBLEMS INHERENT AND INEVITABLE

To begin with, it should be noted that the question of organizational effectiveness is inextricably linked with one's subjective judgment concerning the substance of policy. If one is generally content with substance, he has little need or impulse to criticize the arrangements under which decisions were formulated and actions implemented. A given organizational arrangement easily can be categorized as good or bad depending on the observer's reaction to and judgment of the substantive kind of policy it tends to produce. Nevertheless, an objective observer should be able to distinguish between good policy output and bad process. The nature of policy substance is not the subject of inquiry in this discussion. In order to assure a maximum amount of objectivity, this critique of existing organization is fashioned purely on the basis of organizational and procedural processes.

A balanced criticism of the international economic policy organization of the United States should include, along with the good and bad, a recognition of the inevitable. Certain forces are inherent in the process and cannot be dismissed. The overriding fact of the U.S. penchant for pluralism has already been alluded to. A broad political-philosophical decision to undemocratize the various legitimate viewpoints and interests currently listened to in the policy making process would permit an extensive erasing of bureaucratic boxes on the organizational chart. The resulting centralization of authority would facilitate swifter, more unequivocal decisions. On the other hand, such an approach runs the risk of dogmatism and biased policy that serves only a minority interest. The increasing role of Congress in this area, the rise of consumerism, and the sophistication with which business and labor interests are presented in Washington suggest that rather than a contraction of the international economic policy debate, an expansion is more likely.

The global leadership role of the United States is a second inherent factor in organizational considerations. A broad political-philosophical decision to retreat from our international commitments would also permit a tidy consolidation of bureaucratic boxes. A major diminution of this country's foreign commitments could permit a concentration of international economic policy authority in one of the domestic economic departments, for example, Treasury. However, the American view of international morality, perceived needs for American leadership and military strength, and the fear that Russian external policy presents a threat to our intents all suggest that national security considerations shall continue to enter into the international economic policy-making calculus. The vulnerability of the industrialized world to embargoes of raw materials, especially oil, by developing countries provides another argument on behalf of the continuing need to temper pure economic logic with political considerations.

The limits of organization per se are another inherent factor that must be recognized. These limits apply on two levels. The first is the academic. Organizational theory has not been developed to the point whereby anyone has demonstrated conclusively that certain organizational arrangements have important, predictable effects on national actions and decisions.

There are also operational dimensions to the limits of organization. The only valid universal guideline is a generalization: bad organization will hinder but not destroy an operation run by first-rate people; good organization can help, but not fully overcome a weakness in personnel. The proof of effective business organization can be measured in terms of profit and loss. The definitive means of testing effective governmental organization is still being sought. At best, a streamlined organizational system merely limits the U.S. government's propensity to ignore its own capabilities for rounded thought and concerted actions. One observer has suggested: "Among mankind's happiest perversities is the propensity to achieve satisfactory results despite seemingly impossible organization. . . . Rational paper organization is never a sufficient condition for sound policy and often appears not even to have been a necessary condition."[1]

The operations of the U.S. government have been, and probably always will be, influenced heavily by the cult-of-personality syndrome. To a large degree, strength of character, ambition, and relationship with the president are the factors that determine power and influence, rather than specific titles and positions. Organization and procedures can, and should, be designed to ameliorate the worst excesses of this system by guaranteeing a minimum opportunity for all interested bureaucracies to be heard and for major dissents to reach the president on equal terms. If agency jurisdictions and duties were to be fixed immutably, the personality factor would be diminished, but at some cost in flexibility. However, once again the possibility for change is limited. The presidential system in this country uniquely bestows appointive power on a more flexible basis (for example, cabinet members need not be members of Congress) and on a deeper basis (no other chief of a democratic state can make political appointees in the bureaucracy as far down as the equivalent of the deputy assistant secretary rank). The net result of this latter fact gives the president the potential to load the bureaucracy with senior officials of a similar ideological persuasion, thereby introducing a formidable intellectual bias into even the most rationally designed bureaucratic organization.

Finally, and by no means least, the nature and scope of U.S. international economic relations properly dictate a large number of individuals and institutions be involved. On any contentious issue, sophisticated nuances of domestic economic and political priorities, and international political and economic considerations must be reconciled. This process of trade-offs and reconciliation is not taking place in a monolithic unit. International economic policy is composed of a number of interrelated but separate sectors—trade, finance, investment, resource transfers, and so on. A semblance of policy consistency is required within and among each of these sectors.

## WHAT'S RIGHT WITH THE SYSTEM

A number of positive things can be found in the organizational structure. The lack of rigidity in the system can work against good, consistent policy, but it is also a strength. Agency jurisdictional dominance, coordinating techniques, and other organizational procedures are continually changing. The inevitability of new presidents being inaugurated, as well as the fondness for perpetual reorganizational tinkering that is peculiar to the American psyche, results in perpetual change. The resulting shifts can compensate for perceived weaknesses, prepare for newly emerging issues, or adjust to a president's individual style. Although good may be discarded with the bad, no one need despair that any organizational problem is necessarily permanent and unalterable or beyond the purview of the inevitable organizational study commission that springs up from time to time.

The organization also has demonstrated repeatedly the ability to coordinate viewpoints in an effort to reach an acceptable trade-off point between domestic and international priorities. There is a fairly well ingrained appreciation of the need to provide an airing, even if not a sympathetic hearing, for the views of all agencies with a direct interest in the matter under discussion. Bureaucrats of all levels may disdain the viewpoints and goals of others, but very few would question their legitimacy as part of the policy formulation process. It is this very diversity of interests and needs that has served to produce balanced policy more frequently than stilted or stalled policy.

A final strength of the organization is the caliber and diverse expertise of its personnel. The civil service of the United States may not receive the domestic prestige accorded its counterparts by some other nations, but the substance of the work, the spiritual rewards, and (except at the very senior level) the monetary compensation have attracted, on the whole, a very capable group of bright, dedicated people. The sheer size and diversity of the international economic policy establishment has also fostered a broad range of expertise on virtually every aspect of the subject. The technical ability to collect and literally interpret data is not disputed. Problems arise when low-level specialists operating in a narrow field are unable to appreciate and convey to senior policy makers the complexities, nuances, and competing values inherent in most international economic issues.

## WHAT'S WRONG WITH THE SYSTEM

A good starting point to evaluate the deficiencies of existing organizational arrangements for international economic policy making and policy implementation is the four broad criteria suggested as desirable standards in the 1975 Report of the Commission on the Organization of the Government for Conduct of Foreign Policy:

1. Foster a consistent general framework for policy making responsive to and integrated with vital considerations of domestic and foreign policy.

2.  Permit and even encourage a broad sharing of authority and responsibility for the formulation of policy, while preventing narrow and isolated views from becoming dominant.

3.  Foster greater foresight in perceiving, analyzing, and attacking problems at an early stage.

4.  Provide adequate assurance that, once decisions are made, they are followed up and implemented in the spirit intended.

Except for the fourth criterion, existing organization does not measure up very well.

In general, the U.S. government has not responded well to a number of the challenges and opportunities of contemporary international economic relations. Because these factors directly affect our domestic economy and are coming to play a dominant role in this country's external relations, U.S. leadership in this area is now as important to our foreign policy as was military leadership in World War II and in the period immediately thereafter. Nevertheless, the lack of coherence and consistency in U.S. international economic policy attracts extraordinarily harsh criticism from almost all scholars in this field.

In 1972, Harald Malmgren, formerly a deputy special representative for trade negotiations for the president, stated: "Widespread confusion exists as to who is responsible for what. Both policy and daily decisions seem to be aimed in several different directions simultaneously . . . the fact is that there is no coherent, overall foreign economic policy."[2] Three years later, following one more high-level stint as a trade negotiator, Malmgren's views had changed little. In congressional testimony, he lamented that there was little indication that the diffusion of responsibilities and proliferation of conflicting or inconsistent policies had been brought under reasonable control. Indeed, he opined that the confusion was "greater than ever," adding:

> The disarray in policy management hurts us domestically, because our economy is badly served by conflict and confusion in the management of our economic relationship with other nations. The disarray hurts us in our dealings with the governments of other nations, because they sense the inconsistencies and the lack of domestic consensus in support of our international initiatives, which leads them to wait us out, while we wrestle with ourselves at home.[3]

The theme of organizational disarray producing incoherent policy was echoed at the same 1975 hearings by another international economic policy expert, C. Fred Bergsten. In his view, the usual bureaucratic battles have become far more intense and often are common public knowledge, a situation which is damaging both to the substance of policy and to perceptions of it at home and abroad. "There now exists no procedures which can even begin to resolve the issues. . . . The United States is thus defaulting on many of its important economic and foreign policy interests—and is indeed jeopardizing the stability of the entire international economic system, which continues to rely heavily on the United States for leadership."[4]

To return to the Murphy Commission criteria noted above, the current organizational framework is anything but consistent. The virtues of some flexibility notwithstanding, any new international economic issue forces the government into an ad hoc organizational scramble. All serious substantive deliberations on any nonestablished issue are perforce delayed until procedural guidelines are worked out by the affected bureaucratic units.

Indeed, an absolute minimum of fixed organizational guidelines and a maximum of bureaucratic entities, each with a hunger for jurisdictional dominance and a large staff, produce a quasi-automatic delay in governmental responsiveness. Jurisdiction and clout more often than not are fleeting functions of the personalities of key officials and of their relationship with the president, rather than being representative of their organizational positions. The speed with which the role of the Treasury Department has expanded reflects in part the fact that three treasury secretaries in the early 1970s could amass considerable power in the economic policy field because they enjoyed the full confidence of the president. If appointment of a relatively weak treasury secretary in the future should coincide with that of a strong secretary of state with an economics orientation, the trend would be reversed temporarily. In the meantime, one of the most intense modern-day bureaucratic rivalries was waged between State's economic officials and Treasury's international officials from 1974 through 1976, thanks to the relatively unusual circumstance of a strong secretary of state and strong treasury secretary serving simultaneously.

The policy impact of the president's special representative for trade negotiations has had dramatic ups and downs depending primarily on the personality of the job holder. In the early years of the Nixon administration, the job all but disappeared from the bureaucratic map. This was largely because of the personality of the individual chosen to be the president's special trade representative, but partly because great uncertainty exists as to exactly what this official's role is during the intervals between multilateral trade negotiations. Further confusion is caused when responsibility for certain trade issues, such as East-West trade policy, is not organizationally fixed. It wanders to and fro among the Departments of Treasury, State, and Commerce.

The traditional lack of any firm guidelines from the White House and the bewildering array of interagency coordinating committees, working groups, and task forces compound the problem. The result is an uncertain, cumbersome system in which an inordinate amount of energy and time often is consumed in intragovernmental debates, which pass through a multistage process. The first stage is devoted merely to trying to decide which agency is to take the lead in handling a given problem. A necessary second stage requires decisions on the vehicle by which interagency coordination is to take place and who the chairman is to be. Only after the third stage, substantive consensus building, can the United States begin formal negotiations or take a formal position with foreign governments.

The system too frequently has not been able to integrate successfully the vital considerations of domestic and foreign policy. This is best seen in the aftermath of the new economic policy. In this case, the U.S. government lacked an effective mechanism to analyze and integrate the political and economic aspects of an international economic problem.

As to the second of the Murphy Commission criteria, previous and current organizational arrangements cannot be faulted for any systematic limitation of agency participation in the conduct of international economic policy. Bureaucratic end runs are relatively rare, but they persist. The real problem in this instance is centered on the process of the sharing of authority and responsibility. The absence of presidential involvement and the absence of a permanent high-level coordinating mechanism are two of the most critical factors in organizational shortcomings. The location of authority is often all but impossible to pin down.

In the case of the CIEP (the White House coordinating mechanism established in 1970), its impact has been barely visible on major problems in international trade, finance, and resource-transfer policies, where primary jurisdiction has been claimed by State and/or Treasury. Where the CIEP has realized its potential as a White House coordinator and planner, it usually has been on new issues where bureaucratic jurisdiction has not been demarcated (for example, foreign direct investment in the United States), on issues where jurisdiction has become so contentious a dispute that all participants agree to negotiate on neutral territory (for example, expropriation policies), or on issues of no great importance to any individual agency. Although designed to be a central, high-level coordinator, the CIEP has produced no reduction or streamlining in the maze of interagency coordinating mechanisms. In a bizarre perversion of organizational logic, exactly the reverse has occurred: the CIEP has become a member of other interagency groups, thereby enlarging the bureaucratic thicket. The principal factor in the atrophying of the CIEP was the prolonged absence of the presidential attention to it.

The failure of presidents to become involved in and to exert leadership in international economic policy has produced a kind of survival of the fittest among the competing bureaucracies. Only the White House can provide presidential guidelines for making the tough decisions of international economic policy, act as a neutral referee among the line departments, and goad them into producing options for the president or into making decisions on routine issues.

Only the president can arbitrate a policy dispute between the two strongest departments involved in international economic policy; indeed, a major conflict between the State and Treasury departments is of sufficient importance to justify automatic presidential involvement. No one else can resolve what is the ultimate conflict in international economic policy organization, one that is beyond the pale of normal organizational arrangements.

No effective senior-level coordinator mechanism is possible without the president's active participation in it, or the leadership of a strong presidential surrogate, such as Shultz in the 1972–73 period. The absence of presidential involvement has permitted the outbreak of some of the fiercest bureaucratic warfare in Washington. The open disputes between Treasury and State on the questions of international commodity agreements and the oil floor price are classic battles of bureaucratic politics. Clearly, both departments have interests in these areas. But on such questions as international energy and commodity policy, exactly where does authority to make policy lie? No department has obvious jurisdiction, but each has the responsibility to assure that an appropriate American response is forthcoming.

The vacuum created in the absence of guaranteed presidential participation has produced jurisdictional battles not only at the departmental level, but also among cabinet-level coordinating groups within the White House. The competition for jurisdiction as chief coordinating group that has existed between the NSC and the EPB (previously described) means that no single senior-level mechanism for conflict resolution exists above the quarreling departments. Unless the NSC and EPB are cooperating in perfect harmony, no preestablished single channel to the president is in use.

The presidency has lacked for many years a senior adviser on international economic policy with both clout over the bureaucracy and substantive economic knowledge. Without such a person, there is little likelihood that a White House perspective will be relayed to the president when he is considering the options offered by the line departments and agencies. The absence of such a senior adviser is also a major factor in the resulting absence of any internal action-forcing process within the executive branch. In sum, nothing in the previous experience of international economic policy making suggests that the departments operate best when left completely unfettered by White House oversight. And there is nothing to suggest that the president is best served when he has no knowledgeable senior adviser responsible only to provide him with a separate viewpoint and to urge the bureaucracies to be responsive to the needs of the country and of the president.

Competition for international economic policy jurisdiction is a frequent energy-wasting activity of the U.S. government. To the frailty of organizational arrangements is added the catalyst of bureaucratic politics and empire building. It often appears that governmental agencies posture more with one another than with their foreign counterparts. Throughout the 1972–73 period, the special trade representative's office and CIEP were locked in a bitter struggle as the latter sought to absorb the former. At stake was the issue of trade policy leadership within the White House. A second example is the jockeying between the State and Agriculture departments as to which is to be chairman of the interagency groups formulating international food policies. In 1975, Kissinger had consolidated leadership on that issue in State much to the chagrin of the USDA. But in the midst of campaigning in the Illinois presidential primary in the spring of 1976, President Ford announced that the then Agriculture Secretary Butz would head a new cabinet-level committee to coordinate all agricultural policy. With the subsequent creation of the Agricultural Policy Committee and the demise of the International Food Review Group and the Food Committee of the Economic Policy Board, the State Department temporarily lost its chairmanship of international food policy efforts, at least until after the elections.

The tendency for any new international economic issue of import to be met by the establishment of a new interagency group to cope with it is a reflection, more than a cause, of organizational weakness. Excepting the occasional virtue of cosmetics to portray urgency, the resort to an endless string of new committees leads to further confusion and decentralization and implies that existing organization is incompetent to handle any new issue. The frequency of such ad hockery is a barometer of how ineffective organizational arrangements are perceived to be. An effectively functioning high-level coordination mechanism would reduce the rationale for the proliferation of ad hoc coordinating efforts; international investment is a prime example, what with individual groups being formed for developing policies on foreign expropriations, direct investment in the United States, and "questionable" corporate payments abroad.

The stupefying plethora of coordinating groups makes it less likely that major decisions will be consistent with other economic and foreign-policy objectives. Worse yet, there isn't even a reasonable assurance that actions within a given sector of international economic policy will reinforce each other and be consistent. Most coordinating groups are organized on the basis of relatively narrow subject areas, not on the basis of broad function or even on the basis of common sense. All tend to be islands unto themselves, that is, individually managed fiefdoms. Indeed, when the parts of international economic policy are added up, they don't always produce a coherent whole. One example of this is the great palm oil debate between advocates of increased exports of U.S. soybeans and the foreign-aid specialists who have encouraged LDCs to grow oil palm trees. It turns out now that palm oil has begun competing with soybean oil in world markets, driving down prices and displacing U.S. exports. Another example is the continuing series of new interagency groups that materialized as the outgrowth of the State-Treasury disagreement on international commodity policy.

Still another example of this problem involves the numerous groups that formulate trade policy towards the Communist bloc countries. In its 1976

criticism of U.S. East-West trade policy, the GAO concluded that the organization of the government in this area "reflects very little appreciation for, or
adjustment to, the unique and difficult interface between the U.S. and Soviet
economies." The criticism also said that:

> The agencies most sensitive to the balance of diplomatic benefits either have
> no commercial policy responsibility (Defense) or view trade as an instrument
> of foreign policy (State). The agencies that pursue trade as an end in itself
> and have direct commercial responsibilities are preoccupied with market
> access rather than with the balance of benefits (Commerce and Treasury).
> The agency most concerned with commercial reciprocity (Office of Special
> Trade Representative) has not been intensively involved in East-West trade
> policymaking.[5]

The resulting confusion in organization also presents a dilemma to American business. Conflicting information from different departments concerning
U.S. policy and delays in obtaining export licenses are commonplace occurrences. The interagency process was also criticized for not insuring that agency
positions are clearly defined and properly analyzed before decisions or implementation plans are made. "Moreover, once an agency has been given or has
assumed the lead in particular negotiations, there has been no guarantee that
true interagency consultations will occur."[6]

An example of intrasectoral coordinating confusion involves aid, or more
broadly, resource transfers to the LDCs. New interagency forums have sprung
up in response to discussions of the new international economic order, for
example, the Commodities Policy Coordinating Committee. They join an
already crowded field: the Interagency Staff Committee (PL 480 loans), the
National Advisory Council (Eximbank and international financial institutions), and the Development Loan Committee (AID loans). Additionally,
there is the cabinet-level Development Coordination Committee (DCC)
created by Congress in 1973 to "advise the president" with respect to coordination of U.S. policies and programs affecting the development of the LDCs. This
senior coordinating committee, however, has been dormant and is nearly
forgotten, mainly because State and Treasury are mutually uncomfortable with
the fact that the administrator of AID was selected as chairman. A proliferation of groups to this extent suggests an inability to cope with the aid issue on
an integrated basis. The large number of groups should not be equated with
substantial executive branch concern for this issue.

Organizational arrangements are so imprecise, ephemeral, and amor-
phous that no unified theory of policy making appears feasible. The question
of who is to chair an interagency committee can tie the bureaucracy in knots
for weeks. There appears to be no method to predict how the system will (or

will not) handle any given economic issue. A quick, responsive, and creative policy or program is more a matter of luck than anything else.

Whereas there is no shortage of views introduced in most policy deliberations, there is nothing inherent in the system to force a decision. Neither is there anything inherent in the system that serves to force a decision in the direction, not of a least-common-denominator bureaucratic compromise, but of a clear, forceful, and consistent response that is reasonably reflective of the broad interests of the United States. More often than not, decisions are forced by circumstance, for example, approach of an international meeting, congressional testimony, or presidential insistence. Even though a decision usually is reached when the bureaucracy is pressed hard enough, there is a pervasive inability to get the problem identified, articulated, and discussed far enough in advance to have assured adequate preparations and a systematic reconciliation of all the considerations of the issue at hand.

Only the size of the bureaucracy has grown commensurate with the growth in the importance and complexity of international economic relations. An effective management process is lacking. The decision-making process is arbitrary. Except in those relatively few cases where bureaucratic turf has long been clearly delineated—for example, international monetary reform—can a fixed pattern of leadership be determined. Leadership roles are fought for, bartered, shared, or assigned by the president with no particular rhyme or reason. Assignments reflect more the skills of bureaucratic infighting and historical legacy than any system of managerial or organizational logic. Why, for example, is the secretary of commerce the chairman of the energy Resources Council? Why is the secretary of the treasury the secretary of the East-West Foreign Board?

Fragmentation, jealousy, and duplication are endemic in all levels of existing organizational arrangements. Questions concerning international investment and the multinational corporation are not the primary concern of any single department, nor even of any single interagency working group. The group handling expropriation and codes-of-conduct issues is fictionally dubbed a CIEP group to soothe State and Treasury egos. Should the executive branch confront a congressional initiative to change the laws on foreign-source income, a whole new organizational arrangement would have to be conjured up. Any serious effort to initiate a specialized multilateral institution dealing with multinational corporations would lead to yet another group.

At the senior level, the same syndrome can be seen at work by the frequency with which joint NSC and EPB groups have to be formed. Both the NSC and the EPB are White House-level coordinating groups; however, for reasons of history, membership, and bureaucratic fantasy, the NSC is deemed to be a foreign-policy (State Department) operation beyond redemption while the EPB is branded as being a domestic economic policy (Treasury, Agriculture, and others) operation. Neither one, therefore, can be fully trusted by all of the interested line departments and agencies who can be classified as being either foreign-policy or domestic economic-policy oriented. Indeed, one of the major weaknesses of the EPB in its early months was the fact that the State Department conducted a virtual boycott of it; while he wore two hats, as State and NSC head Kissinger presented the foreign-policy perspective directly to the president.

Policy formulation for many major issues has been coordinated at the highest levels by joint EPB-NSC groups. Such an arrangement reduces bureaucratic jockeying, but it does not guarantee an orderly escalation seniority-wise of policy disputes or the approval process. Because of the melange of coordinating groups and the need for White House coordinators to coordinate other coordinating groups, an orderly decision-making process occurs despite the organizational system, not because of it.

The organizational disarray produces a built-in incentive for procrastination and public, prolonged bureaucratic struggles. The absence of presidential involvement or a senior presidential aide with clout and substantive expertise produces a situation in which events external to bureaucratic organization force decisions—for example, international meetings and public speeches.

A final weakness of the organizational structure involves the final stage of the policy process evaluation. The executive branch is devoid of any bureaucratic actor whose job is primarily to examine critically policies actually in place and to do so with a dispassionate point of view devoid of any self-interest or stake in the policy-making process. The OMB occasionally approaches this role. But it tends to approach problems and investigations from the point of view of its narrowly assigned mission: to minimize the waste of public revenues. The GAO, a relatively obscure part of the legislative branch, is in fact designed to evaluate policies and programs from a totally dispassionate perspective, and thus could fulfill the criteria necessary to conduct an effective evaluation effort. But its efforts in international economic policy have been few and generally not of outstanding quality. Partly for these reasons and partly because the GAO is viewed as an outsider, the impact of its critical analyses on the executive branch has been limited. Only a change in administrations augurs well for a full-scale policy review and reevaluation that will separate good, bad, and obsolete policies. Otherwise, once in place, most policies, good and bad alike, survive until political and economic pressures literally embarrass or force policy makers into effecting changes.

The system has proved itself consistently inadequate in fulfilling the third Murphy Commission criterion: presenting policy makers with advanced warnings and analyses of forthcoming problems. All too much of U.S. international economic policy has been in the nature of protective reaction. Policy makers have been mainly on the defensive, putting out a series of brush fires. One cause of this situation is the limited state of the art of economic forecasting. Other causes of a lack of foresight are an insufficient research and planning effort, and secondly, the occasional inability of the analytic level of the bureaucracy to convince the policy-making level of the importance of developing trends.

But the "great grain robbery" of 1972 and the soybean export controls episode demonstrate that the system is fully capable of not understanding an issue even while in progress, and of being unable to collect or interpret empirical data concerning an issue that has no precedent or cannot be foreseen. Even when analysts can foresee a problem, the organizational system still might not function properly. For example, the energy problem had become clear in the minds of technical experts by the early 1970s, but no sense of urgency successfully transmitted to key policy makers until the Arab oil boycott.

The support services provided by international economic research and planning are still inadequate. The amount of output relevant to policy appears to be insufficient; coordination and cooperation between researchers in different agencies are almost nonexistent; and perhaps, most importantly, there is still the perennial problem of a gulf between planners and policy makers. Kissinger's remark that planning is usually a "sop to administrative theory" is a good characterization of the prevailing situation in this area.

The production of economic intelligence (in the broadest sense) has increased in quantity at the producer's end, that is, on the part of the CIA. Although this was done in response to the changing needs and priorities of policy makers, many international economic policy officials still view economic intelligence as having only marginal value, and give such reports a low priority on their reading list. Most of the fault in this instance lies with the policy makers, not the producers of intelligence; the latter, of course, are working for the former.

Proper implementation and follow-up on decisions are the only Murphy Commission criteria listed in the beginning of this chapter that do not capture one of the weaknesses of the current organization. There may be inconsistencies and contradictions in the policy itself that frustrate the attainment of objectives. There may be a high degree of ambiguity or fuzziness in decisions reached. And there may be failures to evaluate objectively policies and programs put into place. However, there is sufficient cohesion and loyalty in existing arrangements to preclude any valid criticism that working-level personnel regularly frustrate or bend the will and intention of policy makers. This is in stark contrast with the national security sector, where instances of bureaucratic inattention or delay in the face of high-level instructions are numerous. The general responsiveness by the international economic bureaucracy cannot be explained with any certainty.

The case of U.S. international investment policy leads to still another criticism of the system: its energies can be channeled at times into secondary matters. An insufficient amount of sophisticated thinking has gone on among government officials and planners as to exactly what are the competitive, production, and balance-of-payments effects on the American economy of vast foreign investments by the biggest U.S. corporations. Nor is there any objective research to speak of on the effects of such investments on the host country's economy and balance of payments. The basic question of how the international investment syndrome is affecting the major objectives of American domestic and international economic policies are still unanswered. The few inquiries into this question have mainly been modest statistical surveys or privately financed studies starting with a preordained view point synonymous with that of the sponsoring organization.

The efforts of the U.S. bureaucracy continue to be devoted to such lesser questions as devising voluntary codes of conduct, compliance with the Arab boycott, and bribery. All are important. Yet all are subsidiary to the questions of the basic effect of multinational corporations and the potential need for the government to negotiate on behalf of U.S. corporations overseas as controls proliferate abroad. American policy is guided essentially by the instinctive trust in the net contribution of multinational corporations. The government presumably is receptive to data that might prove to the contrary, but the burden is on outsiders to develop such data.

In sum, the deficiencies of the organizational process by which U.S. international economic policy is formulated include the following:

There is no good means of constructing a "grand design" to provide basic policy guidelines that will promote consistency, a common sense of mission in the bureaucracy, and a pattern of complimentarity between the numerous sectors of international economic policy. A conceptual grand design would provide a larger pattern into which lower level bureaucrats could relate their narrowly defined responsibilities.

Authority is seized by the toughest bureaucrats; it is not assigned by a rational, centralized authority.

Organizational arrangements, at least at the senior level, are excessively ephemeral. In some periods they work well, sometimes adequately, and at still other times they work poorly. There are absolutely no consistency and traditions in high level international economic policy making.

The content of policy overwhelmingly is a function of the dominating personalities at hand.

The organization is ignoring rather than emphasizing the unique integrating perspective held by the president. His involvement in policy formulation is too little and too late. Additionally, no person has served as a trusted adviser to the president on international economic policy for many years. The resulting absence of presidential leadership has reduced the decision-making system's ability to take a broad, conceptually integrated viewpoint.

There is no internal action-forcing mechanism in the system. Only the intervention of the president, an external event, or bureaucratic weariness can
bring about resolution of a dispute between the bureaucratic "superpowers"—Treasury and State.

The coordination process is extensive if measured in terms of the number of
interagency working groups. Qualitatively, it suffers from excessive "ad
hockery," inconsistency and duplication. Worse still, there is no provision
for a neutral figure to assure that the right officials are assembled at the
right time.

Most of the bureaucracy still views international economic policy as something
to be subordinated either to domestic economic policy management or to
foreign policy, that is, national security objectives. The inevitable jurisdictional fights that result are an additional element in delaying the already
difficult process of weighing domestic versus foreign as well as political
versus economic considerations so as to adopt a balanced international
economic policy.

The bureaucracy remains far too intellectually and physically removed from
the business community to fully understand its needs, motives, and operations. The same description would apply to business attitudes towards the
government.

## NOTES

1. Edward Hamilton, "Summary Report: Principal Lessons of the Past Decade and
Thoughts on the Next," in *Appendices* (to the [Report of the] Commission on the Organization
of the Government for the Conduct of Foreign Policy), vol. 3 (Washington, D.C.: U.S. Government Printing Office, 1976), p. 10.

2. Harald Malmgren, "Managing Foreign Economic Policy," *Foreign Policy,* Spring 1972,
pp. 42, 56.

3. Statement of Harald Malmgren before the Senate Committee on Banking, Housing, and
Urban Affairs, in *International Economic Policy Act of 1975, Hearings,* 94th Cong., 1st sess., p.
91.

4. Statement of C. Fred Bergsten, in Ibid., p. 11.

5. General Accounting Office, "The Government's Role in East-West Trade—Problems and
Issues," mimeographed (Washington, D.C., 1976), pp. 56–57.

6. Ibid, p. 5.

CHAPTER

# 8

## COMPARATIVE
## INTERNATIONAL ECONOMIC
## POLICY MAKING

> One [British] Treasury official remarked on his sense of shock at first seeing a brief to the Chancellor before a Cabinet discussion on foreign policy . . . which began, "This is, of course, partly a moral issue . . ." but then went on to discuss the question entirely in terms of its potential impact on the balance of payments. In the committee structure of Whitehall, however, *this is the Treasury's proper role* [author's emphasis].
>
> William Wallace

The utility of studying how America's major economic partners cope with the unique organizational challenge of international economic policy is threefold. First, the results of these countries' efforts provide potential solutions to existing dilemmas and shortcomings in the U.S. system. There is the potential for the United States to adopt any number of largely unknown foreign organizations or procedures that are used successfully in pursuit of the common objective of good policy. Aside from inherent educational value, an understanding of how this policy is made in other countries has implications for the techniques adopted here. By definition, U.S. international economic policy involves other sovereign countries. We ignore their techniques of policy making at our own peril. The logic and strength of U.S. policy efforts are partially dependent on the existence of a modicum of compatibility between this country's system and its foreign counterparts. Thirdly, a comprehension of foreign organizational process has implications for the substance of U.S. policy. Understanding exactly how decisions are made in other countries and who makes them would place U.S. policy makers in a better position to assess and react to the degree of authenticity and finality of foreign-made pronouncements.

## GENERAL PRINCIPLES

A study of the mechanics of how the governments of various countries are organized to conduct international economic policy can be treated as an interesting end in itself, especially within a larger study examining how the process works in the United States. To appreciate the broader significance of how countries make policy, however, it is necessary to view international economic policy-making organization and procedures as wheels within wheels within wheels. The middle set of wheels is overall governmental organization patterns. No country's government is organized in this area in ways radically different from those employed in national security and major domestic issues areas. If international economic policy making is a microcosm of overall governmental patterns, the latter in turn are manifestations of the national psyche, history, ambitions, and capabilities. The outer wheels are the goals, geopolitics, membership in supranational institutions, and so on, which determine the broad outlines of a country's external policies.

U.S. international economic policy making is based on a desire to promote the benefits of the market mechanism through the establishment of multilateral institutions whose jobs are to negotiate and codify a liberal world economic order. These are objectives clearly synonymous with the needs and objectives of a democratic, capitalist superpower with an inherent preference for the status quo. Given the size of its domestic economy and the extensive worldwide activities of its business sector, the U.S. government concerns itself intensively with all aspects of the international economy. Organizational response reflects the fact that it is wealthy enough to enlarge the bureaucracy whenever issues grow in complexity or new ones arise.

Except to the revisionists perhaps, it appears that U.S. government policy in international economics follows, rather than leads, the wealth, size, and resources of the country. The conscious pursuit of international power by Washington is not a demonstrable national priority sought by a single-minded executive branch. A parallel exists in national security policy. The U.S. system of government remains institutionally marked by its origins. "It is a system built on the open clash of arguments and interests between groups with a broad access to the machinery of government."[1] Within such a system, successful conspiracies do not for long flourish. And so it is that U.S. international economic policy making is characterized by a large, loosely knit bureaucracy besieged by a multitude of opinions, and forever struggling to reach consensus without producing meaningless policy mush in the process. Its greatest asset is the national strength, to whose creation bureaucracy has contributed little.

Similarly, the organizational arrangements established by other countries to produce international economic policy should not be viewed in a vacuum.

To understand them, it is necessary first to understand the country's background, resources, and goals, and secondly to appreciate the overall structure of government organization and procedures.

The examination of each of the national organizational processes profiled below follows a common outline. Initially, the indigenous characteristics and governmental phenomena that influence the substance and organizational processes of international economic policy are treated. The formal organization chart is examined next to portray the nature of ministerial responsibilities and jurisdictions in this field. The final topic is a brief analysis of how each system was unofficially wired together as of late 1976 to coordinate responsibilities and resolve differences. An obvious caveat must be enunciated: the nature of and performance by the system discussed are transitory; all arrangements are subject to obsolescence by changes in priorities, ruling parties, and senior personalities.

## EUROPEAN COUNTRIES

The countries of Western Europe have major historic cultural and economic links with the United States. Along with Japan and Canada, this constellation of first-world, industrialized, wealthy countries is economically welded together by a web of trade, financial, and investment relations.

The organizational arrangements by which France, West Germany, and Great Britain—the three largest economies of Europe—conduct international economic policy are affected in a major way by their membership in the European Communities (EC). In a sense, each country is part of the first great reaction to the growing economic obsolescence of the nation-state. To preserve the ability to attain national objectives and provide a maximum standard of living to their populace, each has surrendered some degree of economic autonomy to a larger, supranational institution. Many observers have assumed that this loss of autonomy will spill over someday into the political realm, causing total integration and a real loss of sovereignty. In the interim, the still sovereign governments of France, West Germany, and Great Britain have had to adopt extraordinary organizational means in the wake of an unprecedented transfer of economic decision-making authority to EC institutions in Brussels. The move towards a common commercial policy is nearly complete; common positions actively are sought in other international economic organizations dealing with financial, investment, and development authority; and a long-term commitment to full economic and monetary union has been made. The exact extent, in real terms, of the transfer of power to the EC that has taken place is difficult to measure. At a minimum, formalities, appearances, and legal considerations have dictated a major organizational response in the governments of member countries.

The organization of the Swedish government has been included in this examination to provide a broader sample. Sweden is the largest, most sophisticated West European economy that is not a member of the EC.

## Great Britain

British international economic policy organization is a reflection of the postwar period and of internal political dynamics. It reflects in fact an evolutionary reaction to the post-World War II decline in the country's role as a world superpower. It is also an outgrowth of the operations of a pure form of cabinet government. Both factors led to a special handling of international economic policy. From the end of World War II through the 1950s, a conceptual dichotomy divided British external policy into two sectors. One sector involved the traditional global political interests of a one-time world leader in the process of dismantling an empire and reducing its overseas military commitments.

The second sector was economic in nature. The reasons for the neat segregation of international economic policy from international political concerns are to be found partly in the dominant economic ideology of British policy making prior to, and after, the Second World War: the equating of the country's interests with free trade and a sound pound sterling. The basic beliefs held that political considerations that could distort the international economy should not be encouraged, and that the government should intervene in the operations of the marketplace as little as possible. Other reasons for the international political-economic separation included the institutional framework within which economic policy was handled after the war, the direct link perceived between domestic economic management and international economic relations, and the distinctive, highly influential domestic interests involved in the field of economic policy in general.[2]

The British cabinet system has differed in practice from the system in most European countries. Tradition and the keen competition for ruling-party status between the Labour and Conservative parties within what effectively has been a two-party system (that is, few coalitions) assured that the feeling of collective responsibility within the cabinet remained at a higher-than-average level by parliamentary government standards. In few other countries have two political parties experienced the revolving-door effect of ruling-majority status swinging to minority status with the frequency demonstrated in Great Britain. The strong ministerial-group feeling that prevails is not unrelated to a survival instinct, especially during the question period in Parliament.

Group feelings and team play reach their apogee in the cabinet, where all important policy is approved and bureaucratic differences are resolved. This fact encourages an outward appearance of a monolithic international economic policy-making organization. In fact, the British system is not exempted from the interplay of bureaucratic politics between foreign and domestic perspectives. Rivalries exist, but they are handled internally with discretion.

> It is part of the style of Whitehall that differences are muted and as far as possible concealed from the public eye, and that interdepartmental disputes are subject to the acceptance of an overriding common interest. Even so, there are clear departmental interests and clear clashes of interest arising from the very nature of large-scale organizations and of human behaviour.[3]

International economic policy making at the present time culminates in one of three standing cabinet committees, Economic Policy, Defense and Overseas Policy, and Europe, or in an ad hoc committee. An example of the latter is the one recently formed to deal with the North-South dialogue concerning the new international economic order. Each succeeding prime minister has the authority to decide exactly what kind of committees are to be formed to handle basic issues and which ministers are to become members.

All of the principal ministries involved in international economic relations participate in the permanent cabinet committees that touch on that subject. The ministries are Her Majesty's Treasury, the Foreign Office, the Department of Trade, the Department of Industry, and the Overseas Development Ministry.

Her Majesty's Treasury, the strongest ministry in the British system, exerts the largest overall influence on British international economic policy. Historically, the chancellor of the exchequer has enjoyed a special status, one that puts him just under the prime minister in terms of power and prestige. The international financial role played by Britain's currency and the Foreign Office's concern with high-policy issues, such as the British Empire, assured the Treasury a high degree of autonomy in the financial sector. The department that has been at the heart of British international economic relations is the Overseas Finance Sector. An outstanding feature of it is the relatively small number of professional-(administrative-) level civil servants. Less than 40 persons handle international monetary policy, European economic cooperation, foreign-exchange controls, balance-of-payments policy and reserves management, economic aid policy, export finance, and the other financial concerns of Treasury. This trim operation (about 20 percent of personnel in OASIA, the comparable bureau in the U.S. Treasury) is a conscious design to retain optimal internal direction and communication. Despite the department's control over the budget and its central direction over the British civil service, the Treasury has actively resisted increasing the number of either its domestic or international economic policy officials. The Overseas Finance Sector does supplement its resources by drawing heavily on the ministry's chief economic adviser and his staff.

More importantly, the international sector is augmented by the larger personnel resources of the Bank of England. Much of the economic data and analysis used by the Treasury comes from the bank's Economic Intelligence Department (which analyzes the impact of the external sector on the British economy and collects data) and from the Overseas Department (which involves itself in the entire gamut of international economic relations through a professional staff of well over 100). Given its more generous staffing, and given the fact that legally it is part of the government, charged in its founding legislation to advise the Treasury, the Bank of England is more than an agent to implement Treasury policies. It participates in numerous interdepartmental working groups and is not reluctant to offer suggestions on actual policy. The prestige and size of its staff suggest that its advice is not taken lightly. The role of London as a major international financial center further enhances the bank's international economic responsibilities. It has actively advocated a laissez faire British policy towards international banking transactions with the country.

The evolution of the Foreign and Commonwealth Office (FCO) clearly reflects changing priorities and shifts in Britain's overall international position. In 1947 there was a merger between the India Office and the Dominions Office to form the Commonwealth Relations Office, which in 1966 also absorbed the Colonial Office. But as the empire disappeared and the commonwealth dissipated, the Commonwealth Relations Office in turn was merged with the Foreign Office to form the FCO. Today, it is a decentralized ministry composed of 60 specialized departments and offices, most of which have a relatively narrow responsibility. In lieu of an overall economic division, eight of these departments are concerned with the FCO's interests in international economics. Among them are Financial Relations, Trade Relations and Exports, European Integration, Energy, and Economists departments. The FCO also has responsibility for all overseas commercial representation and overseas export promotion services.

The FCO only in the late 1960s, and not without the reluctance of diplomatic traditionalists, became actively involved in British international economic policy. Opponents of this trend agreed that it would produce a duplication of other ministries' duties and would detract from the chief mission of the FCO—the conduct of traditional diplomacy. As late as the 1960s, the foreign minister was not sufficiently interested to attend meetings of the cabinet committee on Economic Policy on a regular basis.

> The gradual realisation, from 1964 onwards, that an independent foreign policy was impossible without the backing of a viable economy, and the experience gained in the successive approaches to the European Communities, were reinforced by an appreciation among some Diplomatic Service officials that the FCO would increasingly lose out in Whitehall unless its members were able to contribute effectively to economic discussions.[4]

The subsequent economic consciousness raising in the FCO, as seen in part by its sending its people to the Treasury, the Bank of England, and commercial banks in London, has diminished the traditional antagonism felt by the Treasury towards the involvement of the Foreign Office in International economic matters.

The Department of Trade is the lead actor in the foreign-trade sector. To understand its role and internal organization, it is necessary to appreciate its evolution from the historically powerful Board of Trade. From the eighteenth century until the Conservatives returned to power in 1969, the Board of Trade dominated British foreign commercial policy. In that year, the board was merged with the Ministry of Technology to form the department of Trade and Industry, which was given responsibility for domestic industrial policy as well as trade. But in the spring of 1974, the returning Labourites completed a dismembering process that produced four separate ministries: Trade, Industry, Energy, and Consumer Protection.

The Department of Trade's mandate in mid-1976 expands beyond trade matters on only a very narrow basis, for example, into industrial law and shipping and civil aviation. The Commercial Relations and Exports Division handles basic bilateral and multilateral trade policy formation. Three other divisions operate within the country various export promotion efforts, including the British Overseas Trade Board operated cooperatively with representatives of business and labor. Various industrial aspects of Britain's EC membership, including advice to the private sector on its implications, are placed in a separate European division. The latter is operated jointly with the Ministry of Industry, a throwback to the period when the two were one ministry. The Department of Industry presently has no international department as such; it participates in interagency trade policy deliberations on a sectoral basis, that is, how individual industries would be affected by changes in trade policy.

The pattern of coordinating British international economic policy parallels the general penchant for cooperative relations among ministries. On the working level, interagency groups meet on an informal basis for consideration of most issues. At the ministerial level, coordination is made somewhat more systematic through the efforts of the Cabinet Office. The increasingly interdepartmental nature of policy making has broadened the office beyond its original core, the Cabinet Secretariat, whose duties centered on calling for and circulating papers, being the secretariat for cabinet committees, and serving as chairman of the committees' subordinate groups. Today, the professional civil service staff numbers 90. It has added three additional units, two of which touch on international economics. One is the analytically oriented Assessments Staff.[5]

The other is the European Unit, established in the Cabinet Office subsequent to Britain's EC membership application being accepted in June 1971. It serves as the focal point for formulating and coordinating all British policy involving issues of European economic cooperation and integration. The staff of the nine-person unit is all on assignment from economics-oriented departments (including the Foreign Office). By tradition, it is headed by a civil servant from one of the domestic economic ministries. It supplies a centralized organizational capability necessitated by what British officaldom saw as four extraordinary characteristics of EC membership: the intensity and diversity of the issues involved, the need to disseminate vast amounts of information on EC activities to interested ministries, the fact that the geographic locale of EC decision-making activity was physically located outside of London, and the increased blurring between the foreign and domestic policy ramifications of membership.[6] Additionally, the fear existed that an individual ministry easily could inadvertently act at variance with policies established in Brussels on any of a multitude of things. Furthermore, a cabinet office coordinator was seen as precluding subtle bureaucratic devices to attain certain ends, for example, pointing to an urgent, quickly approaching deadline for a policy paper in order to garner a quick interdepartmental concurrence.

Unlike its French counterpart, the British European Unit occasionally relinquishes the chairmanship of interdepartmental working groups to the representative of a line ministry when technical or laborious efforts are called for. The European Unit, again unlike its French counterpart, does not itself directly transmit instructions to Brussels.

The British system is a careful balance between a centralized coordinator and a retention of responsibility in the ministries. The means of coordinating EC policy was systematically and carefully programed for the British system. Immediately prior to accession to membership, the government conducted an analytical evaluation of how the original six EC members were organized internally to coordinate EC issues. The only serious alternative to the present coordinating system was a brief experiment in 1973 with a separate minister for Europe, who had no bureaucratic support. Unless other member countries adopt a European Ministry, it is probable that the administratively created system within the Cabinet Office will continue under subsequent governments.

## West Germany

For an understanding of the contemporary objectives, perceptions, and values of the Federal Republic of Germany (FRG), the key date is 1945, the year of total military surrender and the partition of what had been the Third Reich. Only two factors that shape West Germany's performance in the world economy antedate the end of World War II: the historical efficiency of the German people and the abhorrence of inflation born of economic collapse in the interwar period. The government of the FRG has a solid socioeconomic foundation on which to operate, but fundamental historic and political forces heretofore have constrained the government from pursuing an aggressive leadership role in world affairs. There is an unfriendly counterpart German government in the East. And memories of Germany's role in instigating two world wars reinforce lingering anxieties and suspicion of Germans throughout the European continent. The following passage captures feelings that prevailed in the FRG through the 1960s: "West German attitudes remain marked by the deep insecurity of a country whose sovereignty, borders, and former capital city are all in doubt, whose national identity has been shattered by the Nazi experience, the ordeal of defeat, and the trauma of partition."[7] Today (1976), the FRG uses its international economic power with circumspection only to avoid accusations of hegemony. The government of Chancellor Helmut Schmidt does not practice the politics of guilt or insecurity, nor does it worry about being perceived as "overly aggressive."

Since the onset of the 1960s, West German international economic policy might best be characterized as speaking softly and carrying a strong currency. The West German economy, the largest in Europe and the one with the lowest inflation rate, has yielded persistently large trade surpluses and a favorable balance-of-payments position. This situation has permitted the deutsche mark to experience the most rapid appreciation in value of any currency in the world since 1960. Possession of one of the world's strongest—and most chronically undervalued—currencies is demonstrated by the fact that the FRG's monetary reserve holdings were the world's largest at the end of 1976.

Germany's economic strength is superior to that of France, but its pursuit of nationalistic aggrandizement is less intense than that of its neighbor. Germany has used its wealth to finance, not force, achievement of its two major international objectives: To preserve good relations with the United States, it has cooperated with many U.S. economic demands, the most obvious being the making of offset payments to defray the balance-of-payments costs of this country's stationing troops there. And to promote the economic integration of Europe, Germany supports EC's agricultural policy, which is financially disadvantageous to German taxpayers, and it repeatedly has provided emergency financing for other EC member countries facing economic difficulties. Given both the economic problems in France, Italy, and Britain in the 1976–77 period, and the EC membership applications of lesser developed countries (for example, Greece and Turkey), West Germany is rapidly becoming the EC's lender of last resort.

The formal organization by which the FRG conducts international economic policy is dominated by two strong economics departments, the Ministry of Finance and the Ministry of Economics. The role of the Finance Ministry in overall economic policy is limited to dominance involving monetary, credit, and currency questions. Dealing literally with financial issues, the Finance Ministry does not have the pervasive clout on nonfinancial international issues that some other finance ministries have. Its leverage is further circumscribed by the absence of an integrated foreign bureau. International responsibilities are divided between the Financial Relations Bureau (which handles questions regarding the EC budget and international economic organizations) and the Currency, Money, and Credit Policy Bureau (which is responsible for international monetary policy and European monetary questions). The latter has less than ten professional civil servants.

The lack of Finance Ministry dominance is partly attributable to the independence, influence, and personnel resources of the central bank, the Bundesbank. The German phobia concerning inflation was instrumental in assuring that the critical question of monetary aggregates would be kept away from the politicians. Symbolically, the bank is physically located in Frankfurt, not Bonn. The finance minister may participate in the deliberations of the Bundesbank's Council, but he cannot vote. He merely has the power to postpone for two weeks the implementation of a decision, in a gesture of extreme dissatisfaction. Compared with the Finance Ministry, the much greater number of economics experts employed by the Bundesbank, as well as its high reputation, make for great similarities with the Bank of England's standing. The big difference is that the German central bank is distinctly independent of the government policy-making machinery.

The fact that the German Ministry of Economics possesses a broad jurisdictional mandate is the second reason that the Finance Ministry's jurisdiction is circumscribed. For a brief period in 1971–72, the two were in fact joined to form a bureaucratic colossus. The sheer size and power wielded by the merged departments encouraged a quick return to the traditional setup, however.

The Ministry of Economics has primary responsibility for domestic industrial policy, energy and raw materials, general economic policy, technology, and the periodic economic forecasts required by law. It is also responsible for international commerical policy, and its European Affairs Bureau has been a focal point for the coordination of day-to-day EC economic matters. The concerns of the Bureau of International Economic Relations go beyond trade to include foreign investment policy, bilateral economic relations, economic relations with Communist bloc countries, and development aid, including the new North-South dialogue. The broad and diffuse responsibilities of the Economics Ministry have led to extensive internal bureaucratic politics. The result is a self-confessed inability to reach an agreed position within the Economics Ministry.[8]

Although the German Foreign Ministry was entrusted with external representational duties as part of an agreement with the Ministry of Economics, the former has not been a major force in the overall formulation of German international economic policy. There is one major exception to this assertion: the European theater. In addition to the economic aspects of *Ostpolitik,* the Foreign Ministry has played a key role in the FRG's policy towards the economic integration process in the EC. The ministry's presence in the latter instance was enhanced organizationally by the creation in 1973 of the position of minister of state, specifically responsible for EC affairs. The minister of state is a political appointee, a member of the Bundestag, and holds cabinet status. The leverage of the Foreign Ministry on EC affairs has been enhanced further by the inner politics of the current German coalition: whereas the ministers of economics and the foreign minister are members of the Free Democrats, the junior party of the ruling coalition, the two persons who have held the post of minister of state dealing with European affairs have been influential members of the dominant Social Democrats and have had close ties to the chancellor. The Foreign Ministry also provides the economic and commercial officials in West German embassies. Furthermore, the Foreign Trade, Development Aid, and European Integration Bureau frequently has assumed a role as mediator on foreign-aid issues between the very generous, activist policies of the Ministry for Economic Cooperation and the fiscally conservative stance of the Finance Ministry.

The processes by which coordination is accomplished and ministries debate one another in a constructive spirit have some parallels with the British system. First, the dynamics of a bitterly contested battle for the right to govern between two leading political parties and the collegial dynamics of the cabinet system exist in both countries. Secondly, the Germans also have initiated a number of interministerial committees to deal with international economic issues at the working level.

The Chancellor's Office, a rough equivalent to the British Cabinet Office, plays an active role in coordinating efforts at the senior level in both domestic and external economic policies. The internal organization of the Chancellor's Office assigns responsibilities on the basis of coordinating the work of specified ministries. One section is responsible for foreign policy, that is, the work of the Foreign, Defense, and Development ministries; a second monitors economic policy and therefore works with the Ministries of Finance, Economics, Agriculture, and Labor. The senior officials who head these sections, like their small staffs, are assigned to the Chancellor's Office for tours of duty ranging from three to five years.

Most international economic policy responsibilities fall into the economics section of the Chancellor's Office, whose job is to bring a "prime-ministerial" perspective to the policy-making process. Being familiar with the chancellor's points of view and priorities, the economics section communicates them to the ministers and advises the chancellor on the practicality of his own views. The economics section also serves as the secretariat for the two cabinet committees dealing with international economic relations: Europe and Economics.

Whenever the chancellor holds a cabinet meeting with an economics item on its agenda or participates in a meeting of an economics-oriented cabinet committee, his economics adviser will have forwarded to him the papers to be discussed, along with either a covering memo or a verbal briefing. The responsibility for preparation of the papers to be discussed remains fully with the line ministries. The Chancellor's Office advisers merely act as a central conduit for and independent source of advice to the head of government. This can be an important assignment, for the FRG has had chancellors with economics skills who have participated actively in the international economic policy-making process. Although the chancellor's adviser on economic policy will attend cabinet committee meetings and the meetings of the Committee of Secretaries of State for European Integration Affairs (discussed below), the Chancellor's Office does not take a firm position on any issue. The normal process is for the ministers to take positions on behalf of their departments and for the office to be fully informed so as to be ready at any time to counsel the chancellor. Part of the latter process is accomplished by communicating directly with the personal aides of ministers.

Below the ministerial level, a systematic, but centralized, process of coordination is conducted among the ministries. It is facilitated by a uniform organizational breakdown, first at the *abteilung* (bureau) level, then the *unterabteilung* (division) level, and finally the *referat* (office) level. Under the generic process known as *federführung,* the leadership role for every issue at hand is placed in an appropriate ministry as judged by line officials. It is there, at the appropriate level of seniority, that the action responsibilities lie: calling the appropriate interdepartmental meetings, circulating position papers, and assuring that the required actions are taken as quickly as possible. In effect, a degree of self-determination is at work here. The ministries coordinate themselves; only rarely do they require a decision at the ministerial level or by the chancellor as to where the leadership role is to be placed.

The success of this approach begins with the German bureaucratic tradition of assigning a high degree of responsibility at the office-director level. It is further enhanced by the tradition of quickly moving a dispute up the line for resolution. The effects of bureaucratic politics are thus not allowed to fester. Disagreements move upwards until consensus is reached. The need for close cooperation between ministries is not taken lightly. Each of the key ministers can claim a strong domestic political base; each is a potential chancellor. The pressure for a cooperative, discreet effort to resolve bureaucratic differences is strong, even if not universally successful.

The German coordination system that stresses a cooperative, self-administered effort rather than centralized, clockwork precision extends to the key component of international economic policy: membership in the EC. The basic vehicle for coordination of EC economic issues is a special Committee of Secretaries of State for European Integration Affairs which is chaired at the present time by the European-affairs minister of state in the Foreign Ministry, and given administrative (secretariat) support by the Economics Ministry. The committee's membership also includes the Ministries of Finance and Agriculture, and the Chancellor's Office. Other ministries, such as Justice and Interior, are invited to meetings when agenda items to be discussed are of direct interest to them. (State secretaries are senior officials, civil servants with political connections, whose rank is immediately below the ministerial level and parallel with the minister-of-state level.)

The German approach to European integration matters is a relatively informal interagency committee with no inherent power. Should the State Secretaries Committee require approval of a sensitive decision or be unable to reach agreement, it would look to the cabinet Committee for Europe chaired by the chancellor. That committee consists of the five-member ministries of the State Secretaries Committee, Defense, and Labor.

As the European cooperation process moves from the purely economic to the political plane, the Foreign Ministry's European Integration Bureau is becoming an increasingly keener rival of the Economics Ministry's European Bureau for policy-making leadership. The rivalry between these two ministries and the absence of centralized direction on noncosmic issues have produced a less-than-ideal coordinating arrangement. Stories of contradictory positions taken by the German delegation in Brussels frequently are heard from economic officials of other EC member countries. That contradictory instructions are in fact occasionally sent to the German EC delegation by the Foreign and Economics ministries is a function of the uncertain division of labors between the two. Policy questions are deemed to be in the province of the former, while technical issues are the prime responsibility of the latter. The nebulous dividing line between such issues precludes any clear-cut delegation of authority.

The process may be administratively challengeable in that it does not concentrate all of the FRG's energies in pursuing unified objectives in the EC and protecting its national interests therein. Yet in political and historical terms, it makes sense. The ideal of European unity is still important economically and politically in the FRG. At least through the early 1970s, its national interests were served more by reaping the benefits of a true community than by preserving the senses of sovereignty and national being that are still so cherished by the French and British. Furthermore, Bonn's economic strength and leverage are obvious; German officials don't have to try so hard to get their views across or to protect their sense of independence.

> Moreover, a widely-felt reluctance to recreate the political and administrative concentrations of power characteristic of the Third Reich has militated against the emergence of strong and centralized policy direction. Brief consideration was given in the early 1950s to the idea of establishing a special agency to handle Community questions, which would have been based on the Marshall Plan Secretariat, but the Economics Ministry and Foreign

Office combined to prevent this. Caution has characterized the German approach to the Communities; the German Government has not exploited its economic strength in Community bargaining, and its voice in the Community debate throughout the 1960's was muted. . . . The coordinating system which evolved did not encourage clarity or consistency in the preparation of negotiating positions. The combination of these two sets of circumstances has meant that the [German] contribution . . . has been less positive than might have been expected. . . .[9]

By European standards, the private sector in West Germany plays an active role in discussing and arguing economic policy objectives. The industrial sector is as well organized as it is export oriented. Its point of view is directly and forcefully articulated to key power centers in the bureaucracy as well as in parliament by such groups as the Federation of German Industry, the German Diet of Industry and Commerce (composed of local and regional groups), and the Joint Committee of German Trade and Industry (composed of industrial- and trade-related services associations). The *Konzertierte Aktion* (Concerted Action Group), a joint group of government, industrial, and labor officials, regularly proposes guidelines for economic policies, mainly in the area of wages. In addition to the retention by the Ministries of Finance and Economics of part-time economic advisers from the academic ranks, the quarterly economic report published jointly by the five major private economic think tanks is widely read. An annual report that also is widely read is issued by the Council of Experts for the Evaluation of Economic Trends.

## France

Among the adjectives that have been utilized by outsiders to describe French foreign political and economic policies are insufferable, pompous, isolated, vexing, and anachronistic. Seldom have the adjectives included the words obscure, unsure, imitative, muddled, or belated. The fact is that the French have used international economic relations brilliantly as foils for their national objectives. French international economic policy has been dramatic, bold, and imaginative, even if not uniformly successful. In all cases, the French have made their presence felt. Whatever failures occurred can hardly be blamed on a lack of effort or poor organization. The usual cause was a lack of conceptual realism or insufficient French power.

France's posture in the contemporary world system has been a quintessential struggle between the limits imposed by encroaching interdependence and a perpetually fierce sense of national identity. The pursuits of grandeur and autonomy became a national priority under Charles de Gaulle, but they still remain elusive targets. More than others, the French have made the concept of international cooperation in Europe and elsewhere conditional upon its serving French national goals.

The French tradition has allowed the government to be especially well equipped to closely manage international economic policy. Today there is a strong central government and a population that is compliant with such an arrangement. The policy objectives established by policy makers are pursued with a vengeance by a single-minded civil service extraordinary in its degrees of power, cohesion, discretion, and professional loyalty. These traditions, as well as the intellectual homogeneity of the administrative-level civil service, are traceable largely to their common experience of having graduated from the Ecole Nationale d'Administration. All senior French officials, including diplomats, are assigned to departments following graduation. It is their diploma, not party affiliation, that allows them to rise to the highest echelons of their respective ministries.

The economic sector is particularly fertile ground for the influence of the bureaucracy. There is a longstanding tradition of governmental planning known as *dirigisme*. There is also the large-scale presence of governmental intervention in the economy through extensive national ownership in the industrial and financial sectors, indicative economic planning, and a close network between officialdom and business elite groups.[10]

Since the internal turmoil of 1968, international economic policy has ceased to be subordinate to de Gaulle's foreign-policy priorities: French independence, reduced privileges for the United States, and so on. Since then, the imperative has been to make the existing international economic order serve domestic economic needs, not to restructure the system according to a French global blueprint. But whatever the direction, French organizational arrangements assure a high level of official presence and control. And the organization will be unusually insulated from outside scrutiny. Like other European countries, the parliamentary process assures a complacent legislative branch when laws, treaties, or additional budgets are requested. Public opinion, except for business leaders, is not a force. Little policy influence is exerted by academic or research economists. The French civil servants' traditional distrust of the relevance of private observations translates into all economic analysis and research being done in house by the major economic departments.

The strongest department in all of France is the Ministère de L'Economie et de Finances (Ministry of Economics and Finance). It has extraordinary control over the conduct of the French economy through its direction of credit and monetary policies, the budgetary process, nationalized industries, and international commercial and financial policy. Owing to the degree of French intervention in economic intercourse and the subordination of the Bank of France, the ministry probably would still be more powerful than the German Ministries of Finance and Economics combined.

In formal international economic policy terms, the Ministry of Economics and Finance is one large unit. In practice, though, an extraordinary separation means that two ministries exist. The Direction du Trésor (Treasury), whose historic roots go back to the late eighteenth century, has two of its six main departments devoted to international financial and monetary affairs. One handles multilateral affairs, multilateral-development banks, and balance-of-payments and foreign-exchange policies; the other, bilateral affairs.

The Direction des Relations Économiques Extérieures (DREE) directs French foreign-trade policies. It has had an in-and-out historical relationship with the Ministry of Economics and Finance. Today, this bureau-level organization is still literally a part of that ministry, but reports to two different ministers. To instill a greater sense of official concern with the performance of the trade sector, the position of minister of foreign trade was added to the cabinet. The Foreign Trade Ministry that was created under him features the DREE (on a de facto organizational basis) as its exclusive policy-making unit and the operational French Center for Foreign Trade (which handles overseas marketing intelligence and export promotion). In discharging certain responsibilities, for example, allocation of export insurance, the DREE's civil servants still report directly to the minister of economics and finance.

The DREE was set up not to solve any organizational shortcomings, but to elevate international trade issues directly to the full-time attention of a cabinet member. The DREE is responsible for the full range of multilateral and bilateral trade policy, including the country's input into the European Community's common commercial policies. It is also responsible for all trade and commercial functions of overseas French missions.

The Ministry of Foreign Affairs (Quai d'Orsay) is a source of foreign political expertise, not leadership, in most of the trade and financial sectors of French international economic policy. It has many parallels with the experiences of its British and German counterparts. All have emphasized the traditional aspects of foreign policy, while limiting economic efforts to the EC and foreign assistance and to providing the political input into high-level, nontechnical economic negotiations. Like other foreign ministries in Western Europe, the Quai d'Orsay is reconciled to seeing the powerful economic ministries handle the detailed conduct of most French actions in this area, but demands to be consulted and to participate in the broader aspects of policy making because of its unique foreign political expertise and perspective, as well as its negotiating prowess.

The French are organized methodically in their foreign-aid efforts. Bilateral aid in the French-speaking countries of sub-Saharan Africa is administered by the Ministry of Cooperation. The modest programs elsewhere are administered by the directorate General for Cultural, Scientific, and Technical Relations in the Foreign Ministry. Overall budgetary direction falls to the Ministry of Economics and Finance. The DREE is influential in the selection of recipient countries because much of French bilateral aid is dispensed on a tie-in basis to countries deemed to be good customers for French exports.

The coordination process is a critical element of French international economic policy making. One aspect of the process is to be found in the designation of one of the ten personal counselors to the French president to oversee international economic policy. A senior civil servant, usually assigned from the Ministry for Economics and Finance, this adviser provides the requisite guidance and suggestions to assure that a presidential perspective is introduced to the international economic policy-making process. Ministerial position papers are routed to the president through him, and he may attach a personal note to them analyzing or criticizing ministerial proposals or positions.

The president's international economics counselor is removed from the operational process. He cannot issue instructions to ministries and cannot call for an interagency meeting to be convened. Neither can he block any papers from reaching the chief executive, for the latter has weekly meetings with his finance and foreign ministers. Nevertheless, he can be an intangible force in the policy-making process. Besides his proximity to the president, he normally is invited to participate in cabinet meetings at which the president discusses international economic relations with his senior advisers. He represents the Elysée Palace at senior interagency meetings organized by and held in the Prime Minister's Office. Finally, he is in regular communication with the personal staff (cabinet) of ministers having an international economic responsibility. All of the above are designed to achieve his two basic objectives: protecting the interests of the president and encouraging the bureaucracy to consider and resolve pressing international economic issues.

Weekly meetings held by the four senior working-level officials involved in this area are a second vehicle for coordination. The directors of the Treasury, the DREE, and the economics bureau in the Quai d'Orsay, and the secretary general of the interministerial committee on Europe (discussed below) convene in each other's office on a rotating basis. The host serves as the de facto chairman of the meeting; the group has no permanent chairmanship. The objective here is an informal, but regular exchange of ideas and bureaucratic perspectives.

The ultimate marriage of organizational process with policy substance and the personification of the French affection for centralization are found in the Interministerial Committee for Questions of European Economic Cooperation (hereafter referred to as the Comité). It is formally charged with handling all questions arising from the country's treaty obligations to the EC, preparing French government positions, and assuring the full execution of all decisions. Actual meetings of the ministerial-level Comité have become rare. Issues of great import are normally handled by cabinet meetings at the Elysée Palace. The actual coordination of European issues is centered in the Comité's General Secretariat (commonly known by its French acronym, SGCI), which convenes two regular weekly meetings. One involves heads of divisions (directors), while the second includes the *cabinets ministériels* (personal staff)—ministers whose departments have an interest in an agenda item. The DREE and the Treasury, of the Ministry of Economics and Finance, and the Ministry of Foreign Affairs, always participate; the other departments, such as Agriculture, attend when appropriate. Convened and chaired by the appropriate official of the SGCI, these meetings may lead to a reconciliation of views on an issue, a determination of further study by a responsible ministry, or the preparation by the secretariat of final instructions. The secretariat may also call a meeting in order to glean a sense of a problem, its dimensions, or a reading of the ministries' positions.[11]

The Comité and its General Secretariat represent the only instance of an EC member country establishing an exclusive bureaucratic agency, nominally independent of the ministries, to coordinate all EC activities. Technically, the SGCI is responsible to the prime minister, but it operates as an independent agency. Its clout was further enhanced in the past by the occasional designation of its secretary general to serve also as a counselor to the president. When a final French policy emerged from the SGCI, there were no doubts, no dissents, no deviations, and no mistaking the French position on an EC issue. Few, if any, coordinating groups anywhere have matched its record of bringing together and keeping together the views of interested ministries. "The result has been an enviable record of cohesion and decisiveness which the French delegation has been able to turn to its advantage in the EC where its performance has contrasted with the degree of preparedness and/or even occasional contradictions shown by its partners."[12] The exact clout of this extraordinary bureaucratic actor appears to be a function of the personality and contacts of its secretary general, a situation not unlike that faced by White House offices such as the NSC or CIEP. The fact that not since 1975 has the secretary general enjoyed the dual status as a presidential counselor has coincided with a temporary reduction in the SGCI influence.

The pursuit of a coordinated French position by the SGCI goes beyond convening interdepartmental meetings, calling for position papers, and brokering a consensus. It writes all final instructions to the French delegation in Brussels, transmits them, and is the recipient of telex messages sent from the delegation. Furthermore, French officials must clear all travel orders to Brussels with the SGCI before leaving Paris. The SGCI has also expanded beyond its immediate EC mandate to include multilateral economic organizations where an informal attempt is made to present a unified EC position. The OECD and, to a lesser extent, the Conference on International Economic Cooperation are examples of other SGCI efforts at coordination of the French government's position.

Officials of the SGCI argue that since they are administratively neutral and take no position on issues, they have no conflicts with the ministries. They describe their mission as being that of neutral coordinators who merely attempt to assure that internal bureaucratic differences are insulated from EC discussions, a goal instinctively shared by all French bureaucrats. They also point to the small size of the professional staff in an effort to deny that they themselves make or create French policy. The number of SGCI professional (administrative-level) officials is small, the exact number fluctuating between 12 and 20. All are up-and-coming civil servants assigned for a two-to-four-year tour of duty after selection by an elaborate process. The internal organization of the SGCI assigns a broad area of responsibility to each of its senior officials. By having only one or two officers staff each of its subdivisions, there can be no usurpation of the line ministries' prerogative of providing all of the technical expertise in the policy-making process. Most of these subdivisions are concerned with the Common Market, and have broad designations such as commercial policy; agriculture, and monetary and financial problems; and energy. There is one subdivision each concerned with the European Coal and Steel Community and the OECD.

The heritage of this highly centralized coordinating mechanism is the peculiarly French predisposition towards administrative centralization and the urgency that the European Community serve France's national purposes without draining away its sovereignty. Without an SGCI-like operation, the French would have been weakened, first, in their relatively successful efforts to present an organized, unshakably unified negotiating posture, and, secondly, in their pursuit of isolated, protracted positions. The intransigence that has forced all of the other EC members to accommodate French views has been demonstrated on such issues as EC voting procedures, reform of the international monetary system, and agricultural policy.

## Sweden

Sweden differs in several respects from the three European countries previously discussed. It is not a member of the European Community. Its population of 8.2 million people is relatively small. It makes no pretense to big-power status, in either international political or economic terms. The foreign policy of the country is based on the principle of neutrality, a fact that has been instrumental in the country's being able for almost 200 years to avoid involvement in European wars. Until the 1976 election loss, the longevity of Sweden's ruling political party was also unique by European standards.

Attainment of the high Swedish standard of living is directly associated with a moderately sized, but industrially sophisticated economy adhering to the doctrine of international specialization of labor through minimal trade barriers. The country pays for a large volume of imports mainly by exporting a wide array of manufactured goods; the equivalent of one-half of the value of total industrial production is exported annually. The government's erection of a vast welfare state complex (the figure for tax revenue as a percentage of GNP was 43.5 percent in 1973, well above the figure for other countries examined here) creates a widespread misconception among outsiders that socialism is rampant. The fact is that by European standards, the degree of government ownership of, and involvement in, the economy is relatively low; market-directed production is prevalent. It has been suggested that Sweden is capitalistic in production, but socialistic in distribution. The major exception to an otherwise liberal laissez faire approach to trade policy arises from the neutrality doctrine. Sweden endeavors to be as self-sufficient as possible in strategic materials and to minimize import dependency on any single country or bloc of countries.

Like the other parliamentary democracies of Europe, Sweden's formal organization to conduct international policy centers around the traditional ministries: foreign, finance, trade, industry, and, to a much lesser extent, agriculture. The Finance Ministry's overall strength in the governing process, together with its stewardship of the budget, assures the ministry a completely clear field in the international financial and monetary sectors. There is neither sufficient interest nor personnel resources in other departments to require even a perfunctory system of formal interagency consultations on such issues. The Bank of Sweden (Riksbanken) operates according to directions stipulated by the government; it does not operate independently. The ministry's influence notwithstanding, its international bureau's professional staff of eight is minuscule by U.S. standards. This figure is equivalent to about 4 percent of the U.S. Treasury's international affairs bureau.

The Ministry of Industry is the newest department, having been established in 1969. Its role in international economic policy is limited to an assessment of the impact of foreign trade on the Swedish industrial sector. Its participation in trade policy is on a selective, low-profile basis. For example, when a U.S. delegation came to Stockholm in the spring of 1976 to discuss voluntary export restraints covering sales of specialty steel products to the U.S. market, the ministry did not directly participate; it apparently did not feel the need to do so. The explanation offered by an official in the ministry, extraordinary by U.S. standards, was that it couldn't contribute very much to the discussions. He explained that Swedish trade officials knew everything they needed to know about the ministry's position from interdepartmental discussions held before the negotiations started. The Ministry of Trade had made its views clear in those meetings, and its leaders felt no compulsion to reiterate them or to monitor their colleagues' performance at the actual discussions. Besides its trade interests, the Ministry of Industry manages the country's energy policy and represents Sweden in the IEA.

The principal structure for formulating and managing trade policy is a unique organizational creature: the Utrikes Handels Departementet (UHD), which was formed in June 1973 to resolve the jurisdictional problem of how to divide the foreign-trade responsibilities of the Foreign Affairs and the Commerce (often translated as Trade) ministries. The struggle to find the right dividing line had led to an arrangement whereby the Commercial Department of the Ministry for Foreign Affairs effectively was placed under the authority of the minister of commerce on questions of foreign trade. Dissatisfied with the red tape resulting from this maneuver, the government felt that it was better to integrate the two departments. The trade policy officials of these two ministries in this way could work side by side, yet preserve intact the other functions and duties of the respective ministries.

> As these new departments consist of officials from both Ministries and, consequently, are larger than the old divisions, and as they have been placed under the concurrent supervision of both Ministries we have a more flexible organization than before. We believe efficiency will be improved partly by a more adequate division of labour and duties that minimizes the risk of duplication of work, and partly by formalizing the means of effective cooperation which, before last May [1973] depended on the personal relations between the officials of the two Ministries.
>
> Officials from both Ministries now working in the departments and the Negotiating Secretariat remain in the service of their respective Ministry. In other words, the officials of the Ministry for Foreign Affairs remain in their diplomatic career, and the officials of the Ministry of Commerce remain in their career in the Ministry of Commerce.[13]

Supervision of the UHD is jointly exercised by the deputy director general of the Foreign Affairs Ministry and the undersecretary for commerce. It is divided into three departments. One deals with economic relations with the EC, the European Free Trade Area, and with Nordic cooperation matters. Additionally, it is responsible for bilateral economic relations with West European countries who are members of these organizations. A second department handles bilateral economic relations with all other countries. A third department handles questions relating to GATT, OECD, UNCTAD, and other international economic institutions.

Since the country's negotiation position in the Tokyo Round is managed by the UHD, it chairs an informal interagency group, which allows input from all other official organizations with an interest in trade policy: Finance, Industry, Agriculture, the National Agricultural Marketing Board, and the Board of Trade (discussed below). In all cases, interagency coordination is done on an informal basis with a very few key officials getting together when necessary.

Besides its trade policy role in the UHD, the Ministry of Commerce chairs an informal interagency group concerned with multinational corporations; in this case concern is mainly with the subsidiaries of foreign-owned companies operating domestically. The ministry also has the lead on economic issues pertaining to defense, for example, economic self-sufficiency and stockpiling of strategic goods.

The Ministry of Foreign Affairs administers the relatively generous Swedish foreign-aid program through a specialized agency called the Swedish International Development Authority.

One of the outstanding features of the Swedish bureaucratic process is the small number of professionals concerned with policy formulation in the ministries. The compact size of the Finance Ministry's international section has already been alluded to. The UHD currently consists of 45 professionals, while the international secretariat of the Ministry of Industry operates with but five professionals. The main reason for this situation is a unique system of two distinct levels of bureaucratic entities. The top level consists of ministries who are charged with the basic functions of policy management: planning, decision making, relations with the parliament, instructions to operating agencies, and administrative matters (appeals, pardons, and so on). The second tier of bureaucratic actors includes the agencies and boards who independently execute the directives and policies previously promulgated by the ministries. With the agencies being left to interpret and apply programs and legislation, the ministries remain tightly knit policy-making units. Various agencies operate to support all of the ministries with international economic policy responsibilities: the Board of Trade (under the Ministry of Commerce); the Swedish International Development Authority (under Foreign Affairs); the National Institute of Economic Research (under Finance); and so on.

The Board of Trade complements the trade policy-making responsibilities of the Commerce Ministry by providing experts to analyze all major industrial sectors, collect data, and consult with the private sector about changes in trade policy. The major contact points are the Federation of Swedish Industries (whose membership accounts for 80 percent of domestic industrial production) and the Swedish Confederation of Trade Unions. The board's factual analyses and sense of private sentiment are channeled to the Ministry of Commerce for use in policy formulation.

The veil of harmony that characterizes the international economic policy-making process in Sweden is impenetrable to an outside observer. Requests made in 1976 by the author for examples of bureaucratic politics in action uniformly produced shrugs and assurances of the symmetry of a small, manageable bureaucracy where everyone knows everyone else. Bigness is branded a drawback, not a virtue. Swedish law explicitly stipulates interdepartmental cooperation; ministries are required to extend the hand to each other. Feelings of intense rivalry and prolonged disputes may not exist, but different ministerial perspectives inevitably produce different viewpoints. The latter apparently are politely and easily resolved in most instances.

This state of alleged bureaucratic harmony begins in the unusual political circumstance whereby the Social Democrats continually controlled parliament between 1932 and September 1976. An unparalleled degree of cohesion and shared values has resulted from the fact that until that party's defeat after almost 45 years of rule, all of Sweden's cabinet ministers in the post-World

War II period have come from the same factionless party, one with a tradition that ministers do not quarrel among themselves in deference to their collective responsibility for government policy. Another contribution to harmony results from the fact that promotion to senior posts within the professional civil service was usually predicated on membership in the Social Democratic party. With serious parliamentary opposition to governmental policy being unheard of, a tightly-knit bureaucracy engendered a true team spirit.

That a uniform set of bureaucratic perspectives dominates Swedish international economic policy is demonstrable in two ways. First, there is no one on the minuscule personal staff of the prime minister with responsibilities in this area. The ministries are completely left to their own devices for coordination. Secondly, the classic pattern of bureaucratic divisions associated with the new-international-economic-order debate does not apply to Sweden. The country is one of the very few industrialized countries where there is consensus that the extraordinary (and costly) new measures demanded by the LDCs are justifiable and necessary.

The Swedes have enjoyed one of the more friction-free systems of international economic policy making, thanks to political circumstances (now terminated) peculiar to the country. They are enjoying the procedural fruits of an incestuous milieu of values growing in a garden of unborn bureaucratic instincts for empire building.

# PACIFIC COUNTRIES

## Japan

All considerations of Japanese international economic policy structure must begin with this essential fact: Japan is the first non-Western society to become an industrialized economic power. The relationship between government and the private sector, the relationship between laborers and employer, and attitudes towards the international order must not be measured in Western terms; they must be understood in Japanese terms. The country's historic isolation, its oriental heritage, and its occidental economy have combined to produce unique political and economic practices and attitudes.

The imperatives of Japanese social organization, psychology, and business practices, the government's indicative economic planning and the country's growing economic impact on other countries have caused many problems for the Japanese. The result is that on one side they have suffered a barrage of criticism for not having liberalized their protective trade and investment controls commensurate with their growing strength. On the other side, they continue to hear demands that they curb their export zeal. In no other country has the speed of economic maturation been so great as it has been in Japan since 1960. But nothing in the nature of the Japanese experience has caused them to radically redesign either their international economic policy or their decision-making institutions in order to better cope with the inscrutable foreigners.

The most important Japanese ministries in international economic relations are the Finance Ministry and the Ministry of International Trade and Industry (MITI). The former is the strongest ministry in the government, not only for the usual reasons of having key responsibilities in domestic economic policy management and the government's budget. It also has special significance because of the unusually heavy debt structure of Japanese business and the ministry's important economic-planning responsibilities. Not unexpectedly, it dominates the Bank of Japan and, hence, monetary policy. No other ministry impinges on its supremacy over international financial and monetary issues.

It is within MITI that the close ties between government and big business come to the fore. Although the Western concept of "Japan, Incorporated" is exaggerated, the continuing official influence on the rationalization and long-term development of the economy and the official emphasis on economic growth make for an unusually strong ministry. In formulating domestic industrial policy, MITI is influential in the allocation of economic resources. It is also the lead ministry in conducting international investment and foreign-trade policies, including all official export promotion activities. The two MITI bureaus with international economic responsibilities (International Trade Policy, International Trade Administration) have generally operated in the shadow of the very influential domestic industrial bureaus. The potential here for bureaucratic politics within MITI has not developed, owing to the clear national priority of industrial policy over trade liberalization policy.

The major voice in the government for international economic liberalization traditionally has come from the Ministry of Foreign Affairs, the third factor in formulating Japan's external economic policy. Japanese postwar foreign relations have been heavily weighted away from politics and towards international commercial relations. The Foreign Ministry therefore is no stranger to international economics, either in Tokyo or in overseas missions. In terms of bureaucratic politics, it has served as a de facto trade department, chairing the Japanese delegation to all major international negotiations and taking the position that a failure to liberalize would have adverse external economic repercussions. The main problem faced by this ministry is its lack of jurisdiction and subordinate status compared to the two all-powerful economics ministries plus the politically potent (and highly protectionist) Ministry of Agriculture.

The potential for effective, swift international economic policy decision making afforded by a relatively neat division of responsibility between MITI and the Finance Ministry is drained by the overwhelming social prerequisite of consensus and cooperation. Decisions are simply not made by powerful mandarins, be it at the bureaucratic, cabinet, or prime-ministerial level. Decisive intervention by senior officials is not part of the process. Many decisions in effect make themselves as they progress up the bureaucracy through lengthy discussions and a continuing series of subtle, mutual accommodations. Sometimes, there is tacit agreement to delay a final decision. Throughout the policy-making process, there is a pervasive reluctance by everyone concerned to ever express an unequivocally negative reaction to another's position. At times, the linguistic vagueness of the Japanese language is employed to assure courtesy and the sense that everyone's views are being taken into account, thereby avoiding any head-on confrontations. Throughout the coordination process, the emphasis is on informality and a polite endeavor to reach unanimity.

Aside from ad hoc interdepartmental meetings, which are convened (and usually chaired by the Foreign Ministry) whenever consensus is not immediately forthcoming, two permanent series of high-level meetings are held by interministerial committees to consider economic issues. Regular meetings are convened by senior career officials of MITI, the Ministries of Foreign Affairs, Finance, and Agriculture and Forestry, and the Economic Planning Agency; the chairmanship belongs to a Foreign Ministry deputy vice minister (the approximate equivalent of an under secretary in the United States). Once a month, the ministers of these organizations meet as a cabinet committee on economic affairs, along with the governor of the Bank of Japan, to discuss both domestic and foreign economic problems.[14] Most international economic policy is decided upon by senior civil servants. Cabinet members delegate an unusual amount of policy-making authority to their senior career aides.

Big business and agricultural interests carry a great deal of weight with the long-standing ruling party in Japan, the Liberal Democrats. To achieve a maximum political impact, they are tightly organized. At the top of the pyramid is the Federation of Economic Organizations, the Keidanren, which in effect is a group of trade associations. Along with the other important national economic groups, the Keidanren is a quasi-member of the Japanese policy formulation, that is, consensus-making, process. Another source of private sector input on economic policy stems from the country's preoccupation with economic growth. A number of influential private economic research institutions have been spawned, most notably the Japan Economic Research Center.

## Australia

The far frontier of the industrialized world, Australia views the world order from several extraordinary angles. In the first place, for only a relatively brief period has the country promulgated its own foreign policy on a fully sovereign basis, that is, not taking its cue from the mother country, Great

Britain. Australian economic policy has reflected an anomalous resources position: the country cannot be classified neatly as an industrialized country or as a developing country. It has the standard of living and traditions of the former, but has a raw materials-to-industry ratio similar to that of an advancing LDC.

The weak international competitive position of its manufactures sector has been the source of a great debate internally for many years: What is the appropriate rate of import protection to protect immature industries and to promote an import substitution policy in general? Further exacerbating the dilemma has been the nature of the coalition government that has dominated the political scene for most of the postwar period. The larger Liberal party is relatively broad in outlook, but the junior member of the coalition, the Country party, is rural and inward looking. Superimposed on all of this is well-to-do, white Australia's geographical proximity to the poorer, yellow-skinned continent of Asia.

Organizational changes have been relatively frequent. Incoming prime ministers have shuffled with regularity the composition of departments and ministerial portfolios to meet shifting political exigencies. Today, international economic policy responsibilities are widely distributed. Highest in the pecking order is the Treasury. Through its Overseas Economic Relations Division, it dominates international monetary and financial policies, as well as policies towards new foreign investments within the country. The Treasury also maintains a low-keyed presence in foreign-trade matters.

The Department of Overseas Trade is the prime actor in formulating export policy, including international commodity agreements (of great interest to this resource-rich country). It is the leader of Australia's delegation to the Tokyo Round of Trade talks, and its Trade Commissioner Service is the source of all economic and commercial representation in embassies and consulates. Overseas Trade also administers export promotion efforts at home, as well as export finance programs.

The domestic business perspective is provided on a specialized basis by three ministries. The Department of Industry and Commerce handles the industrial and services sectors. Until early 1973, it was known as Trade and Industry and incorporated what is now Overseas Trade. In addition, there are the Departments of Primary Industry (agriculture) and Natural Resources (minerals and energy resources). Primary jurisdiction in import policy, that is, tariff levels, now resides in yet another ministry, Business and Consumer Affairs. Created in 1975 and yet to settle in, this department represents a neutral territory for determining the politically charged question of how much import protection is appropriate. As part of the attempt to sharpen the tariff debate within the bureaucracy, the Department of Trade and Industry was split in 1973. It was expected that Overseas Trade would articulate the liberal trade approach, while Industry and Commerce would be free to articulate the domestic perspective. In practice, the prime minister's office has taken the lead on the tariff issue.

To further intellectualize the trade policy debate, the old Tariff Board was expanded into a new statutory body, the Industry Assistance Committee. Not unlike the ITC in the United States, the committee's main function is to respond to government requests for an impartial finding as to whether a business or agricultural applicant is sufficiently efficient to justify relief from import competition. Its publicly released findings on the need for import relief in given circumstances are not legally binding, but it is politically embarrassing for the government to ignore its findings with regularity.

The fact that Australia has been a high tariff country is related, at least indirectly, to an extraordinary organizational phenomenon: It was only in November 1974 that the Department of Foreign Affairs established an Economic Relations Division (equivalent to a U.S. bureau) with about 20 foreign-service officials assigned to it. Prior to that, an all but invisible foreign-policy perspective in the international economic policy-making process had come from an organizationally insignificant branch in the department. It was only after the OPEC-induced energy crisis, Australia's acceptance of full OECD membership, and the initiation of the North-South dialogue that the foreign ministry reordered its priorities and began to exert a meaningful presence in the bureaucratic process of international economic policy. Only since the mid-1970s has it begun a full-scale process of recruiting people with an economics background into the foreign service. The attitude of the rest of the bureaucracy towards the Department of Foreign Affairs' belated entree is mixed. Some don't appreciate additional competition or a potential liberal trade bias, but one economic ministry official avers that it is clearly "in the national interest" to consider the foreign-policy aspects of international commercial relations.

The Foreign Affairs Department's prolonged absence is mainly historical in nature. It was not until World War II that Australia ceased riding piggyback on Great Britain's Foreign Office. First as a colony and then as a member of the Commonwealth, the country entrusted the British to represent its interests in other countries and set the broad outlines of its foreign policy. When an independent policy-making process began in the late 1940s, the foreign ministry's energies and resources were directed first at establishing traditional diplomatic capabilities and secondly to opening new embassies around the world. The growth period has ended only in the 1970s. In the subsequent period of consolidation, a priority has been placed on the expansion into international commercial and economic assistance policies.

The coordination of Australian international economic policy has been overshadowed by the enormity of the soul-searching debate on basic industrial trade policy and the changes in governments. The major trade policy move—a 25 percent across-the-board reduction in tariffs in 1974 as an antiinflationary device—was handled by the Department of the Prime Minister. Otherwise, the coordination process is exactly what would be expected of a small parliamentary government. Collective cabinet responsibility for decision making demands cabinet committees and provides the inevitable forum for top-level policy making. An all-purpose secretariat, which includes senior civil servants expert in economic policy, services these committees from the Department of the Prime Minister and Cabinet. On the working level, most interdepartmental committees are informal or ad hoc. A very few permanent committees have been formed, mainly because of special circumstances. Examples include one dealing with foreign corporate takeovers, another with economic relations with Japan; a third is responsible for monitoring and controlling the composition of all delegations going abroad on official business.

## CANADA

America's neighbor to the north and its biggest trading partner has an international economic policy organization reflecting Canada's parliamentary democracy and its stark economic mix of a rich natural resources sector and a sophisticated, but narrow industrial base. A number of specialized considerations must be handled. Canada's vast energy and mineral reserves give its Department of Energy, Mines, and Resourcres a key role to play in certain areas of export policy. Concerns for the foreign (U.S.) takeover of its industrial sector led to the quasi-independent Foreign Investment Review Agency being created to deal with a narrow, but sensitive international economic policy issue. Finally, still in the shadows is a quietly emerging political factor: the rising influence and power of the provincial governments.

On an across-the-board basis, Canadian international economic policy is dominated by the standard trio of the finance, foreign, and commercial ministries. The External Affairs Department, like so many of its counterparts, is concerned with diplomatic and developmental factors, but has minimal primary authority in the international commercial and financial sectors. Long established in the realm of bilateral foreign-aid policies, it supervises the Canadian International Development Agency. As usual, the Department of Finance is sovereign in international financial and monetary affairs, but it also has responsibilities in commercial policy. A unique organizational wrinkle, traceable historically to the period when tariffs were primarily a revenue-raising device, places tariff-setting authority within the financial ministry. An official from the Department of Finance in fact heads the Canadian delegation in the Tokyo Round of trade negotiations.

The Department of Industry, Trade, and Commerce (DITC) represents the integrated approach to domestic business and international trade questions. As in other Commonwealth countries, there has been organizational indecision as to whether there should be one department or two. In 1963, the department was in fact divided into a Department of Trade and a purely domestically oriented Department of Industry. The two were reunited as the DITC in 1968, but it appears that administrative problems still exist from the mating of concern for domestic business with international trade functions under one roof; "the marriage has not yet been fully consummated," is the phrase used by one Canadian official. An academic observer calculates that DITC has so many elements that overall bureaucratic effectiveness is diminished. In any event, the DITC has prime responsibility for Canada's export policies and programs, including supervision of the Trade Commissioner Service, which provides commercial personnel for overseas missions.

The Canadian system is replete with coordination techniques. Given the fact of cabinet responsibility, the ultimate forum for policy making is of course the cabinet. International economic policy making is undertaken in one of four competent committees: Economic Policy, External Affairs and Defense, Priorities and Planning, and Government Operations. The choice of exactly which committee to use is based more on scheduling convenience than on procedural maneuvering. The committee system is serviced by the Privy Council Office, a small group of civil servants who usually are assigned to temporary duty from the line ministries. No specialist in international economic affairs is permanently assigned to this staff or to the small personal staff of the prime minister. The Privy Council, which reports to the prime minister, coordinates international economic policy through its Economic Policy Secretariat and the External Policy and Defense Secretariat of its Operations Division. Under the direction both of the clerk of the Privy Council and the secretary to the cabinet, the Privy Council Office undertakes the following: preparation of the agenda for cabinet meetings, production of cabinet documents, circulation of agenda and documents to ministers, and recording Cabinet decisions. The Privy Council provides support for interdepartmental committees, including on occasion the provision of chairpersons and secretaries, and the preparation of papers for and on behalf of such committees. It also produces special task force studies for the cabinet and the prime minister. Each cabinet committee is assigned an assistant secretary by the Privy Council; but with only a small staff, he is not in a position to influence the substance of the ministerial-level discussion.

Coordination at the working level is handled by a few standing interdepartmental committees and several ad hoc ones. Examples of the former are committees dealing with international investment policy (mainly within Canada), economic relations with LDCs, and commercial policy. There is also an Interdepartmental Committee on External Relations, which annually establishes specific programs and initiatives Canada hopes to establish in foreign countries. By doing so, it also establishes the personnel composition of Canadian embassies. A number of special committees have been established in connection with the Tokyo Round of trade negotiations to channel information to the cabinet: the Canadian Trade and Tariffs Committee, the Trade Negotiations Coordinating Committee, and the Federal-Provincial Committee of Deputy-Ministers of Industry.

In all cases, working-level coordinating groups decide whether ministers should be brought into the decision-making process through the cabinet committees. The priorities in passing issues up the line are new legislation, new budgetary commitments, direct impact on existing policy, a matter to be discussed in a major multilateral forum (especially if a minister is to attend), and the possibility of a sensitive or publicly debated issue arising during the parliamentary question period. As in the case of European parliamentary governments, the collegial feeling among ministers discourages (but does not prevent) the long drawn-out manifestations of bureaucratic politics all too frequently evident in the United States.

## NOTES

1. Stanley Hoffmann, *Gulliver's Troubles, or the Setting of American Foreign Policy* (New York: McGraw-Hill, 1968), p. 253.

2. William Wallace, *The Foreign Policy Process in Britain* (London: Royal Institute of International Affairs, 1975), pp. 156–57.

3. Ibid., p. 9.

4. William Wallace, "The Management of Foreign Economic Policy in Britain," *International Affairs*, April 1974, p. 257.

5. Wallace, *The Foreign Policy Process in Britain*, op. cit., p. 49.

6. Interview with a senior British civil servant. Several statements of fact and interpretation contained in this chapter were obtained in similar interviews held with officials of the various countries examined, in May and June 1976.

7. Hoffman, op. cit., p. 424.

8. Atlantic Institute for International Affairs, "Problems in the Organization of United States Foreign Policy: Comparative Foreign Practices," in *Appendices* (to the [Report of the] Commission on the Organization of the Government for the Conduct of Foreign Policy), vol. 6 (Washington, D.C.: U.S. Government Printing Office, 1976), p. 385.

9. Helen Wallace, *National Governments and the European Communities* (London: Chatham House, 1973), p. 29.

10. Edward Morse, "Foreign Economic Policy in France" (mimeographed), p. 39.

11. Atlantic Institute for International Affairs, in op. cit., p. 386.

12. Ibid., p. 385.

13. Bengt Dennis, "The New Organization for the Administration of Trade Policy" (paper delivered to the Commercial Counsellors of the Embassies, Stockholm, June 18, 1973), pp. 3–4.

14. U.S. Department of State, "Japan: Making Foreign Economic Policy," mimeographed (Washington, D.C., n.d.), p. 5.

PART

III

PRESCRIPTION

CHAPTER

# 9

## A FRAMEWORK FOR
## PROPOSING REORGANIZATION

[Government] is neither business nor technology nor applied science. [It is] one of the subtlest of the arts . . . since it is the art of making men live together in peace and with reasonable happiness.

Felix Frankfurter

There are no lessons learned from past experience when it comes to systematically reorganizing the means by which the U.S. government formulates and implements international economic policy. The reason, very simply, is that no such effort has ever taken place. Sheer growth to accommodate the burgeoning effects and demands of international economic relations is the only change the system has experienced. The time has arrived to take stock and explore prospects for a rationalization, but there are no preordained rules of the road to follow. Common sense, basic administrative principles, and empirical research concerning U.S. and foreign practices provide generalized, underlying guidelines of how to proceed.

## IMPLICATIONS OF INTERNATIONAL ECONOMIC
## POLICY-MAKING ORGANIZATION IN OTHER COUNTRIES

It should not be surprising that every country's organization and procedures for international economic policy making are sui generis. No two countries have exactly comparable priorities, geopolitical situations, history, patterns of government, and so on. The process by which this policy is made is a dependent variable—dependent on larger political, historic, and socioeconomic forces. The success or precision of any one method of setting ministerial jurisdictions or any one process of coordination provides no assurances of being considered appropriate, or even desired, by other countries. Looked at in broad terms, a study of comparative international economic policy making reveals more about individual national situations than principles of administration.

The conclusions relevant to a study of the administrative aspects of American policy making are to be found in the organizational constants that are detectable in other countries' techniques. The most obvious universal experience is a groping to meet the challenges of the dynamic world economy by utilizing existing organizations, namely, the ministries of finance, foreign affairs, industry, trade, and agriculture, and at times the personal staff of the head of government. No country has introduced sweeping organizational changes or created a major new ministry with a comprehensive mandate inclusive of all major sectors of international economic policy. No government treats the subject as a fully independent one.

Another conclusion is that bureaucratic politics are universally inevitable in a policy jointly produced by the managers of domestic economic policies and the manager of foreign policy. The need to reconcile internal and international objectives is unavoidably the central task of international economic policy. The basic question here is the means by which the foreign ministry, outnumbered by three or four key economic ministries, assures that its perspectives are given attention in the reconciliation process that produces policy. Foreign ministries vary in their impact mainly because they vary in their concern with economic issues and in their levels of professional economic competence. Everywhere the heart of the reconciliation process is an extensive formal and informal system of interdepartmental groups to provide a forum for all relevant viewpoints. Except for the widespread monopoly of finance ministries over international financial and monetary policies, coordination is the name of the game. Efforts to achieve a quick and discreet resolution of bureaucratic disagreements appear generally to have a higher order of priority (and success) in countries other than the United States.

The classic demonstration of the bureaucratic politics of international economic policy is the response of the industrialized countries to the economic demands of the LDCs collectively known as the new international economic order. The main difference in the State-Treasury Department feud in the United States is the degree of its public display. Finance ministries everywhere have looked at the economics of the problem—rational resource allocation principles and budgetary costs—and have come up negative. Foreign ministries have looked mainly at the politics of the situation and have come up positive. They prefer to be accommodating and to construct a useful dialogue, and they emphasize the desirability of taking initiatives in international discussions.

One foreign ministry official in Europe suggested that his country's ability to contribute positively to the North-South dialogue had been eroded by the termination (mainly because of bureaucratic jealousies) of a special interde-partmental committee in which the foreign ministry could debate new policy ideas with the economics ministries. A finance ministry official elsewhere confided details of problems encountered by his department regarding the warm embrace of the North-South dialogue concept by the foreign ministry; the latter's position advocated a positive response to initiating wide-ranging discussions with the LDCs, and deciding only later how far to go in granting concessions. In this fashion, the need to flatly reject LDC demands would be postponed. When he added an anecdote about a positive foreign ministry statement prepared for delivery at the January 1976 IMF meeting in Kingston, Jamaica, but offered to his ministry for clearance only at the last minute, the sense of deja vu materialized strongly. His story is a virtual copy of the mechanics of the State-Treasury dispute; the only real difference is that by breaking the code of silence, his closely guarded remarks are newsworthy and revealing.

The constraint against vicious, public, and prolonged bureaucratic poli-tics posed by the collegial aspects of a parliamentary government is still another organizational constant. Except in France, ministers are selected on the basis of their leadership in the ruling (or coalition) political party. They are powerful people in their own right, with a strong domestic political base, and they feel a strong sense of collective responsibility for official policy. The head of government and the ministers must cooperate very closely, thereby creating a system that strongly discourages bureaucratic dirty tricks or pro-longed confrontations. Ministers are not hired guns like U.S. cabinet members, who can be disposed of, or ignored, at the pleasure of the president.

A fourth constant is the organizational implication of the fact that for all other countries, domestic political-economic priorities usually supersede for-eign-policy considerations. The result is twofold. First, international economic policy issues overwhelmingly are channeled into cabinet committees on eco-nomics, not foreign policy. Secondly, the finance ministry (joined with the Economics Ministry in West Germany) is primus inter pares in the making of international economic policy. No other foreign ministry equals the level of influence possessed by the U.S. State Department as an omnipresent and powerful force in international economic policy making within the councils of government. But then, no other nation studied herein plays a global leadership role commensurate with this country's efforts. The intensity of bureaucratic politics in international economics is due partly to this unique clash between U.S. foreign and domestic priorities.

A general lesson to be learned from this comparative study is the double-edged revolution in policy making wrought by the economic integration pro-cess in the EC. The central government of each member country has had to develop extraordinary organizational arrangements in view of the fact that some aspects of international economic policy are being decided in a supranational mode and being administered in Brussels by international civil servants. The other edge affects nonmember countries, who have to negotiate with a complex supranational authority deeply committed to a free movement of goods, services, capital, and labor within the EC, but ambivalent on how liberal a posture to assume externally.

An interesting result of the comparative study suggests that in countries who have not joined the free trade-oriented EC, there is a correlation between industrial ministries being dominant in tariff and nontariff barrier policy and a relatively high rate of import protection. Japan and Australia clearly demonstrate this connection. But in the low-tariff countries, the United States and Sweden, the foreign ministry has had a strong trade policy voice. In the case of Canada, the Department of Finance has primary jurisdiction, and again the average tariff level is relatively low.

The potential incompatibility of placing domestic industrial policy responsibilities under the same ministerial roof as foreign-trade policy responsibilities is a final conclusion to be drawn. In most cases, there have been reorganizations making what are two separate ministries into one, separating them once again, and then repeating the cycle. Today, separate ministries for industry and trade exist in Great Britain, France, Sweden, and Australia. But in Canada and West Germany, internal coordination problems between domestic and external affairs bureaus appear to plague the Department of Industry, Trade, and Commerce, and the Ministry of Economics, respectively. But in every case save the United States, the lead role in trade policy is clearly assigned to a single ministry.

What, then, are the implications of policy making in other countries for a potential reorganization of the U.S. international economic policy-making process? An overriding implication is that this country should heed the universal characteristics of policy-making techniques abroad. To be radically different is to risk either insufficient compatibility with the broad structures of other governments, a repetition of other countries' mistakes, or both. Organizational proposals should heed the following specific principles:

1. The process of international economic policy formulation should be the culmination of discussions between several different ministries, all of whom have the diverse and distinctive perspectives, goals, and expertise that balanced policy requires. No single department anywhere can adequately carry the load of being an all-round international economic policy maker.

2. The cabinet system of decision making in parliamentary governments presupposes the active participation of the head of government because major international economic policy decisions emanate from the cabinet itself or special cabinet committees.

3. Foreign ministries everywhere do not have the clout or level of primary responsibility that domestic economic ministries do. In every case, they mainly

are called upon to provide the foreign political perspective and negotiating skills. Although foreign ministries are following the State Department's lead in enhancing their economics competence, domestically minded ministries dominate the coordination and formulation of international economic policy. Those in the United States who would restore the State Department's dominant pre-World War II role risk a lack of symmetry in the world's international economic policy making.

4. Unless there is a tradition of unusually close harmony among the bureaucratic actors, systematic coordination is a necessity. Whether formal or ad hoc, it is paramount to assure that the right people are brought together and make a decision at the right time. In larger governments, the coordination process includes an international economics expert on the personal staff of the head of government to act as an adviser and buffer between the leader and his ministers.

5. Some of the virtues of foreign organization and procedure will remain alien because of the peculiarities of presidential-congressional government and an absence of certain traditions found abroad. These include a reduced impact of personalities at senior levels determining the relative standing of departments in the policy-making process, reasonable assurance that the legislature will not defeat a government commitment, a reluctance to air publicly bureaucratic differences, and not having political appointees at subcabinet positions.

6. Bureaucracies everywhere eschew the U.S. fetish that size equals power. Unless it can be demonstrated that deficiencies in U.S. policy making are inversely related to what appears to be excessive size, more responsive, coherent, and consistent policy could be facilitated by a smaller, more manageable bureaucracy.

The final implication is that the United States is missing a good bet by not examining closely some of the better organizational arrangements discussed previously. Properly modified to the U.S. situation, some of them can be keys to a better overall system of making U.S. international economic policy.

## GUIDELINES FOR RECOMMENDING CHANGE

Proposals for any reorganization can derive a sense of legitimacy and coherence by adhering to some broad philosophy and by conforming to a preestablished plan of action. To avoid the twin maladies of ennui and impracticality that have attacked the dozens of earlier, parallel studies dealing with the State Department and foreign policy per se, three fundamental approaches are advisable. First, one should not become entangled in the old-fashioned, oft-repeated administrative solutions that all but ignore the real effects of bureaucratic politics. Secondly, a careful assessment as to what the executive and legislative branches, along with domestic constituencies, are willing to tolerate in the line of organizational change ought to take precedence over the theoretically ideal. Thirdly, full appreciation must be given to the subtleties and complexities of international economic policy. There is need to reconcile its unique characteristics with standard principles of governmental administration when contemplating changes in organization and procedures by which such policy is made. This consideration minimizes the risk that recommendations for reform do not in fact favor domestic over international priorities, or vice versa. Additionally, failure to appreciate all of the subtleties and complexities probably will produce recommendations barely treating the symptoms and ignoring altogether the physiological roots of bad policy.

A number of specific guidelines, or principles for proposing organizational change, have been followed in the hope that the proposals discussed in the next chapter will avoid the numerous pitfalls of the imprecise science of reorganization. In moving towards a meaningful set of proposals, the first specific guideline followed was that ultimately the president is going to shape the real—as opposed to the apparent—lines of command in the policy-making process to conform to his workstyle, philosophy, priorities, and personal feelings towards his senior advisers. A detailed organizational plan is likely to be more of a hit-or-miss effort than a document to be embraced by future presidents. Provisions of ample organizational flexibility and a minimum of procedural specificity may be academically unsound, but they may introduce longevity to the proposals by allowing those in power at any given time a leeway to fashion details.

A second guideline is not equating federal government organization with that of private purveyors of goods and services. The former is not in business to make a profit; it should not exist to extol a particular value or point of view. It does justify itself by producing well-researched, well-balanced initiatives, not readily or efficiently available from private sources, which are in the interests of the majority of the citizens of this country. To accomplish this end, a time-intensive, personnel-intensive process is usually necessary, one that is usually far beyond the levels appropriate to an efficiently run private enterprise. The "provider of goods and services of last resort" in a democracy must be organized and must operate in such a way as to subordinate the concept of managerial efficiency to civil effectiveness.

To a certain extent, the absence of the profit-making ethic has created an oversized leviathan in the international economic area that has grown too large and cumbersome to be either radically altered or shrunk. Vested interests supportive of the status quo have matured not only within the executive branch, but in the Congress and private sector as well. Revolutionary proposals for organizational change are likely to take themselves too seriously. They are more likely to hit a stone wall in terms of acceptance and actual implementation.

Organizational changes branded as panaceas are as much manifestations of naivete as are revolutionary proposals. The worst shortcomings and excesses of the policy-making process can, and should, be reformed. Yet international economic policy making will never be perfectly sound and smooth. Executive branch structure in general and international economic policy organization in particular reflect the values, conflicts and competing forces inherent in a pluralistic society. "The ideal of a neatly symmetrical, frictionless organization structure is a dangerous illusion."[1] Friction in the right degree is a necessary component of the policy-making process for a complex subject like international economic relations where legitimate needs and interests perpetually compete with one another.

The granting of adequate respect and weight to the sensitive triangular relationship between formal organization, the informal behavior patterns wrought by bureaucratic politics, and the substance of policy is a reorganization guideline of major import. The design of an organizational chart is not inherently strong enough to dictate the final form of policy or to neutralize the dynamics of bureaucratic politics. The latter, however, can and do influence a good number of international economic policy decisions. They are also inevitable.

It is therefore not appropriate to divorce recommendations for organizational changes from an appreciation of the inevitability of informal bureaucratic behavior. In his innovative study of organizational and procedural effects on foreign-policy making, I. M. Destler has suggested that reformers continue to mistakenly circumvent the need to come to grips with the gap between overt organizational designs and the covert bureaucratic behavioral patterns by which governmental business is actually transacted. Whereas organization per se finally has been accepted as a factor in policy making, Destler argues that contemporary would-be reformers resort to one of three fallacious devices to cover up their failure to comprehend or admit how bureaucratic process affects the real world of policy:

> The first is to treat organization as just part of the foreign affairs governmental story, but an important part worthy of investigation on its own terms. A second is to recognize political phenomena, but as problems which organization should overcome. A third is just the opposite: to see politics as the "reality," but organizational jargon as a convenient means of disguising it ... [that is] putting forward organizational changes for political reasons but talking about them in terms of "good management."[2]

Failure to appreciate the importance of bureaucratic politics in their broadest sense inevitably leads to yet another recitation of the standard organizational solutions that have been offered repeatedly in the numerous studies of U.S. foreign-policy organization produced since the end of World War II. All are appropriate to international economic policy in literal terms. But modifying some or even all of them for the economics field is not sufficient to get below the surface and impose systemic changes in the policy-making process. Such an effort would merely provide thin disguises for proposals recycled to the point that they are ready to be enshrined as cliches. Destler lists 11 of them:

1. The separation of "policy" from "operations";
2. The joining of "authority" and "responsibility";
3. The creation of a new central official;
4. The strengthening of career services;
5. The elimination of "over-staffing";
6. Coordination from the White House;
7. Coordination by the State Department;
8. Bringing other government foreign-affairs activities into the State Department;
9. Foreign-affairs programing;
10. The establishment of general interagency coordinating committees;
11. The use of central policy staffs.[3]

The relevance of these palliatives to real, structural changes in the means by which foreign or international economic policies are formulated is open to challenge. All are sound and at least mildly useful. But they do not neutralize the dynamics of bureaucratic politics. Nor do they redefine the essential reconciliation process that characterizes international economic policy. The civil servant's mentality is not swayed by such tinkering. An optimal combination of some of the above mentioned reforms can influence and bend the means by which international economic policy is made, and they can be employed to improve or modify. But they cannot revolutionize this process. It is simply incorrect to look for a panacea or to expect that the policy-making system "can be fundamentally reshaped by decisive formal action supported by administrative energy, whether it be a strengthening of career services, a restoration of the authority of the executive, or a breaking of the policy process into neat components like 'policy making' and 'operations'."[4] Convenience and simplicity would abound if the task of organizing the government for international policy making could be reduced to one of designing an explicit system where all officials and units played a preassigned role in a preordained way.

The facts of bureaucratic life are unfortunately not conducive to any neat compartmentalizations.

For in all these cases we are dealing not with "policy machinery" that can be restructured if we have the proper technical expertise, but with relationships among flesh-and-blood individuals and organizational groups who have their own particular interests and ambitions, and who must deal with problems not as they would appear "in the large" to an ideal, rational top-level executive, but as they arise piece-by-piece at various levels of the bureaucracy.[5]

To conclude the explanation of the need to appreciate the interrelationship between form, process, and substantive policy, a quote from Destler is appropriate. A general improvement in the means by which policy is made cannot occur unless an approach is used "which forces the organizational reformer to consider explicitly how the changes he proposes will affect the decision-making process. Nor is this likely to be achieved unless we can develop a set of concepts which provide a useful general view of the real policy-making world, and can compete effectively with the discredited, but far from extinct, formal concepts."[6]

Acceptance of the need to appreciate the impact of the bureaucratic process on policy making leads to the espousal of three criteria for what not to do. The first is not to rely very much on the creative ideas and advice of bureaucrats, past and present, for reorganization recommendations. A broadly based survey of senior public servants on the question of organizational change will produce conservative responses that have nothing in common with one another. The only consistency in the recommendations would be a high correlation between the ramifications of a suggestion and the organizational affiliation of the source. Members of line departments want to enhance the institution with which they identify. White House coordinators point to their era and their techniques as the high-water mark of effective coordination. In an otherwise thoughtful article on the process of international economic policy making, a retired foreign-service officer unabashedly advocates that a "properly reorganized" State Department be given overall coordination responsibility. Such a recommendation is a natural outgrowth of his bureaucratic experience, which, in turn, is intermeshed with his straightforward, but oversimplified assertion, in the beginning of the article, that "foreign economic policy is foreign policy."[7]

Recommendations by bureaucratic players will also tend to be restrained and discreet. Some will deny altogether the significance of organization, pointing instead to the impact of personalities. This is not surprising; they are more used to adapting to different temperaments of political appointees than they are to pondering the subtleties of organizational influences. Furthermore, senior officials are used to witnessing only minor adjustments in international economic policy making. They have not experienced or contemplated a radical or comprehensive redesign. Then too, bureaucrats demonstrate reluctance to rock the organization boat. Subconsciously, there is the realization that major changes could prove either uncomfortable or damaging to the ambitions of friends and colleagues—past, present, and future.

Any radical proposal by an insider will not only connote dissent, but it may well breed hostility and bad feelings among those fellow insiders who perceive their interests adversely affected by a proposed reorganization. The timid recommendations of the Murphy Commission in international economic policy and elsewhere were in part a reflection of the difficulty of gaining consensus in a 12-member group, and in part a reflection of the establishment's disinclination to substantially realign authority. Attitudes towards reorganization are themselves functions of bureaucratic politics.

The second thing to be avoided is a wholehearted embrace of one of the two alluring models of government that ostensibly would greatly simplify the reorganizer's task. One model is that of the strong White House, whereby a great deal of duplication of effort and imprecision in lines of command would be eliminated. The locus of responsibility for all major decisions would be concentrated in an office in the White House. In this case, the U.S. international economic policy-making apparatus would resemble the 1969–74 Nixon-Kissinger NSC system that was responsible for all major policy planning and policy formulation in the national security field. The line departments become essentially advisory and support bodies administering policies and programs decided elsewhere.

Alternatively, the leadership powers of policy formulation and coordination responsibilities could be bestowed upon a strong department, which in this area would be State or Treasury. Once again, the model is simplistic. Whereas apparent bureaucratic tidiness would result from the adopting of either model, there are counterarguments that suggest that such tidiness would not be cost effective. For example, in the White House model, an administrative logjam is likely (unless a huge bureaucracy is quickly assembled), as is a feeling of alienation in the bureaucracy. In the strong departmental model, unbalanced international economic policy is the likely fallout from excessive power being exercised by the holder of a narrowly parochial viewpoint.

One final avoidance criterion involves resisting the temptation to propose the creation of a Department of International Economic Policy into which would be consolidated all of the international economics responsibilities and personnel of the State, Treasury, Commerce, Agriculture, and Labor departments, as well as selected White House offices. There are several arguments that could be offered against such a proposal. In the first place, international economic policy is not an independent phenomenon. Administration of such a department would probably err on one of two extremes. If run too tightly, it would weaken the tricky process of balancing and reconciling the domestic and international priorities of different departments; if run too loosely, it would do little to structurally improve the policy-making process. Furthermore, any lapse in this new department's presidential mandate would lead to a quick and powerful counterattack on its authority by the State and Treasury Departments.

Perhaps the most forceful negative argument, however, is the resiliency and strength of the U.S. bureaucracy's powers of regeneration when limbs are clipped. Stripped of all their responsibilities and existing hierarchies, the current international economic units initially would demand and receive a skeleton crew to serve as policy advisory watchdogs. Fairly soon thereafter, these few advisory officers would request and receive funding, first to hire junior assistants as staff and eventually to retain consultants. This staff buildup would then lead to requests for at least observer status on the internal coordinating committees of the Department of International Economic Policy. Ultimately, much of the old bureaucratic order would be restored, and an even larger, thicker layer of bureaucracy would be the end product.

A final guideline adhered to is that the U.S. policy-making process in this area is by definition intertwined with its counterparts in those countries with which this country conducts economic relations. Major practices and trends in foreign organization and procedures should be taken into consideration in evaluating the evolution of organization in this country. These practices and trends can also be looked on as a source of ideas for organizational improvements in the U.S. government.

## THE REQUIREMENTS OF AN OPTIMAL U.S. SYSTEM

There appears to be no such thing as the single perfect or utopian system for the making of U.S. international economic policy. Beauty is, after all, in the eyes of the beholder. The system outlined in the next chapter does not purport to be the ultimate system. It does purport to conform to the prerequisites of a system that would perform as well as could be realistically expected —optimal even if not perfect.

An optimal organization, broadly speaking, is one that develops international economic policy first through a full, orderly presentation and understanding of the relevant facts and then a balanced consideration of both domestic and external factors. It is an organization that articulates all options and forces decisions on a quick, well-defined, well-greased, and responsive basis. It must have the foresight to anticipate, not merely the reflex to react defensively. It is an organizational system that successfully walks the tightrope so as to avoid both sudden, unnecessary variations in policy and an inability to respond to changing political-economic realities. It is an organization that chooses operational policies most likely to achieve broad objectives, not stifle dissent. It eloquently enunciates decisions and forcefully implements them. An optimal organization would not easily succumb to the blandishments of special-interest groups at the expense of either the overall public welfare or essential U.S. responsibilities in world affairs. Last and far from least, such a system would clearly establish responsibility for policy formulation and management.

The key to implementing such a system begins at the very top, with the president. He must demonstrate his interest, his leadership, and his presence. The U.S. government is geared to function effectively by responding to his articulation of a general policy direction. It needs his unique ability to make decisions on difficult matters, on issues that involve overlapping bureaucratic boundaries, and on prolonged disagreements in the bureaucracy.

Not even the best-constructed organizational and procedural model will hold up in action without the commitment of the president to use and support the arrangement that he has established. Hence, the first specific requirement of an optimal system is increased presidential involvement. The president of the United States needs to better appreciate the need for his participation and leadership in international economic policy. Presidents already have accepted such a role in other high-priority areas, such as domestic fiscal policy and the dramatic issues of national security, especially detente and the Middle East. The president must be involved in international economic policy to a degree commensurate with its increased importance to the national interest and sufficient to keep the bureaucracy responsive to that interest.

The structure of the organization and the pattern of its procedures should be designed to enhance the strengths of a decentralized system, while ameliorating the defects. An atmosphere of creative tension among bureaucratic actors with relevant responsibilities can be a very efficient means of arranging the reconciliations necessary for balanced international economic policy. The virtues of decentralization must be protected by opportunities to thrash out the relevant bureaucratic perspectives and by assurances that the left hand always knows what the right hand is planning. But the size of the bureaucracy must be kept manageable, despite its remaining decentralized. Duplication of effort should be minimized and assignment of responsibilities should be made sufficiently clear so that a specialized expertise is not necessary to discern where exactly the official U.S. position can be explained.

A simplified, but comprehensive system of coordination is a sine qua non of an optimal policy-making system. A coordinator is needed to hold the system together by insuring that it communicates within itself and speaks with a unified voice to the outside. In lieu of line responsibilities, the coordinator must police the policy-making system to insure first that all relevant departmental and agency views have been factored in—the immediate ones of the executive branch as well as those of the Congress and the private sector. The coordinator must also insure that when policy is finally agreed to, it is in fact carried out as planned. Thirdly, the coordinator must arbitrate appeals. And all of these responsibilities must be carried out in a timely fashion.[8]

To fulfill these responsibilities, the coordinating mechanism must be one that guarantees fair participation for the relevant departments and agencies, provides a fixed and recognizable forum for debate, assures that the right issues are being discussed at the right time, resists domination by a particular bureaucratic set of interests, precludes the White House staff from manipulating the levers of power in the line agencies, and has direct access to the president and the cabinet when there is prolonged disagreement or when final approval is needed for major decisions. A White House-oriented system of checks and balances is required to minimize bureaucratic parochialism. But, at the same time, the coordinating system must respect the proper role of the line, or operating, departments and agencies. A very fine line must be tread between central direction and bureaucratic participation.

The coordinating mechanism should treat international economic policy as distinctively as possible, so as to prevent it from being subsumed into the coordination machinery designed primarily for foreign policy (the NSC) or for economic policy (the EPB). In this way, the connotation of either State or Treasury Department domination is avoided. The optimal mix is a coordinator with a bureaucratically neutral White House franchise, but managed by operational officials in the line departments.

Finally, the coordinator's mandate should be comprehensive, its responsibilities encompassing the full sweep of all the policy sectors of international economic relations. There should be one exclusive coordinator. In no case should it participate as a bystander in the real coordinating process taking place in other forums. The prestige and reputation of the coordinator ought to be sufficiently solid so that consensus is reached quickly and at a stage as far down the bureaucratic ladder as possible, and so that bureaucratic dirty tricks could be given the stigma of a gross violation of conduct.

An optimal organization must be alert enough to assemble all of the relevant material of international economic policy: statistics on prices, sales, trade flows; data on international trade and capital restrictions, the performance of major international markets; covert intelligence; and forecasts of economic problems, trends, other countries' economic outlooks, upcoming events. The system must be sufficiently well oiled to distill these data into understandable and relevant analytic pieces that will be read regularly by policy makers; technical problems are brought to the attention of policy makers long before they reach serious proportions. An optimal system will have good communications with the governmental expertise on those domestic factors that are relevant to international economic policy, be it the internal energy supply and demand situation or the workings of the soybean futures market.

The ability to adapt is a further requirement in a subject area that is as fast moving and complex as this one. Flexibility and diversity should be such as to allow the organization to handle routinely all but the most extraordinary exigencies without a knee-jerk recourse to forming new agencies or additional interagency working groups and task forces. In this respect, an optimal system is geared to the challenges of the future. It is not based on arrangements compatible with the simpler, halcyon days of the past.

Still another requirement is a system that operates with a full appreciation of the soundness of cooperating and communicating with the key forces outside of the executive branch. They are the legislative branch, the maker of the laws and allocator of the budgets that support international economic policy, and secondly, the private sector, on whose behalf the majority of policy is conducted. Better communications in both cases should increase the executive branch's understanding of others' needs and of operating dynamics.

The need to keep pace with developments in the proliferating number of international economic organizations and continuing conferences poses yet another demand for good organization. The advantages of maintaining a consistent, mutually reinforcing U.S. position is an obvious reason for a comprehensive systems-analysis approach to the flow of international economic negotiations. Less subtle are the needs to keep track of the trade-offs between the different negotiations and to resist attempts by foreign nations to exploit an inconsistent U.S. posture. "There is danger our trading partners will let the U.S. fumble around the [international economic negotiating] circus we've set up and just pick up the deals they like," former trade representative deputy Harald Malmgren has warned.[9]

A final trait of an optimal system is avoidance of a great concentration of power in any individual institution. The reorganization recommendations that follow are all predicated on a decentralized authority model being adopted. The models of a strong White House or a dominant department presuppose a relatively closed policy-making process where diversified participation is neither encouraged nor welcomed. Both tend to suffer from inevitable flaws and contradictions (for example, bottlenecks in the White House and excessive power exercised by a narrow parochial interest) that offset the virtues of a neatly constructed line of command. In contrast, the third model is most conducive to fostering sound organizational and procedural guidelines that include:

1. Reliance on diversified organizational structures, each with specialized resources and abilities, that are responsible for the implementation of policy and the administration of programs;

2. Encouragement of a competitive marketplace of ideas, one based on a broad participation of viewpoints in the decision-making process and a sharing of authority and responsibility;

3. Adaptation to congressional interests and authority, as well as compatibility with decentralized congressional committee jurisdictions;

4. Responsiveness to the private sector's viewpoints and welfare.

# NOTES

1. Harold Seidman, *Politics, Positions, and Power* (New York: Oxford University Press, 1970), p. 13.

2. I. M. Destler, *Presidents, Bureaucrats, and Foreign Policy* (Princeton: Princeton University Press, 1974), pp. 42–43, 47.

3. Ibid., p. 17.

4. Ibid., pp. 38–39.

5. Ibid., pp. 39–40.

6. Ibid., p. 51.

7. Sidney Weintraub, "The Process of Making Foreign Economic Policy," *Foreign Service Journal,* June 1976, p. 8.

8. Statement of Harald Malmgren before the Senate Committee On Banking, Housing, and Urban Affairs, in *International Economic Policy Act of 1975, Hearings* p. 95.

9. Quoted in Boyd France and John Pearson, "Getting Ready for the Tokyo Round," *Business Week,* January 19, 1976, p. 64.

# CHAPTER
# 10

**PROPOSALS FOR
ORGANIZATIONAL AND
PROCEDURAL CHANGES**

Every new truth which has ever been propounded has, for a time, caused mischief; it has produced discomfort, and often unhappiness . . . sometimes merely by the disruption of old and cherished association of thoughts. It is only after a certain interval . . . that its good effects preponderate; and the preponderance continues to increase, until at length, the truth causes nothing but good. But, at the outset there is always harm. And if the truth is very great as well as very new, the harm is serious. Men are made uneasy; they flinch . . . old interests and old beliefs have been destroyed before new ones are created.

Henry Thomas Buckle

The discussion of the substance of international economic policy, the examination of the policy-making process at work, and the promulgation of a theoretical framework for reform culminate in this chapter in a series of recommended changes in the U.S. policy-making process. The proposals that follow are designed to be consistent with the ratiocination that preceded them. Rather than purporting to represent unassailable logic, these reforms are deemed to represent the most likely means of producing an optimal policy-making system. Alternative variations or refinements might produce equally satisfactory results. Nevertheless, there is no reason to assume that another system would produce better results. Bureaucrats' enthusiasm or gratitude were not criteria for the recommended changes. Compatibility with a fresh look at existing organization and existence of a strong commitment by senior officials to act where necessary were criteria. Change for the sake of change is avoided. Organization can, and should, be built around the existing institutions.

A critical caveat must be emphasized: the mechanics of the reforms proposed below are a necessary, but not sufficient precondition for assuring an improved policy-making process. The other precondition is good people who will manage the restructured bureaucracy in an efficient, effective manner, one which is supportive of the objectives of the reorganization. In other words, how the new institutions and procedures are run can assure, or frustrate, achievement of the intent of the reforms.

The proposals for changes in existing organization and procedures have been divided into two categories. The first includes those proposals designed to structurally affect policy making by changing (1) the means by which different perspectives and recommendations are introduced, discussed, and evaluated, and (2) the level or locus of actual decision making. The second category encompasses the procedural element: mechanical techniques designed to streamline the policy machinery, make its management more efficient, provide better support to policy makers, and generally upgrade professional skills. Both categories have the common purpose of improving the end result, but they are two different means of achieving better international economic policy.

## STRUCTURAL CHANGES

### Establishment of a Department of International Commercial Policy

To consolidate the inefficient, haphazard scattering of responsibilities in the international trade and investment sectors, a Department of International Commercial Policy (DICP) should be established. Its primary objective would be to give greater focus and coherence to these sectors. Policy-making primacy and all of the trade and investment operational responsibilities in Washington of the State, Treasury, and Commerce departments would be absorbed by the new department. The new department would be created by legislatively retitling the Office of Special Representative for Trade Negotiations and giving the office enlarged responsibilities and a cabinet department designation.

The DICP is designed to overcome the administrative deficiencies produced by the most massive melange of operating responsibilities in U.S. international economic policy. Imports, exports, and direct investment capital flows today represent a quarter-of-a-trillion-dollar business in the United States. Existing government organization, however, is more befitting a cottage industry. It is needlessly disjointed, illogical, and duplicative. It is confusing to all observers, except perhaps to the shrewdest Washington lobbyists and civil servants.

Trade policy organization reflects historical and personality considerations only, not organizational common sense. The heart of trade policy—the special trade representative's office—presents a number of organizational problems. It is one of the very few operational units within the Executive Office of the President; its activities ebb and flow depending on the existence of multilateral trade negotiations under the Trade Agreements Program; its trade policy responsibilities overlap with the purported duties of the CIEP; and a number of specialized trade issues are handled in State, Treasury, and Commerce, thereby placing them outside of the operational authority of the special trade representative's office. The result is a string of narrowly focused fiefdoms, which only occasionally work together harmoniously to produce a coherent, comprehensive trade policy.

U.S. trade policy is linked closely with foreign investment policy. At the bottom, there is the conceptual link of their being the two principal market-oriented phenomena with the common business objective of increasing sales to foreign consumers. A technical link results from the fact that a very significant proportion of U.S. exports of manufactured goods presently consists of intracorporate transfers; that is, arms-length sales directly to foreign buyers are not involved. On the import side, the mounting tide of foreign direct investment in this country inevitably will alter the composition and level of U.S. imports, just as export patterns have been affected by U.S. corporate foreign direct investment. Demands by LDCs for increased transfers of technology, as well as the outlook for tighter host-country control over the production and trade patterns of multinational corporations, suggest additional longer-term effects of overseas investment on the U.S. export sector.

The United States is unique among industrialized countries in not having a single ministry or agency charged with the overall direction of trade policy. There are three explanations that immediately present themselves. The first is that this country knows something (or does something) that nobody else does. If so, it is a well-hidden secret. The advantages of a single designated spokesman for trade policy when dealing with foreign governments is obvious. Dismissing this answer, we come secondly to the possibility that the U.S. internal situation is so extraordinary that a trade ministry is wholly inconsistent with reality. While one can argue that the more powerful models of such a ministry (for example, the MITI in Japan) are inappropriate to the tenor of U.S. government-domestic business relations, the abstract notion of a trade ministry is not at odds with the U.S. experience. This leaves a third explanation: U.S. international trade and investment policy organization has grown piecemeal, influenced by historical circumstances and the chance presence of strong personalities in the executive branch and Congress. Existing organization is accepted and tolerated because "that's the way we've always done it." Since passage of the Trade Expansion Act in 1962, no one has publicly taken a long, hard critical examination of U.S. trade policy organization, which did not take the status quo for granted. The time has come to resist simple momentum. Basic assumptions should be challenged.

The establishment of a DICP need not involve the drama, expense, and dislocations normally associated with creation of a new department. The fact is that virtually all of the requisite parts for the department already exist and are budgeted. This situation is well hidden because the components are so widely dispersed that their linkage is all but invisible. It is a situation analogous to the children's picture game in which close examination of the illustration of a forest scene will reveal outlines of a number of animals or whatever, which have been blended cleverly into the drawing.

To minimize the need for acquiring massive new supporting facilities and personnel, the administrative structure of DICP is modeled on the French Ministry of Foreign Trade. Since the latter's operating heart, the DREE, is still a part of the Ministry of Economics and Finance, the ministry's staff consists entirely of professional civil servants engaged in trade policy. All administrative services and support facilities are provided by the Ministry of Economics and Finance. No new bureaucratic layer was created.

In terms of jurisdiction, DICP would have no domestic responsibilities whatsoever. Its mandate would involve entirely overseas commerce, like that of the British Department of Trade, but unlike that of Japan's all-powerful MITI or Canada's DITC. Creation of the French Foreign Trade Ministry involved mainly a redistribution and consolidation on paper of trade duties. The major organizational innovation in that instance was the designation of a single new cabinet official to head it and thereby provide more high-level attention to trade affairs within the upper echelons of the French government. Since the president's special trade representative already has cabinet rank, it would be necessary only to rename the position and broaden its authority.

The new department could have its offices physically located in an existing building, perhaps the one housing the Commerce Department or the Treasury Department. Personnel, budget and supply officers, a library, security, and all other support services could be handled by the most modest of increases in the resources of the host department. Beyond initial start-up costs, the only significant budgetary impact of the proposed reorganization would be the possible hiring of no more than ten to 15 specialists to look at issues not currently covered. If creation of DICP is accompanied by the OMB review of personnel needs discussed below, a net budgetary savings of modest proportions is very possible. Total personnel of the new department would be well under 750, including officials stationed abroad.

To provide a more tightly run trade policy through a clearer delineation of responsibilities, better coordination, and reduced duplication of efforts, the international trade and investment offices of the State, Treasury, and Commerce departments, and the Office of the Special Representative for Trade Negotiations would be merged into DICP. A sensitive political decision would have to be taken on the otherwise administratively sound contingency of also incorporating the foreign-trade responsibilities of the Agriculture Department.

Although the special trade representative's office would be formally abolished, State, Treasury, and Commerce would continue to have a role to play in the interagency policy-making process. In deference to the fact that DICP is to be the lead department, sizable reductions of existing trade and investment staffs in these three departments is required. The trickiest administrative question associated with creation of the proposed new department is the extent to which a nonoperational trade and international investment policy oversight, or watchdog, capability should be retained by the three older departments. Very small staffs are appropriate to retain the purely foreign-policy, balance-of-payments economic policy, and domestic business perspectives in the policy-making process. The question of exactly how much is enough should be settled by an OMB evaluation jointly held with the three departments. Suffice it to say, without a thorough and permanent cutback of international trade and investment specialists in State, Treasury, and Commerce, the logic and effectiveness of the DICP proposal are diminished.

A major staffing innovation should be the hallmark of DICP personnel policy from the beginning: between 10 and 20 percent of its professional staff at any given time should be assigned for temporary duty from the other departments with interests in the trade and investment issues: State, Treasury, Commerce, Labor, Agriculture, and so on. Such personnel should be eligible for positions in DICP through the assistant secretary level. The rationale behind this arrangement is the recognition that U.S. trade policy can never be made exclusively within one cabinet-level department, no matter what its mandate on paper. The specialized domestic economic, international monetary, and foreign-policy expertise resident in other ministries must enter into the policy-making process on an advisory basis even if primary jurisdiction is centralized within DICP. Utilization of professionals from other departments not only would broaden DICP's expertise, it would provide invaluable trade policy experience for these professionals when they returned to trade policy-related positions in their home departments. Such an arrangement would have the additional pragmatic advantage of softening the bureaucratic jealousies in the existing departments, which instinctively would oppose creation of a new international trade and investment department. The result would be a modification of the Swedish UHD model of a foreign-commercial ministry joint venture. Since the State Department will continue to be responsible for economic representation overseas, it is advisable that the majority of outside personnel assigned to DICP be foreign-service officers. (For related personnel proposals, see the later section on personnel exchange programs.)

The leadership of the new trade and investment ministry would be vested in a secretary who, in current organizational terms, would be the president's special trade representative. The new department would have two undersecretaries; their positions can be created by simply renaming the two existing deputy special trade representative posts. Under the Trade Act of 1974, both positions were upgraded to executive-grade levels equivalent to departmental undersecretaries. The undersecretary for multilateral trade activities would supervise two bureaus (each managed by an assistant secretary); conceivably, he would spend most of his time in Geneva as de facto head of the U.S. delegation when multilateral trade negotiations were in progress (the secretary would formally be the head). The first bureau under his direction would be concerned primarily with trade policy issues considered in the GATT and OECD and with those involving U.S.-EC trade relations. This proposed Bureau of Multilateral Trade Negotiations would approximate the current operation of the special trade representative's office. Its main function would be the formulation and coordination of the strategy and tactics employed by the U.S. government in multilateral trade talks. A second bureau, for trade policy planning and private sector liaison, would be charged with congressional relations and overall supervision of the public advisory committees on trade policy mandated in the Trade Act of 1974. This bureau would also be responsible for the department's trade and international marketing research.

Four other bureaus, each headed by an assistant secretary, would report directly to the second undersecretary. The first would supervise all bilateral relations with industrial countries and with the Communist bloc countries, that is, America's East-West trade policy. Trade relations with the poorer countries of the third and fourth worlds would be the responsibility of a second bureau. Trade policy in this case is distinctive because of its general subordination of free market principles to the feeling of obligation to provide economic assistance (equity over efficiency) and the need to assure access to supplies of raw materials at reasonable prices.

A third bureau would oversee the various policy aspects of international investment issues associated with the multinational corporation phenomenon, and, in addition, international business practices. Inclusive in this bureau would be the primary responsibility for possibly considering creation of international investment organizations, for expropriation problems, for policies concerning foreign direct investment in the United States and technology transfers to LDCs, and for advice to U.S. businesses with limited foreign investment experience. It would also deal with overseas U.S. business activities that contravene U.S. laws, for example, bribery, and compliance with certain Arab boycott demands. And for the first time, there would be a full-time effort to quantify the effects of international investment. An increased level of knowledge should emerge from a close examination of the plethora of scattered data that have become available concerning multinational corporations. This would involve extensive macroeconomic research on international tax policies and on the impact of foreign investment on employment, prices, competition, and so on, in both the United States and host countries.

All of the operational processes associated with international trade programs would be combined into a fourth bureau neatly divided into export and import activities divisions. The bureau would administer export control procedures and manage all export promotion activities, both domestically and at American embassies, consulates, and trade fairs abroad. It would also be responsible for devising and administering policies related to the overseas transfer of U.S. technology.

DICP would be responsible for all commercial activities involving direct contact with the private exporting sector. But it would not assume any of the overseas economic functions—analysis and forecasts, and representation to and negotiations with host governments—currently belonging to the Department of State. The purely business promotion function overseas is at odds with the four primary missions of the State Department: policy formulation, articulation of what American interests are abroad, the conduct of traditional diplomacy, and the assessment of foreign governments' attitudes and needs. Although the State Department has avoided involvement in all program management, it inexplicably has jealously guarded its role in the trade promotion program. The energies of the American Foreign Service should be channeled where they are most needed and effective.

A sharp distinction can be made between overseas economic and commercial functions as practiced by the U.S. government. The latter are concerned with assessing local economic trends and dealing directly with a foreign government. Commercial activities consist of the general promotion of American business activities abroad, assistance to the American private sector by extensive data reporting, notifications of business opportunities, and assistance to businessmen on the spot. Specifically, commercial activities include the development of export sales opportunities and the dissemination of information on such opportunities to American business, the preparation of purely business publications (for example, *World Trade Data Reports* and *Market Share Reports*), operation of trade centers and fairs, provision of agent-distributor services, and extension of foreign investment advice and support services to American businessmen. At present, these roles in Washington are handled entirely by the Department of Commerce. In the field, however, these roles are usually performed by State Department foreign-service officers working in the commercial branch of an embassy's economic section.

Assistance to businessmen and product promotion are efforts that naturally complement DICP's mandate. The business support function is too specialized to appropriately be left to foreign-service officers whose career goals and talents typically lie in the finer arts of diplomacy, as well as political and economic reporting and assessment. Far from downgrading the role of commercial attaches, the transfer of responsibility for trade promotion efforts to DICP, a move which would include direction of professionals to staff the commercial sections of overseas missions, would improve the quality of performance and eventually the reputation of the effort. Such a transfer should in no way diminish the authority of the ambassador or operating patterns of an embassy. The ambassador would oversee and assist the commercial counselor with the same emphasis given to the other embassy sections—political, military, economic, cultural, and so on. Foreign-service officers should continue to be eligible to be commercial attaches under the new system.

Two further innovations should accompany the assumption of overseas commercial responsibilities by DICP. First, to add an additional career incentive to the overseas commercial service, any of its officials who had served an overseas tour of duty in a U.S. mission should be eligible to become a consul general. Such an arrangement would also encourage the posting of business specialists to cities that are industrial centers, but not capital cities. Secondly, the ranks of the DICP and foreign-service personnel serving abroad as commercial counselors should be augmented by an experimental program of temporarily retaining people directly from the private sector on a fixed-term, contractual basis. They would serve one or two tours (of two to three years each) as an overseas commercial officer. Other countries have successfully used this technique to make official efforts more relevant and alert to commercial sector needs and interests. DICP also should assume the responsibility for assigning international trade specialists to those Commerce Department domestic field offices located in major industrial cities.

The import activities division of this fourth bureau would absorb the Treasury's investigative responsibilities carried out in response to allegations of certain unfair foreign-trade practices (dumping and countervailing duties). Currently, investigations of charges that such practices exist are assigned to that department's assistant secretary for enforcement, operations, and tariff affairs. The U.S. Customs Service, currently under Treasury jurisdiction, might also be placed here, even though it has no policy responsibilities. In addition, the division would absorb several import-related offices within the Commerce Department, such as those that administer adjustment assistance programs, and import control programs for textiles and other manufactures.

If agency consolidation is a favored concept in the White House, the Eximbank could be included in DICP as a semiautonomous financial unit, similar to the CCC's relationship with the Agriculture Department. Such a move would have at least two marginal impacts: first, assuring maximum compatibility of Eximbank operations with overall trade policy; secondly, reducing the costs of administrative overhead. Similarly, the Overseas Private Investment Corporation, also a smallish agency dealing exclusively with the private sector, could be incorporated as a semiautonomous unit.

## The Assistant to the President for International Economic Affairs

The occasional post of presidential assistant for international economic affairs should be filled on a permanent basis. The person selected for this senior post should be hired on a nonpartisan basis and ought to score high in terms of vigorous personal and professional standards. These include a broad substantive knowledge of international economics and a familiarity with domestic economic constraints and foreign-policy objectives. He needs access to and the confidence of the president. At the same time, he must be trusted and respected by the Cabinet to minimize end runs by department heads to the president. And he must be selfless. The latter is defined as keeping a low profile and remaining immune from the wretched excesses of "Potomac fever." To the extent he publicly upstages or builds a competing power center vis-a-vis the line departments, he complicates the policy-making process. Neither should he impose his personal will or views on the bureaucracy.

The assistant should have no operational authority. He should refrain from being an open advocate for a particular course of action. His job is to advise the president on issues as needed; assure that the options and judgments sent to the president for a final decision reflect all appropriate bureaucratic viewpoints and do not ignore the best interests of the president; advise affected agencies of presidential decisions; and make certain that those decisions are faithfully implemented in the manner and with the speed intended. A final task is to monitor discreetly the issues under review by the departments and then involve the president, if necessary, in ordering acceleration of the timetable for reaching consensus, or in ordering initiation of a new approach entirely. In short, the assistant's main function is to provide first a constant feeding in of information and guidance to the president and, secondly, a feedback of the president's views to the line departments and agencies.

He should have a small staff of at most five assistants, each of whom would be experienced in at least one of the major sectors of international economic policy. In addition to backing up the assistant to the president, the staff would act as the White House-based secretariat for the central coordinating mechanism described below. While some of the staff appointments could be political, it would be advisable (as long as petty bureaucratic jealousies could be avoided) to select some staff members from the ranks of bright young professionals working for the relevant line departments. This would provide a horizon-broadening experience to such civil servants.

Neither the assistant nor his staff should be retained on a long-term (more than four years) basis. Vested interests should not be allowed to develop in this sensitive office designed to enhance the unique perspective of the president, not career opportunities.

## Establishment of the Cabinet Committee for International Economic Policy

To assure the most efficient, comprehensive method of policy coordination, a cabinet Committee for International Economic Policy (CCIEP) should be created with the president as chairman. The executive secretary of this replacement for the CIEP would be the president's assistant for international economic affairs.

The central purpose of the committee is to achieve the noble ends for which the CFEP and the CIEP were created in the 1950s and 1970s, respectively: high-level coordination of all aspects of international economic policy and the attainment of consistency between it and foreign policy and domestic economic policies.

The CCIEP is to have three functions: to coordinate the high-level activities of the operational departments and agencies; to serve as the link, or channel, directly to the president when his approval or his resolution of a bureaucratic disagreement is necessary; and to spotlight the locations of responsibility for every issue falling under the rubric of international economic policy.

Organizational innovations are necessary if this effort to achieve these long sought-after goals is not to prove futile. One innovation is to pattern the CCIEP on the cabinet economics Committee system used in European parliamentary governments. The EPB-NSC rivalry within the White House, as discussed in Chapter 5, suggests that bureaucratic jealousies would preclude international economic policy from being placed squarely in a cabinet economics committee, as is the case in West Germany and Great Britain. Nevertheless, the principle of face-to-face discussion between the head of government and his cabinet officers should be utilized in the American model. A separate cabinet committee devoted exclusively to international economic policy is the ultimate in neutral territory. A presidential commitment to use it is a necessary crowning touch to preserve and protect bureaucratic respect and participation.

The formality with which the committee is created is incidental; an executive order would suffice. Looked at literally, a name is not even mandatory. For the president to meet with a select group of his cabinet, only a few telephone calls are necessary, not a formal organization. Titles and membership lists in this instance are ornaments. The critical consideration is that the president and appropriate members of the cabinet convene for the express purpose of considering international economic policy. If members are to be formally selected to a committee, then the permanent participants should consist, at a minimum, of the secretaries of state, treasury, and international commercial policy, a member of the CEA, and the assistant to the president for national security affairs. The secretaries of agriculture, commerce, and labor, the director of the OMB, and others would participate whenever any meeting had an agenda item that touched on their institution's responsibilities.

Meetings of the committee without the president in attendance should involve only preliminary discussions; efforts to reach final decisions without his presence should be discouraged, lest the loss of the presidential imprimatur lead to a repetition of the CIEP's unhappy fate. Meetings should be scheduled only on an as-needed basis; regularly scheduled sessions would not be productive. A committee meeting could be requested by the president, his assistant for international economic affairs, or a cabinet member. The president would have to approve such requests made by his aides. Scheduling, preparation of an agenda, dissemination of position papers, and announcements of results would be handled by the executive secretary, that is, the president's international economics assistant.

Although the CCIEP could easily be created by a presidential memorandum or an executive order, it might be good politics to obtain prior congressional approval, informally or formally. On the one hand, it is designed simply to guarantee that the appropriate officials in the line departments are convened at the appropriate times. Not being designed to acquire or duplicate any of the authority of these organizations, it would have no specific or separate power. On the other hand, there can be an implied authority in being a central coordinator. The CCIEP, furthermore, is designed to replace a congressionally legislated body, the CIEP. More importantly, the ideal companion to creation of the CCIEP would be a parallel rationalization of congressional committee assignments to bring them into alignment with the responsibilities of the subcommittees of the CCIEP.

The main source of day-to-day CCIEP activity would be centered in five specially created subcommittees. Each would be chaired by a presidentially designated official of subcabinet rank. Each of the five would have an executive secretary who would come from the professional staff of the assistant to the president for international economic affairs. The full CCIEP would need to meet only in crisis situations, in cases where the subcommittees could not reach consensus, when the president had to give formal approval to an important policy initiative, and for occasional briefing sessions to pull together at one time the major strands of U.S. international economic policy. While the CCIEP is a presidential system, the subcommittees are an interagency coordinating mechanism.

The subcommittees should operate on that fine line that minimizes bureaucratic parochialism and at the same time respects the proper role and abilities of the line departments. Consequently, the five chairmen each would be designated a deputy or associate member of the CCIEP. This designation would be a second hat for all of them, since their chairman status would devolve from their full-time position as a subcabinet official in one of the line agencies principally concerned with international economic policy. Unlike existing coordinating arrangements, all of the coordinating efforts associated with the new cabinet committee formally would be held under the aegis of a bureaucratically neutral White House mechanism and chaired by officials formally acting on behalf of the president, not a department or agency.

A logical sequence of subcommittees would consist of the following:

1. International Trade and Investment Policy, chaired by one of the undersecretaries of the proposed DICP.

2. International Financial-Monetary Policy and Economic Interdependence Issues, chaired by the undersecretary of the treasury for monetary affairs.

3. Economic Relations with Less Developed Countries, Natural Resources, and Technology, chaired by the undersecretary of state for economic affairs. Food and oceans policies would be included here, as would North-South issues.

4. Economic Analysis and Forecasting, chaired either by the CEA member with international responsibilities or by a special deputy assistant to the president for international economic affairs. Members of the economic research offices of non-executive branch and non-policy-making agencies such as the CIA, ITC, and the Federal Reserve Board would participate in the subcommittee. Economic intelligence would also be supervised here.

5. International Energy Policy, chaired by an undersecretary (or equivalent) of a department or agency with major energy policy responsibilities. If no centralized energy entity is created, it might be appropriate to incorporate such responsibilities in the Commerce Department, which would then chair this subcommittee.

The additional time and effort required of these officials to meet their CCIEP responsibilities should be nominal. In most cases, there would be little if any net increase in the interagency coordinating efforts in which they are engaged already. The real difference is the ambiance of the White House that will flavor all coordinating efforts. The CCIEP and its subcommittees are to play the role of the president's eyes and ears to assure that the bureaucracy is functioning smoothly and in the president's (and presumably the country's) best interests. It would involve the president's time and physical presence only periodically, in cases of crisis, great import, or bureaucratic deadlock at the cabinet level. Similarly, it is presumed that the undersecretary-led subcommittees would need to involve cabinet officers only for sensitive, important issues and in cases of bureaucratic deadlock.

When decisions have to be moved up the line for final approval, the exact technique would depend upon the working styles of the principals involved. For example, a verbal discussion in the Oval Office could secure the required presidential decision or approval. If the situation required a written memorandum, it would be prepared by the appropriate subcommittee. The paper would list all of the options, and as appropriate, agency positions and points of disagreement. The paper would then be sent to appropriate cabinet members of the CCIEP for either final disposition or transmission to the president through his assistant for international economic affairs. In all cases, the White

House secretariat would apply pressure for whatever efforts were necessary to obtain consensus on a final policy.

One further structural change is required to assure the success and rationale of the CCIEP. Each and every one of the existing interagency committees, working groups, task forces, and other such units should be abolished. All of their duties and activities that cannot be buried forever would be reassigned to one of the CCIEP subcommittees. Interagency coordination in international economic policy would very simply be composed of the president and appropriate cabinet members overseeing the continuing operation of the five subcommittees charged with routine coordination in every sector of international economic relations. For example, in the foreign-assistance sector, the situation would be ended whereby one interagency group handles multilateral aid (the NAC), one considers bilateral aid (the Development Loan Committee), another handles food policy (Agriculture Policy Committee), a fourth considers international commodity agreements, a fifth approves PL 480 loans, and still another doesn't seem to coordinate anything (DCC). Instead, the subcommittee responsible for economic relations with LDCs single-handedly would look at all development policy issues on an integrated basis; that is, there would be horizontal integration. (Military aid programs would remain within the national security hierarchy.)

The broad coordinating mandates of each of the subcommittees would necessitate the establishment of specialized working groups on the appropriate level of seniority (assistant secretary or office director) either on a continuing or ad hoc basis. The importance of the issue under discussion would dictate the seniority level at which an interagency working group would meet. The group's chairman would be selected by the chairman of the subcommittee to whom the working group reports. Selection would be made on the basis of which department had prime responsibility for a specific subject matter. For example, in the Economic Relations with Less Developed Countries, Natural Resources, and Technology Subcommittee, a debt rescheduling working group might be chaired by Treasury; tariff preferences and corporate technology transfers, by DICP.

By systematically incorporating all coordinating groups in the larger CCIEP effort, clearer lines of responsibility would be drawn, a better system of checks and balances of bureaucratic interests would be achieved, and fewer interagency meetings would be required. Indirectly, an American adaptation of the German style of *federführung* would be established. The locations for coordination activity and policy-formulating responsibility would be clearly delineated by the creation of the five subcommittees. Excessive size, lack of tradition, and intensity of bureaucratic rivalry in this country preclude a successful overnight recourse to the German system of allowing the ministries to decide directly among themselves how to coordinate honorably and efficiently. Too much jealous bickering before and backbiting afterwards would exist in this country to foster a system with no central direction, but one which automatically assigns a powerful role to a specific office in a specific ministry, all without recriminations or discontent. In effect, the CCIEP is a halfway house that utilizes the majesty and neutrality of the White House to fix responsibility at the same time that ministerial officials are in fact doing the job.

One minor procedural spin-off from the creation of the CCIEP could be a reduction in the numerous scattered international economic reports submitted at regular time intervals to Congress (but seldom read). The five CCIEP subcommittees could submit the definitive report on their policy sectors in lieu of the submissions of the CIEP, the Office of the Special Representative for Trade Negotiations, NAC, Commerce (on export controls), DCC, and so on.

After creation of the CCIEP, the Executive Office of the President would be streamlined in terms of international economic responsibilities. The special trade representative's office and CIEP would be terminated altogether. The NSC would sharply narrow its activity in economics to those issues bearing directly on national security (for example, access to critical raw materials, international petroleum policy). Dozens of narrowly focused interagency committees would be terminated. On the other hand, the CEA and OMB would continue their highly selective participation in the international area in partial fulfillment of their assigned domestic economic responsibilities.

The ultimate justification for the creation of the CCIEP is the demonstrated slippage of White House coordinating groups whose primary jurisdictional concern is foreign policy or domestic policy. The NSC on occasion—for example, in the early Nixon years—has ignored international economic issues, while the EPB encountered difficulties in managing external economic issues. The reasons vary. In the first case, it was the inattention and economic inexperience by the head of the NSC staff; in the EPB case, the nonparticipation of the Department of State. But the results are similar: there is no guarantee that international economic considerations will not be relegated to second-class status or managed in an unbalanced way unless there is a separate White House coordinating mechanism fully respectful of the unique and separate nature of international economic policy.

As indicated above, there is no compelling reason to establish an elaborate or formal organization to convene members of the president's cabinet. The ultimate objective is merely to assure a regularized meeting between the president and the senior agency heads of both the foreign-affairs and economic policy bureaucracies. On a literal basis, such a convocation could occur within the context of an NSC or EPB meeting or a purely informal gathering called by the president. The CCIEP is necessary because its very existence symbolizes, and therefore indirectly supports, the concept of a distinct, balanced, and sharply focused policy-making process. Creation of a CCIEP per se would cost absolutely nothing. Whether or not such a name is utilized is not the important consideration. Gathering the cabinet into a meeting is a formality. The creation of a comprehensive sub-cabinet coordinating mechanism is a desperately needed innovation. The key reform is the establishment of the office of presidential assistant for international economic affairs and the five subcommittees. They are the ones that clearly would offer the means to better methods of formulating and managing U.S. policies in this area. The logical supervisory body for the operation of these two specialized White House activities is the concept embodied in the CCIEP.

## PROCEDURAL AND PERSONNEL CHANGES

Unlike the direct impact that these three organizational changes would have on the structure of policy making, procedural and personnel changes have the more modest objectives of improving the quality of and speeding up the support provided for senior policy makers, of permitting the system to better anticipate future problems, and of making the routine conduct of international economic relations more attuned to the interests and needs of the Congress, the private sector, and other countries.

### Strengthening the State Department

The organization, staffing, and role of the State Department must be commensurate with the overarching importance of foreign-policy considerations in virtually all international economic relations. The department has come a long way towards remedying its basic internal shortcomings and those of the foreign-service personnel system. These reforms have improved State's performance in the management of foreign policy in general and in international economic policy in particular. Since it must continue to be a superpower in the latter area, pragmatism must triumph over the subculture of the foreign service. For example, limitations should be eased on the hiring of economics specialists outside the foreign-service system.

Specifically, the role of the undersecretary of state for economic affairs should be expanded by having two bureaus report directly to him. One would be the existing Bureau of Economic and Business Affairs that has a reduced trade policy role, but an increased competence in food and development policies. The second would be the existing Bureau of Oceans and International Environmental and Scientific Affairs. Such an arrangement would eliminate the existing anomaly of there being no formal relationship between the undersecretary for economic affairs and the Bureau of Economics and Business Affairs. Under the present organization no one outside of his personal staff reports directly to the undersecretary. The resulting economic-technological complex, directed by the renamed undersecretary for economic and technological affairs, would serve two principal functions: providing the department's technological and economics capabilities and supervising U.S. participation in all multilateral organizations and conferences considering specialized economic or scientific issues, for example, the United Nations Development Program and the Law of the Sea Conference.

If this new group within the State Department is to provide the most effective input into the international economic policy process, further progress must be made in upgrading its economic and technological expertise. Three methods for doing so have been advanced several times in the past, but bear repeating here: increased appointment of career ambassadors and deputy chiefs of mission from the ranks of the economic officers; occasional recruitment of specialists without requiring their inclusion in the foreign service (lateral entry); and further improvements in economics and technical training programs for career foreign-service officers. The existing reflex prejudice against appointing people who are not political specialists to senior diplomatic posts should be ended. To further raise State's economic consciousness, there should be a phased-in requirement that appointment as deputy chief of mission of U.S. embassies follow at least one overseas tour as an economics or commercial officer.

## Strengthening the Treasury Department

As the department with the major responsibilities in macroeconomic policy, the Treasury must also be organized and managed in a manner befitting a superpower. The conduct of international economic relations needs to receive a sharp focus and high-level attention.

The Treasury's responsibilities in international economic relations should be concentrated into a single bureau. The prime shortcoming of the existing internal organization is that the prime overseas unit, the OASIA, is deprived of responsibility in some key issue areas and includes a few unneeded domestic responsibilities. The reasons for this situation are historical, and OASIA in 1976 is still suffering from the aftereffects of organizational gerrymandering. It has been split asunder and then put back together with additional pieces inserted. In both instances, change came not in pursuit of administrative soundness, but to parcel out a reward to a particular protege of Secretary Simon. The streamlining of OASIA should begin by removing domestic energy responsibilities. At least two of its three energy offices (Energy Policy Analysis, and Energy Regulation and Legislative Policy) currently in OASIA are oriented to domestic policy and should be transferred to Treasury's domestic operations or outside to a centralized energy department. The remaining Office of Financial Resources and Energy Finance should have its international focus shifted to the deputy assistant secretary with international monetary policy responsibilities, while the domestic focus is shifted out of OASIA.

The five divisions of OASIA, each headed by a deputy assistant secretary, already are sloppily apportioned. Their organizational rationality would be further eroded by the creation of DICP. A more rational structure would begin with a deputy assistant secretary for international monetary affairs whose domain would include policies and programs concerned with the U.S. balance of payments, international monetary reform, gold, exchange-rate crises, the IMF, and so on. Industrial nations' financial issues, both bilateral and multilateral (for example, the OECD and the EC), would be handled by a second division. It would also include Treasury's reduced oversight of first- and second-world foreign-trade-and-investment issues. A third deputy assistant secretary would head a developing nations' finance division, which would be concerned with bilateral and multilateral aid and with the whole gamut of issues and institutions concerned with the North-South dialogue and the new international economic order.

The fourth division would supervise all international financial research efforts and, in addition, would direct all of the national security affairs responsibilities (including liaison with the intelligence community) currently headed by a special assistant to the secretary. The office or offices formed under this deputy assistant secretary would also be in a position to furnish in-house foreign-policy expertise. These shifts, combined with the transfer of trade investigation responsibilities to DICP, would consolidate all of Treasury's international economic policy responsibilities under one assistant secretary. The one exception is international taxation. But this subject is so technical in nature and so closely linked with domestic legislation that it is best left with the assistant secretary for tax policy.

Full consideration also should be given to the creation of a new office in OASIA to deal with the increasing manifestations of international economic interdependence. The office would have two main functions: to handle the technical preparations for future economic summits and to explore more fully the economics of interdependence—movements in the world business cycle, the possibility of increased coordination of national economic policies, the interrelationship of the trade, monetary, and investment sectors, and so on.

## Personnel Practices

To reduce the gap in viewpoints between the State Department and the domestic economic agencies, a systematic personnel interchange program should be established at the middle-grade levels (GS 11 through 14; FSO 5 and 4) among all departments and agencies with international economic policy interests. To put teeth into the program, real incentives and sanctions must exist to assure that all persons appointed to senior posts (perhaps office director and above) have spent at least a two-year tour of duty "on the other side of the street." Neither State Department economic officers nor domestic-agency international economists should be promoted by their personnel offices to specified senior-level positions under normal circumstances without service in a domestic economic agency or in the State Department (at home or abroad), respectively. Once DICP or its equivalent is created, an assignment there would fulfill the interchange requirement for both State and Treasury career personnel. When the exchange program matures, it could serve as the de facto launching pad for an approximation of the all-inclusive Foreign Affairs Executive Corps suggested and explained in detail in the chapter on "Personnel" of the Murphy Commission's report.

## Research, Analysis, and Intelligence

Improvements in the information gathering and analysis process can contribute to better policy making by assuring that policy makers are getting relevant data quickly and in the forms desired. A large number of bureaucratic organizations have capabilities in this area, but the non-capital-intensive and imprecise nature of the effort required suggests that the existence of numerous analytic sources should be perpetuated. Nevertheless, several changes within the existing organization need to be made.

The informal and haphazard communication among the various research operations (a situation which can also exist within a single department) should be better coordinated to assure that all relevant data, reports, and planning papers automatically are either made known to, or distributed to, those analysts and policy makers with the need to know. Oversight responsibility for this coordination effort should belong to the CCIEP's Subcommittee on Economic Analysis and Forecasting. The latter should be empowered to direct any number of research offices to provide inputs into a major project involving scattered or overlapping areas of expertise.

Much of the research and analytic work done in the departments necessarily is devoted only to short-term phenomena of immediate importance to bureaucratic responsibilities. The forecasting subcommittee should retain a small number (three to six) of international economic experts on a full- or part-time basis to serve as senior advisers. Their raison d'etre would be to focus on longer-term international economic trends and problems. Attaching them to this subcommittee would serve the purpose of enhancing their reputation for being free of bureaucratic bias. This would also relieve these economists of all operational responsibilities and short-term concerns, except possibly for their having to give an additional opinion where the conclusions of departmental analysts disagree with one another.

To improve communications between the producers and consumers of economic intelligence, the activities of the Requirements Advisory Board should be revived within the CCIEP's Subcommittee on Economic Analysis and Forecasting. The board was begun in the CEP in 1973 to articulate economic policy makers' needs and priorities to the intelligence community. It further allowed a feedback process in which an evaluation was made of the economic intelligence being forwarded to policy makers.

This same subcommittee should develop a new, comprehensive analytic paper to be distributed on a regular basis to all luminaries in international economic policy making. It would identify, explain, and monitor economic-political developments and trends that have, or are likely to have, a bearing on the international economic relations of the United States. Written properly, the papers would not only inform, but also stimulate the imaginations of policy makers. Sample topics to be handled include a correlation between the trade performances of major countries and the movement or nonmovement of their currencies' exchange rates; the debt structures of selected LDCs or Communist bloc countries; and current monthly data on the key economic indicators of larger industrialized countries.

## Establishment of a Presidential Advisory Board for International Economic Policy

There is considerable merit in the Murphy Commission's recommendation that a high-level International Economic Policy Advisory Board be created. As envisioned here, the Board would provide advice directly to the president and cabinet from a senior, representative group of persons with expertise in this field. Being able to establish specialized ad hoc groups and to commission studies, it should replace most of the advisory groups currently dealing with narrowly defined aspects of international economic policy. The logical channel of communications between the board and the president is the proposed CCIEP.

## Shrinking the Bureaucracy

The bloated size of the bureaucracy that manages U.S. international economic policy prompts one to suggest a sweeping proposal for an across-the-board personnel reduction of a given percentage. This is a tempting, but simplistic proposal. The problem is far more subtle. Increased efficiency through tighter lines of command is a highly probable effect overall. Still, the shrinkage process involves the extremely sensitive reality of depriving people of their jobs and the equally sensitive bureaucratic perception of being deprived of influence, prestige, and the other wherewithal needed to fulfill a bureaucratic mission. A universal force-reduction formula also is inconsistent with the fact that the degree of overpopulation or underpopulation varies with different sectors and departments.

The OMB, perhaps in cooperation with the congressionally oriented GAO, should initiate a study of the personnel requirements of every bureau of the bureaucratic organizations in the international economic policy-making process. It should be conducted in conjunction with any of those reorganization recommendations contained herein that are actually implemented. The final force-reduction report should pinpoint where transfers of new personnel are needed and where reductions in force could be phased in. A reduction of international economic policy personnel cannot begin to make a meaningful savings dent in the $400 billion-plus federal budget of this country. Since international economic policy cannot be classified as capital intensive (except for foreign-aid disbursements), the overriding logic of a reduction in the bureaucracy's size is administrative, not financial, in nature.

## More Effective Inputs from the Domestic Policy Organization

Good international economic policy is often dependent on good domestic policy and on a full understanding of what and how things transpire in the domestic sectors of the economy. Ignorance concerning large-scale transactions by the grain-trading companies led to the Russian wheat fiasco, while one year later ignorance concerning the significance of soybeans futures contracts led to the sorrowful export controls effort. A lack of appreciation for the deteriorating international competitiveness of American industry associated with the exchange-rate rigidity of the late 1960s led to a prolonged refusal to consider dollar devaluation as a remedy. And the absence of a sound domestic energy policy makes a sound international energy policy tenuous at best. The international economic policy-making process could not effectively absorb domestic economic expertise without a power grab and a diversification effort that would increase its size and thereby further reduce efficiency.

Attainment of better domestic policy, as well as better coverage of the workings of the domestic economy and its future evolution, must be attempted through a strengthening of the domestic bureaus of the economic departments and agencies. No longer should the intellectual gulf between government and business dynamics match the geographic distance that separates Washington, D.C. from U.S. industrial and agricultural centers. The economic policy-making process should be less enamored with broad policy issues and more concerned with a finer understanding of how business decisions are made, how markets actually operate, the impact of governmental policy, and so on. This objective could be pursued by expanded programs of analytic coverage and applied research and by better contact with the key communities in the private sector.

The international economic policy-making organization needs to be plugged into this increased awareness and expertise on the contemporary and evolving domestic economic scene. Conversely, the international economic policy makers should be at the ready to provide complementary support to the needs of the domestic economic policy-making process.

Specifically, the Commerce Department should expand the capabilities of its Bureau of Domestic Commerce to provide comprehensive expertise on the industrial and service sectors. The department might more appropriately be renamed the Department of Industry and Commerce. Since the department would have lost a number of its international economic duties to DICP, consideration should be given to centralizing in it all domestic energy policy-making responsibilities. Such responsibilities would complement its domestic economic functions and permit termination of the FEA and other specialized energy-related agencies.

The Department of Agriculture should increase its comprehension of the economics of the food cycle once commodities have left the farm, that is, events involving processors, trading companies, commodity options trading, and so on. Like the Commerce Department, this increased expertise would come from reoriented personnel priorities and a limited hiring of specialists to augment the current professional staff.

### Increased Multilateral Meetings of Finance Ministers

The well-deserved reputation for conservatism and niggardliness attached to finance ministries, enhanced by the experiences of the North-South dialogue, masks their potential contribution to pursuit of a liberal world economic order. Belatedly, most have discovered the virtues of floating exchange rates in comparison to artificially pegged rates and to capital and trade controls. Their commitment to fight inflation and seek a rational allocation of economic resources means that most finance ministries are liberal traders at heart (short of a balance-of-payments crisis, at least). The continued process of interdependence and the prospect of slower world economic growth suggest the imperative of better communications among senior officials of finance ministries— those that dominate international economic policies in most countries. Just as the dynamic of trade negotiations makes resort to unilateral trade barriers highly distasteful and embarrassing to a participating trade minister, regularized face-to-face contacts among finance ministers would stimulate peer-group pressures against unilateral resort to beggar-thy-neighbor trade restrictive policies.

To regularize contacts between finance ministers, the annual OECD ministerial meeting should be held twice yearly. The meetings should emphasize the coordination of domestic and international economic policies among the industrialized countries themselves and externally vis-a-vis second- and third-world countries. They should relate closely to the lower-level discussions—multilateral surveillance—held in Working Party Three of the OECD.

The economic summit meetings, bringing together the heads of government of the major industrialized countries, should continue on a regular basis, being held at least annually. The resultant symbolism and the high-level attention required when presidents and prime ministers sit down to discuss economic policy among themselves are sufficient justification for holding these meetings. The potential for increased mutual understanding and substantive agreements are desirable objectives, but not prerequisites for successful summit meetings.

## Government-Private Sector Relations

In addition to the proposed establishment of the presidential-level International Economic Policy Advisory Board, better communication between government and the business, labor, farm, and consumer sectors is desirable and could be fostered in four ways:

1. The State Department and the international bureaus of each of the domestically oriented economic departments should appoint a private sector officer to act as a specific and identifiable liaison with business, labor, farmers, and consumers. This position would be enhanced in DICP by its tie-in with the advisory groups created in connection with the Tokyo Round.

2. A regular series of semiannual government briefings on international economic policy matters should be held on the road with key regional private sector groups in the Northeast, South, Midwest, and Far West. These briefings would be conducted by senior-level (office director through assistant secretary) personnel of the major departments concerned with international economic affairs.

3. The now very limited personnel exchange program between the private sector and the federal government should be expanded in the area of international economic policy. As in the case of intragovernmental exchanges, care must be taken to assure that objectives are carefully thought through, good positions made available; and that career benefits will accrue to government officials who have a one-to-two-year tour of duty in the private sector, and vice versa.

4. The State Department's existing program of economic policy briefings in Washington for businessmen and academics should be broadened to include presentations by the other major international economic departments.

One further area where federal liaison needs to be improved is with state and local governments. An office should be established (probably within

DICP) to deal with their needs and problems in the area of international economic relations, such as foreign direct investment in the United States, state laws affecting imports, and trade promotion activities.

The industrial, agricultural, and labor sector advisory committees established pursuant to the Trade Act of 1974 should be retained in more modest size and scope after termination of the Tokyo Round. They should serve as the prime vehicles for imparting to policy makers specialized private sector views on trade issues. Overall trade policy guidance, including the consumer's viewpoint, would be provided by the proposed International Economic Policy Advisory Board. The federal government ignores private views at the risks of later obstructionism in the policy-making process by irate groups, or of governmental favoritism towards one group over another.

## Energy

The organizational means to conduct international energy policy merit separate discussion on the basis of the issue's importance. The high cost of petroleum and the growing U.S. dependence on imported oil necessitate a massive internal and external policy effort to respond to urgent economic, political, and national security considerations. But the organization associated with energy policy, like that supporting economic development policy, must follow, not precede, policy objectives. For example, if the United States is content to follow the liberal trade option and to increase energy imports according to supply and demand, an organization designed to pursue a rigorous energy independence effort is inappropriate. Furthermore, an effective international energy policy is a function of an effective domestic energy policy that reduces consumption and increases supply in the short run.

Although the importance of and domestic base of international energy policy are extraordinary, this is not an extraordinary policy issue from a management point of view. The same essential procedures are appropriate here as elsewhere in U.S. international economic policy: good data collection and analysis, introduction and appropriate weighting of specialized bureaucratic perspectives, clear lines of responsibility, and so on. Only one structural change appears needed, again in the context of domestic energy policy. A consolidation of the decentralized, far-flung bureaucracy that formulates, implements, and manages the many components of energy policy appears to be a necessary organizational reform. Whichever department or agency is chosen to provide central leadership on energy matters should serve as the chairman of the International Energy Subcommittee of the CCIEP. International energy policy can be managed efficiently and effectively by the chairman and his department working closely with other interested bureaucratic actors within the machinery of the central coordinating mechanism established for international economic policy.

## Development Assistance

The myriad of motives, techniques, and dispensers of U.S. development assistance to LDCs has presented an especially vexatious organizational problem for many years. The fact that organizational reform never really caught up with the complexities of the foreign-aid program has been transcended by a larger fact: U.S. economic relations with LDCs today go far beyond aid per se into the larger issues of international economic reform as articulated in the new-international-economic-order dialogue between the countries of the North and South. The components of aid policy have become extremely disparate. The traditional vehicle of congressional loans, that is, foreign aid in its strictest terms, has been joined by demands for changes in the international trade, monetary, and investment systems. Organizational arrangements must reflect the diluted operational link between development programs, as well as the increasingly active interest in the development sector of the ministries with responsibilities for international trade, monetary, and investment policies.

As a consequence, no compelling evidence is at hand that a centralized Department of Foreign Economic Assistance would either better manage development policy or even find support in the executive and legislative branches. The preferable and more pragmatic organizational procedure to formulate development policy is to install a simplified, comprehensive coordination of the various bilateral and multilateral programs in the proposed CCIEP Subcommittee on Economic Relations with Less Developed Countries.

Bilateral foreign-aid disbursements have become a relatively small component of U.S. economic policies towards LDCs. The funds and expertise provided by the AID have been crowded out by multilateral lending banks and the precepts of the new international economic order. Nevertheless, AID continues to demonstrate a flexibility in adapting to basic redirections in U.S. foreign-assistance strategy. It has responded well to the congressional mandate of 1973 to shift from capital-intensive development loans to technical-assistance training programs (involving, for example, agricultural productivity, health care, or education). The existing AID structure is a realistic, appropriate organization for providing the specialized financial, technical, and human resources it is required to provide within the larger context of U.S. relations with LDCs. Neither the role nor organization of AID should suggest that it be the lead agency in directing resource transfers to LDCs. Coordination and direction of the highly diverse actions and programs undertaken in connection with these transfer efforts must occur at a level above that of AID.

## Protecting the Integrity of the ITC

A relatively unknown independent fact-finding unit, the ITC (formerly the Tariff Commission), performs the sensitive function of recommending or rejecting import barriers in cases where domestic industries claim import-induced injury or threat of injury, as defined by law. The mounting financial stakes in international trade and the simplification of the injury determination process stipulated by the Trade Act of 1974 have transformed a sleepy, venerable institution into one of significance.

The quality and independence of the ITC's commissioners need to be upgraded by terminating the widespread practice of appointments being made on the basis of political patronage rather than technical competence. The Congress should either desist in its zeal to make the ITC more beholden to it (as exemplified by excessively tight budgetary control and Senate Finance Committee-inspired legislation in 1976 for a reorganization that has the ultimate effect of lending support to recommendations for import barriers) or abolish the ITC. The ITC should not become a political football in executive-congressional trade confrontations.

The ITC's technical resources, based on unique expertise and noninvolvement in policy responsibilities, should be upgraded so that it can expand on its past record of producing unique and objective research reports. The economic research office should participate actively in the analytic efforts led by the CCIEP Subcommittee on Economic Analysis and Forecasting.

### Structuring U.S. Representation to International Conferences

The proliferation of international economic conferences is taxing existing coordination efforts to the limit. The intense bureaucratic politics syndrome has made the leadership and composition of the U.S. delegations to these meetings a contentious subject in itself. Therefore, the chairmanship and membership of all U.S. delegations to international economic conferences should be considered and approved in advance by the CCIEP subcommittee having jurisdiction over the policy issue to be discussed, be it trade, development, or other matters. This process should also be directed to reduce the propensity for senior U.S. government officials to travel abroad with entourages of grossly inflated proportions.

### Policy Evaluation

There is no facile means of having the executive branch evaluate its own approved and cherished policies in a detached, iconoclastic manner. One means of improving the evaluation process is to charge the senior economic advisers retained by the particular CCIEP subcommittee to make selective, periodic evaluation reviews. Policy obsolescence could also be detected by occasional recourse to contracts for evaluations with private research firms and academics. The GAO, not beholden at all to the executive branch, should place greater emphasis on producing technically sound critiques of executive branch policy, programs, and organization in international economic policy. A final vehicle for a clear rethinking of policy should be a required biannual submission of a comprehensive international economic policy statement by the executive branch to Congress. Hearings, probably by the Joint Economic Committee, would force an articulation of policy strategy while subjecting it to congressional and public review at the same time.

### Preventing Organizational Obsolescence

The rush of unforeseen developments in the international economy will probably induce considerable obsolescence by 1990 in the executive branch organization outlined above. This lack of permanence is also linked to the anticipation that in response to reorganization, the affected bureaucracies will ingeniously adapt and compensate, thereby neutralizing a portion of the mandated change. Ten to 15 years after reorganization is completed, another outside evaluation of international economic policy organization should be conducted. It should be followed by subsequent studies initiated at similar intervals.

## THE CONGRESS AND EXECUTIVE-LEGISLATIVE RELATIONS

Recommending organizational change in the legislative branch is problematical because of the jealousy with which congressmen guard existing prerogatives. Outsiders with reorganization plans rush in where angels fear to tread. Ideally, there should be a major reorganization of congressional committee responsibilities to provide a parallel alignment with the sectoral composition of the five subcommittees of the proposed CCIEP. This proposal may be valid on its intellectual merits. But for political reasons, it would have little chance of being enacted in the short run.

As a second-best set of recommendations, certain existing trends and innovations in the Congress should be encouraged:

1. Increased use of dual, or joint, subcommittee hearings whenever relatively technical international economic issues are under discussion;
2. Continued presence of congressmen as observers in the U.S. delegation at major international economic negotiations, such as the MTNs in Geneva;
3. The creation of specialized subcommittees on international economic issues, such as have been set up by the House Ways and Means and the Senate Finance committees and in the two committees concerned with foreign relations;

4. Extension to other international economic agreements of the so-called "fast track" procedure initiated in the Trade Act of 1974, whereby Congress must approve or disapprove trade agreements within a specified period of time and without amendment;

5. Upgrading of professional support through a policy of nonpartisan hiring of professionally trained international economists by the staffs of committees, the Congressional Research Service, and the GAO;

6. Convening oversight hearings on a more frequent basis to keep Congress appraised of continuing developments and policy evolution by responsible officials in the executive branch;

7. Reliance on the Congressional Budget Office for cost-effectiveness critiques of international economic policy.

Improving executive branch-congressional relations cannot be more than a procedural art in the absence of massive structural changes in both branches. Attitudes of key officials in one branch about the rights and prerogatives of the other branch are crucial. There are, however, certain behavioral patterns peculiar to the periods in which this relationship has flourished; they should become permanent features for international economic policy making. The keystone of good administration-congressional relations is a sense of shared participation. On the part of the executive branch, there should be a full appreciation of the constitutional role of Congress, not a begrudging tolerance of its intrusion into certain portions of the international economic policy-making process. Prior consultations concerning administration policies and negotiating positions do more than inform and flatter Congress. They can also serve to accommodate extreme congressional dissatisfaction, curb criticism and delaying tactics on the floors of the House and Senate, and reduce the likelihood of a surprise congressional rejection of supporting laws or treaties. The harmony that characterized passage of the Trade Act of 1974 in the midst of the Watergate controversy is proof of how well the two branches can work together.

Creation of the DICP and the CCIEP should enable the executive branch to make clearer to Congress where specific responsibilities and jurisdictions are assigned. Designation of administration spokesmen on key policy issues can be made in connection with the breakdown of responsibilities in the CCIEP. Responsible officials should not only be available to testify before formal meetings of committees and subcommittees, but should aggressively pursue informal working arrangements with leaders of counterpart congressional committees (and perhaps senior professional committee staff members as well). Although open government is a noble concept, there is something to be said for periodic closed-door, informal communications between the two branches. This would provide relief from the inevitable role playing and posturing required by each side when they are in the public spotlight.

A further institutionalization of interbranch cooperation would follow from the creation of the position of congressional relations officer, international economic policy, in the Departments of State and Treasury, and in the proposed DICP. These three officers should be trained economists, but also experienced in dealing with the special world of the Congress. Their job as central contact points would be to assess congressional moods and interests, respond to congressional inquiries, encourage a two-way flow of information, and be intimately knowledgeable on the details and interpretation of international economic legislation. The Treasury and State department officers could be located either in OASIA and the Bureau of Economic and Business Affairs, respectively, or in the regular congressional relations office; within DICP, the bureau concerned with trade policy planning and liaison would be the most appropriate spot for the new officer.

The Congress, for its part, could keep an open mind to a rationalization of committee responsibilities in this area. Party leaders and committee chairmen in both houses should convey an appreciation that the increasing importance and significance of international economic relations are too great to allow their outlook to be dominated by considerations of partisan politics or the efficacy of freely bestowing preferential treatment on special-interest groups pleading for special dispensation. Good leadership, good procedures, and good information can and should discourage obstructionist attitudes and protectionist policies.

A rationalized committee system, upgraded professional international economic expertise on Capitol Hill, and a forceful, continuing, and respectful dialogue with the executive branch are the priorities to be sought. Collectively, they would provide the momentum and pressure required to deflect the Congress from its instinctive drives to respond to the demands of vocal, albeit minority, constituent groups by edging towards an inward-looking, isolationist attitude towards other countries.

Congress was never intended to be a superslick decision maker. The Founding Fathers did not construct a friction-free relationship between the executive and legislative branches. Still, goodwill and willpower can make the system work well.

# 11

## THE NEED FOR REFORM:
## A FOLLOW-THROUGH

We make [international economic policy] . . . in the most disorganized, fragmented, and incoherent way imaginable. If there is consistency among decisions we make in our relations with less developed countries, trade negotiations, selling agricultural products abroad, and so on, this is purely coincidental. . . . We now have a non-system.

Sidney Weintraub

A "non-system" for formulating and conducting something as important as U.S. international economic policy cannot be an acceptable state of affairs. Improvements are needed now. There is no guarantee that any reorganization, even one that exactly replicates the recommendations in the previous chapter, would produce better—or different—policy. But guarantees are neither necessary nor appropriate requirements to come to grips with obvious weaknesses and the need to impose change. What is needed is the presumption that new organizational procedures can provide the most probable means of achieving the best and most consistent policy possible.

The virtues and promise of the aforementioned structural and procedural changes cannot be appreciated without a deep insight into the policy-making dilemma facing this country. A lot of pages have preceded a solitary chapter of recommendations; not all were exciting. But collectively, they formed the outline of a three-part exercise, which is the prerequisite for solving the international economic policy-making problem: acceptance of international economic policy as a distinctive phenomenon and a separate subject matter; identification of the dynamics and shortcomings of existing organization; embarcation on an objective, dispassionate effort to redesign existing institutions and ways of doing business.

If we have successfully passed through this multifaceted process, then the proposals, if enacted, will effectively make positive changes in the substance of policy. But this is still not enough. In addition to being intellectually sound, the recommendations must also be capable of implementation within acceptable magnitudes of effort, time, cost, and discomfort.

## WHY THE RECOMMENDATIONS SHOULD BE ADOPTED

International economic policy must be intellectually liberated from the shadows of foreign-policy and domestic economic policy management. It is a policy area that can never erase its mixed heritage, but one that can and must demand an equal share of attention and respect for its individuality. The organization by which it is made must be custom fitted to accommodate its unique nature and its importance. The United States and the world can ill afford to continue allowing this country's international economic policy machinery to fester as a metaphor for the value struggle between foreign-policy and economic policy ideologies and priorities. The current organization fails primarily because it encourages the worst excesses of bureaucratic politics; it too often is a house divided against itself. As the challenges and complexities grow, as they inevitably must, the existing organization is becoming increasingly hard pressed to cope. It becomes increasingly dependent on luck and benevolent dictators to impose efficiency. An unbiased exegesis cries out for a change in the organizational status quo.

U.S. international economic policy should be made not by roving street gangs of freelance operators, but in oak-paneled conference rooms where an appreciation is possible for the seamless web that this policy has become. Policy should continue being made as a result of the adversary process, which the U.S. government has developed far more than anyone else. However, the overall effort must respect the extent to which congruence has developed between the major functional areas—trade, finance, investment, and aid—of U.S. international economic relations. Similarly, it is increasingly difficult to escape the interconnections of U.S. regional policies: relations within the first world increasingly assume the shape of a European-Japanese-American triangle. Policies vis-a-vis the communist and developing countries increasingly assume a shallowness if not coordinated with the other two sides of the first-world triangle. The policy-making process must also be mindful of the unique pursuit of global American interests and leadership being eroded by the loss of American international economic hegemony.

A reorganization is needed that can creatively harness the energy generated by a large, diversified, and intelligent American bureaucracy. The energy that springs from the multiple perspectives, priorities, and values relevant to the policy formulation equation, should be channeled into a structured pursuit of balanced policy based on a consensus and publicly supported within the executive branch and the Congress (and, ideally, by the private sector). Energy must be used to identify problems, articulate the options, make decisions, and implement policy. It should not be used for stifling bureaucratic dissent, waging unending wars of nerves on sensitive or sticky issues, or seeking the least common denominator of consensus.

As time and events pass, we can be reasonably assured that the list of demonstrated organizational weaknesses will continue growing. It would not be overly cynical to defend the aforementioned reorganizational proposals by arguing that nothing could be lost. Policy could not be made under much worse conditions, while the possibility of real improvement exists. Unless the natural trend of international economic relations changes course, which is unlikely, improved U.S. policy and leadership can only come from highly qualified leaders and a more rational organization. The alternative is to provide further evidence of the wisdom in the aphorism that warns that those who do not learn from history are doomed to repeat it.

Several structural flaws must be corrected in the organization. A presidential perspective must be made a clear and permanent fixture. Since the president should become personally involved in only the most extraordinary issues, it is important that senior officials in the line departments be clearly designated to have the authority to make decisions on noncritical matters. Since basic policy inevitably emanates from an interdepartmental coordinating mechanism, it is vital that a select number of specified groups be assigned responsibility for specific sectors of policy formulation. Each must be universally recognized within and without the bureaucracy as not being tilted to any particular preconceptions or point of view. No such organization or set of groups exist today. There is not even the means today of coordinating the numerous coordinators so as to assure that policy in one international economic sector complements that in another.

The continuing failure to implement a well-designed cohesive organization, which is methodically geared to make clear, balanced policy, manifests itself in at least two administrative respects. The first is the resurrection of earlier organizational failures. The demise of the CFEP and then the CIEP revealed identical causes and symptoms. The senior coordinating effort in 1976, the EPB, is a relative improvement over past shortcomings, but is still far from an optimal arrangement.

Secondly, the weakness of the American international economic policy structure manifests itself in the opposite time direction, that is, the future. We appear to be approaching the point where the organization's inability to cope with certain international economic complexities can be expressed in an academic model with statistically significant predictive power. Under certain circumstances—for example, the approach of a deadline to publicly explain

U.S. policy on an issue hamstrung by a State-Treasury deadlock—a pending demonstration of policy disarray becomes highly probable.

This model would have accurately predicted the American malaise at the fourth meeting of the UNCTAD in the bicentennial summer of 1976. UNCTAD has become a major forum for the gathering of the industrialized and the developing countries for discussions of the entire range of the North-South economic issues. As noted in Chapter 6, the U.S. government is in singular disarray on the exact approach it is to take on the prime item in the North-South dialogue, international commodity agreements.

It is true that Secretary of State Kissinger made a comprehensive statement of U.S. thinking during the first week of the conference. But the story behind the speech involves a bitter, one-minute-before-midnight quarrel within the delegation, which materially affected the U.S. negotiating position. At the outset of the meeting, the U.S. delegation had to turn its energies inward, for intragovernmental negotiations. The Kissinger speech was finalized only a few hours before its delivery. The reason, very simply, was that bureaucratic politics would not give way to a compromise consensus any earlier on the so-called integrated-commodity-approach issue. This occurred despite the fact that the fourth meeting of the UNCTAD had been scheduled more than a year in advance. Furthermore, this protracted delay precluded any meaningful coordination of positions with the other industrialized countries (a point which Kissinger lamented in an OECD ministerial meeting speech delivered a few weeks later). The fact that the rich countries encountered a united group of poorer countries with clearly articulated demands further increased the cost of nonexistent U.S. leadership. Some of the more astute participants from the LDCs were perplexed that U.S. energies were absorbed on matters not germane to LDC demands.

The source of the dilemma was simply the absence of the will and the machinery to reconcile and consolidate the differences in positions held by the international economic superpowers, the State and Treasury departments. "Up until the end of the conference, there was dispute between various departments within the U.S. government over the details of the U.S. position, details which should have been ironed out before the conference began."[1]

The concentration of State and Treasury department representatives was further dissipated before and during the conference by a fight over the details and wisdom of proposing the creation of an International Resources Bank. The latter would be used to finance private investment in resource extraction projects in LDCs, thereby increasing the supply of critical raw materials. To begin with, the proposal was somewhat incongruous, given the desire of the LDCs to protect prices by restraining production. Worse yet, other delegations were aware that the U.S. delegation was debating ad nauseam within itself about the bank initiative, which at best was tangential to the financial demands placed on the conference table by the poorer countries. Perhaps the greatest value of the proposal was the perverse one of allowing the LDCs to express their dissatisfaction with the U.S. performance by later defeating (33 to 31, with a whopping 89 abstentions) a proposal merely to begin considering developing an International Resources Bank.

In sum, the internecine warfare in the U.S. delegation in this case resulted from a direct link between organizational deficiencies and a weakened negotiating position. Some U.S. officials were asked point blank by other delegation members why the United States would not, or could not, concentrate on the central issues of the meeting.* They undoubtedly had no acceptable answer.

Another test of organizational competence can be made in connection with the fourth meeting of UNCTAD. How did the French handle themselves? Not surprisingly, they submitted a proposal early in the proceedings that was clearly articulated and universally backed by that country's delegation. It was also a unique one, this time not because of French extremism, but rather because it was an imaginative attempt to provide a compromise between the extreme positions taken towards the common fund to finance buffer stocks by its EC partners, West Germany and the Netherlands.

The creation of a CCIEP and a DICP, the permanent establishment of a senior-level assistant to the president for international economic affairs, and the procedural changes discussed previously will have two broad salutary effects. Such an organization would support the strongest possible base for good, timely international economic policy. Secondly, it would make U.S. government organization wholly compatible with the evolutionary effects of the basic trend in international economic relations: increasing quantitative and qualitative interdependence. It would also place the United States in a better position to respond to the central dilemma of the global economy as the 1980s approach: a lack of consensus among countries as to where to proceed to next and the lack of a dominant state to point the way.

International economic policy is no longer a branch of foreign policy. It is close to being a new kind of foreign relations with a distinctive set of problems, bureaucratic actors, chemistry, and protocol. It is a policy that is characterized by harassed national authorities simultaneously pursuing conflicting goals. Policy makers are at once battling to stem the tide of the encroaching obsolescence of the nation-state as a viable economic unit, responding to voter demands, pursuing greater efficiency in the operations of

---

*The sophistication with which some foreigners perceive U.S. bureaucratic politics was demonstrated in the reaction of one Asian official who unofficially confided that he disliked the U.S. preference for linking the proposed International Resources Bank to the World Bank. His reasoning was that such a link would place the U.S. Treasury department in the lead role in formulating U.S. policy and budgetary commitments to the bank. This eventuality, he worried, would encourage a conservative, hard-line posture towards its funding and activities.

international markets, supporting greater equity in terms of international income distribution, and seeking greater economic security in terms of guaranteed access to supplies of critical goods and a disadvantaged economic position for potential enemies.

The completion of the initial phase of liberalization of international trade, financial, and investment restrictions roughly corresponds to the end of the post-World War II era and of cheap energy supplies. Although it is still uncertain whether the momentum of postwar economic growth can be sustained, it is obvious that the next phase of liberalization must touch on very sensitive nerves affecting sovereignty. Jealously guarded national prerogatives —for example, agricultural price supports and required adjustments in exchange rates—are next in line for international codification. This means that an international economics evolution is pointing towards a revolution in domestic policy management. Both evolution and revolution will be managed primarily by finance ministries.

The apotheosis of finance ministries as international economic powers is amply demonstrated by their full-scale intrusion into the North-South dialogue, which in the 1950s or 1960s would have been dominated solely by foreign ministries. The proliferation of finance ministry-controlled international economic organizations—the IMF, World Bank, Common Market, OECD, and so on—merely serves to further prove their diversified jurisdictions. More importantly, the logical progression of worldwide economic interdependence has already progressed to the point of summit meetings to discuss specifically the coordination of national economic policies. By the end of the century, consultations may have to be elevated to joint planning of domestic economic policies. In either case, coordination consultations and joint planning fall into the backyards of finance ministries. In sum, the means by which U.S. international economic policy is made in the 1980s and beyond must respect and compensate for a powerful role by domestically oriented departments, most notably the Treasury. This reflects the ultimate blurring of the distinction between domestic and foreign issues.

By becoming a tightly woven mosaic of domestic economic concerns and foreign relations, international economic policy requires an entirely new negotiating dynamic. The State Department must be the one to provide the vital ingredients of a global political perspective, as well as assessments and forecasts from abroad. However, no foreign ministry any longer can adequately represent the breadth and depth of the domestic sector's sensitivity to external forces. A decreasing percentage of international economic problems will be resolvable solely through the traditional diplomatic exercise of applying good faith to balance or to bridge differences between the needs of two governments. A major element of the problem is the need to manage the domestic political forces inside the United States and appeal to the domestic forces within the other nations. To manage these problems effectively, a substantial portion of economic policy makers' time is being absorbed by bargaining with specific domestic private interest groups, or by neutralizing them with counterbalancing forces.[2]

The reorganization proposals will not only encourage the internal workings of the executive branch to adapt to the expected evolution of the global economy, but they will allow for maximum effective communication between that branch's two key partners. Congress has embarked on a new course of activism in international economic relations in response to the post-Watergate syndrome of reassertiveness and the increased domestic political sensitivities that now are involved in this area. To some rugged individualists in the executive branch, this activism borders on meddling. But to others, it is a proper exertion of the basic separation-of-powers principle. In point of fact, a nonpartisan, intelligently and sensitively handled executive branch-congressional partnership can be a useful device for balanced consensus making. Additionally, the proposed reorganization would make clearer to the private sector where international economic policy power lies in the executive branch. It would also maximize the government's opportunity to communicate with and understand the workings and real needs of American business, laborers, and consumers.

One final justification of this organizational design is that it is not too pat. It does not go too far in assuring a small, tightly knit group of American bureaucrats marching lockstep in single-minded pursuit of detailed objectives. Such an arrangement not only risks unnecessary American isolation from its economic partners, it risks restoration of a "pax Americana" as well. If the Washington policy-making system fully harnessed America's economic, political, and military strength, the critics who allege that this country pursues imperialist objectives might well be proven correct.

## HOW THE RECOMMENDATIONS COULD BE ADOPTED

Justice Oliver Wendell Holmes is reputed to have said that the test of truth is its ability to defend itself in the marketplace. Whatever might be the perceived truths and virtues of the reorganization recommendations, their successful introduction cannot escape that basic American prerequisite for achieving any objective: good marketing. The concept of changing international economic policy organization must be attractively packaged and a sales campaign must be mounted if changes are to be made. Skeptics have to be convinced, Congress has to be consulted, and bureaucratic counterattacks have to be contained. Given the nature of the proposed changes, however, the marketing program need be neither intensive nor extensive.

If senior officials accept the basic logic of the proposals, they need not fear that implementing them would be difficult or exhausting; the American electorate amply demonstrated in the 1976 presidential primaries its fundamental dissatisfaction with Washington's ways of doing things. This is a proposed reorganization that extends the promises, among others, for aiding the performance of the American economy and for enabling this country to better pursue its interests in a highly competitive global marketplace. As such, a favorable public and congressional responsiveness to an articulate sales campaign should easily be forthcoming. The prime potential stumbling block is that part of the executive bureaucracy which either equates reorganization with a presumption of past policy failures or perceives its own interests and power challenged. It is absolutely mandatory that the president, his White House staff, cabinet and subcabinet officers be committed to the changes. Since the proposals do not collectively produce a positive sum gain situation (where everyone gains), the bureaucracy cannot be expected to become eager advocates of the package of its own volition.

A number of other supporting arguments can be mustered. No major expense is involved. The bureaucracy's overall size and the extent of its policy mandate are not significantly affected. Modest reforms, not a revolution, are being proposed. Care has been taken to assure that the major international economic actors retain at least a portion of their existing responsibilities, even to the extent of their supplying senior personnel to the proposed DICP.

Furthermore, a minimum amount of new legislation is required. Most of the proposals could be implemented, in strictly legal terms, through administrative directives and executive orders. Creation of the post of assistant to the president for international economic affairs could certainly be accomplished in this manner, as could virtually all the proposed procedural changes within the executive branch. The proposed CCIEP could also be created in this manner.

However, some consultations with the legislative branch would be advisable. At a minimum, Congress would have to terminate the existing CIEP by failing to renew its periodically extended legislative life, now scheduled to end on June 30, 1977. Congress has demonstrated a concern for the need to coordinate international economic policy, but no real attachment to the CIEP as an institution. In budgetary hearings held in the summer of 1975, Senator Adlai Stevenson III, chairman of the Banking Committee's International Finance Subcommittee, made clear this attitude on several occasions. He said that he didn't question the need for coordination, but he did question the need for the CIEP: "The record doesn't indicate much coordination. CIEP just provides staff support for another agency [the EPB]. . . . CIEP has not fulfilled the coordinating role intended for it by the Congress. It seldom meets and seldom coordinates. Issues are left to be resolved throughout the interplay of personalities seeking the President's ear."

An important statement of congressional attitude towards potential White House reorganization preceded these remarks, when Senator Stevenson said that "I concede the President's right to organize his office as he chooses and if for some mysterious reason [the CIEP] is what he chooses—or to put it slightly differently, if for less mysterious reasons he doesn't want to rock the boat at the moment—then at least on the theory it is transitional, with the next President taking another look at it, I have no objections to going on as we have."[3]

Short of the ultimate ideal of a rationalization of congressional committee jurisdiction, the proposals for change within the Congress and in executive-legislative branch relations have already been implemented in part or could be invoked with only modest administrative efforts. The streamlining of committee jurisdictions and of voting procedures are concepts that can be planted by others, but can only blossom within the halls of Congress. All that can be done externally is for the executive branch to set a precedent by rationalizing its own organization and procedures. At best, a subtle pressure can be exerted by depriving Congress of the excuse that its organizational shortcomings in international economics are but a mirror of the disarray in the administration.

The proposed creation of a DICP in many respects symbolizes the rationale of the proposed reorganization. In terms of overall implementation, the DICP presents at once the great challenge and the great opportunity. The marketing effort therefore must be centered here. Legislation would be required, as would some changes in congressional committee jurisdiction. The legislative and oversight functions associated with the policies and programs shifted to the new department could, at least temporarily, be handled through the existing committee pattern. Nevertheless, a single committee in each house will have to be given the central budgetary authority; that is, one committee will approve the annual spending authorization bill, approval of parts of which currently is shared by the committees on finance, banking, and commerce. Bureaucratic forces will be realigned structurally as authority and personnel are transferred from the Departments of State, Treasury, Commerce, and so on, to DICP. Senior career civil servants in the existing departments, their friends on Capitol Hill, and clients in the private sector will need to be massaged, mollified, and generally convinced first that they will retain trade policy influence, if not power, and secondly, that a better means of formulating and conducting foreign trade is in the offing.

To argue the case for creating a DICP International Commercial Policy is to defend the need for American organizational arrangements that meet the vigorous demands of a dynamic world economy. A centralized focus for trade policy, it should be argued, is the only way to respond successfully to the tough, sophisticated foreign competition—where the alliance between business and government grows even tighter. Such centralization not only would assure that the administration could keep its own act together, but would establish clearer and more efficient two-way communications channels with the Congress and the private sector. The advocates of DICP could also correctly suggest that a more comprehensive, coherent means of making trade policy will assure an incremental measure of governmental efficiency in protecting the interests of the American public, be it through challenging foreign trade barriers or correcting unfair or injurious import competition.

It should be stressed that with the addition of DICP, Congress would not lose the special trade representative's office; that office would undergo a metamorphosis, not dismemberment. Its role would effectively be enhanced; the president's special trade representative, as head of a new cabinet-level department, becomes a man with a new title and wider power over all U.S. foreign trade policy, not merely one dimension of it. The business community is gaining a more powerful entity to conduct policy on its behalf. Consumers are gaining an eclectic agency, one at least as interested in the dynamic of trade liberalization as in protection for the relatively few U.S. firms and businesses injured by a liberal trade policy.

In sum, it's a rough world—government intervention in the business sector is proliferating, as are trading blocs. U.S. competitiveness cannot afford to be eroded either by a disjointed policy-making process or by the current ability of some foreigners to play off against one another the warring factions within the U.S. bureaucracy. To prevent situations of a competitive disadvantage, policy inconsistencies, deadlocked U.S. decision making, and weak, defensive reactions, it is necessary to argue for major changes in the means by which U.S. international economic policy is made.

It may not be fashionable to conclude on a sardonic note, but the following anecdote so poignantly describes the state of this country's policy-making system that it merits retelling. The snowballing of the international economic negotiating agenda in early 1976 convinced certain professional staff members of the Senate Finance Committee, who have international trade responsibilities, that events were moving so fast that they needed a comprehensive briefing to keep themselves fully appraised of the situation. They proceeded, therefore, to visit key executive branch offices and ask what the international economic policies of the United States were, how they were being made, and by what means the executive agencies were coordinating efforts. Admittedly, this was a chaotic period in which many things were happening simultaneously: international monetary reform negotiations, multilateral trade negotiations, international food stockpile negotiations, as well as the North-South dialogue on a new international economic order, which in turn was punctuated by the State-Treasury Department ideological schism.

The Senate Committee staff members' quest for understanding was a complete bust. The doughty inquisitors from Capitol Hill were no less ignorant afterwards than when they started; and they were greatly disillusioned. Conferences with officials in the CIEP, the special trade representative's office, and the relevant departments left them confused and empty-handed. They heard not about specifics or how policy was made, but rather contradictions, disavowals of responsibility, equivocations, and criticisms of other agencies. ("What does the White House know?" was the retort used by one official to dismiss an explanation previously given to the congressional staffers by a CIEP official.) In no case could an office or an official be found who would claim leadership in the foreign commercial, energy, or developmental policy sectors.[4]

Perhaps the Hill people didn't talk to the right people; perhaps they didn't listen carefully enough. In any event, there is something gravely wrong with the system when, in privately reciting their experience, basically nonpartisan professional staff members of a committee very active in this area can look you in the eye and say they concluded that a process to make U.S. international economic policy per se did not exist.

One of them likened his procession of unproductive interviews to peeling off the leaves of an artichoke and finding no heart, that "nothing was there." Adoption of the new organization and procedures advocated above would help to assure that the international economic policy of the United States does have a heart, as well as a brain and a backbone.

## NOTES

1. *Report by Congressional Advisers to UNCTAD IV* (Washington, D.C.: U.S. Government Printing Office, 1976), p. 5.

2. "Statement of Harald Malmgren," in *Congress and Foreign Policy,* hearings before the House International Relations Committee, 94th Cong., 2nd sess. (Washington, D.C.: U.S. Government Printing Office, 1976), p. 210.

3. *International Economic Policy Act of 1975,* hearings before the Senate Committee on Banking, Housing, and Urban Affairs, 94th Cong., 1st sess., 1975, pp. 27, 48. 51.

4. Off the record interviews, July 1976.

STEPHEN D. COHEN is an associate professor in the School of International Service at American University, Washington, D.C. Prior to his appointment in 1975, he served as the senior staff member for economic affairs on the Commission on the Organization of the Government for the Conduct of Foreign Policy.

He is the author of *International Monetary Reform, 1964–69: The Political Dimension* and has published articles on international economic relations in anthologies and journals in the United States and abroad.

Dr. Cohen began his career as an international economist with the U.S. Treasury Department, and served as the chief economist of the United States-Japan Trade Council from 1969 to 1973. He is currently a consultant on international economics to the Congressional Budget Office and to the Washington Analysis Corporation. He holds a B.A. and Ph.D from American University's School of International Service and an M.A. from Syracuse University.

**RELATED TITLES**

Published by

Praeger Special Studies

TECHNOLOGY TRANSFER AND U.S. FOREIGN
POLICY

Henry R. Nau

\* THE ENERGY CRISIS AND U.S. FOREIGN POLICY
edited by
Joseph S. Szyliowicz
Bard E. O'Neill

THE MULTINATIONAL BUSINESSMAN AND FOR-
EIGN POLICY: Entrepreneurial Politics in East-West
Trade and Investment

Jeffrey M. Brookstone

\*FOREIGN TRADE AND U.S. POLICY: The Case for
Free International Trade

Leland B. Yeager
David G. Tuerck

\*THE UNITED STATES AND WORLD DEVELOP-
MENT: Agenda 1977

John W. Sewell and the Staff
of the Overseas Development Council

\*Also available in paperback as a PSS Student Edition